"In the long and proud history of the British Armed Forces, there have been many brave men and many decent men. But few soldiers have combined both qualities to quite the degree of 'Gentleman Jim' Almonds, a founder of the SAS and quite simply one of the most courageous men who has ever served his monarch and his country. Lorna Almonds-Windmill has produced an exquisite tribute to her late father, who was as inventive and practical as he was adventurous and daring. In "Escaping the Ordinary: How a Founder of the SAS Blazed a Trail at the end of Empire", she tells of the incredible exploits of her father after the Second World War when yet again, as in the 1939-45 conflict, he time and again covered himself in glory. The author has produced a quite splendid sequel to her book, "Gentleman Jim: The Wartime Story of a Founder of the SAS and Special Forces". I commend the author for both the diligence of her research and her determination to ensure that her father's immense gallantry is never forgotten."

Lord Ashcroft KCMG PC, military historian/bravery expert

"Fascinating to read of the distant period when the Malayan Scouts became the SAS…it helped fill in gaps for me.

General Sir Peter de la Billière, KCB, DSO, MC & Bar, former Director SAS during the Iranian Embassy siece and Commander-in-Chief of the British Forces in the Gulf War

ESCAPING
THE
ORDINARY

How a Founder of the SAS Blazed
a Trail at the End of Empire

Lorna Almonds-Windmill

Matador
9 Priory Business Park,
Wistow Road, Kibworth Beauchamp,
Leicestershire. LE8 0RX
Tel: 0116 279 2299
Email: books@troubador.co.uk
Web: www.troubador.co.uk/matador
Twitter: @matadorbooks

ISBN 978 1800460 126

British Library Cataloguing in Publication Data.
A catalogue record for this book is available from the British Library.

Printed and bound by CPI Group (UK) Ltd, Croydon, CR0 4YY
Typeset in 11pt Minion Pro by Troubador Publishing Ltd, Leicester, UK

Matador is an imprint of Troubador Publishing Ltd

To our great and gracious God, and for my family

CONTENTS

Foreword by Sir Ranulph Fiennes OBE   ix
Acknowledgements   xi
Author's Preface   xiii
Maps   xv

PART ONE
October 1945–March 1951

Prologue   The Prisoner   3
1   Manhunt   5
2   Escaping the Ordinary   14
3   Ethiopia and the British Military Mission   21

PART TWO
April 1951–December 1952

4   Rise of the Shifta Bandits   39
5   Eritrea Police Field Force   49
6   New 'Wild West'   56
7   The Empire Strikes Back   66
8   Operation Roundup   74

PART THREE
January 1952–August 2005

9	Malayan Picnic	89
10	Deep Jungle Warfare	98
11	Singapore Island	109
12	White Man's Grave: The Gold Coast/Ghana	124
13	Volta River	130
14	Rainforest, Rocks and Rapids	142
15	Treks, Tracks and Elephants	155
16	Those Who Go Down to the Sea in Ships	164
17	Maiden Voyage of the Ketch Kumasi	171
18	Lonely Sea and the Sky	185
19	Wild Atlantic	202
20	A True Viking	214
21	Last Escape	232
Notes and Sources		241
Glossary		255
Nautical Terms		258
Bibliography		261
Index		265
About the author		282

FOREWORD

BY

SIR RANULPH FIENNES OBE, EX-SAS

*Described in the Guinness World Book of Records
as the greatest living explorer*

'Gentleman Jim' Almonds is a Special Forces hero and he is one of mine too.

Almonds didn't talk about himself so I am delighted that his daughter has now written the story of his post-war adventuring. I am also honoured to write the Foreword to this remarkable book.

In wartime, Almonds always ran to the battle. After 1945, in so-called peacetime, he always ran *towards* active service, exploring, adventuring and danger. When there wasn't any, he was driven to create his own. And despite having no formal training, he even designed and made cars, canoes and boats in which to do it! These included a 22 foot sloop and a 32 foot ocean-going ketch.

A great wartime escaper, it is no surprise to me that Almonds was determined to escape from ever having an ordinary job. The story of his role in British anti-terrorism in the Horn of Africa is set in an unreported theatre of operations. As Second in Command of the Eritrea Police Field Force, he hunted (and caught) outlaws with prices on their heads. British justice was swift yet he remained humane, respecting the local officers with whom he served and honouring their customs.

Off duty, often alone, Almonds explored the highlands of Ethiopia, navigated its crocodile-infested rivers by canoe and scoured the bush of Eritrea, West Africa and later the coasts and jungles of Asia. His huntin', shootin', and fishin' exploits are well told – but he only ever killed for the pot.

After leading an exploratory expedition down the Volta River to the sea in one of his boats, Almonds volunteered to rejoin the SAS during the Malayan Emergency, parachuting into the jungle to clear Communist terrorists northwards out of the country. In Singapore, he built more boats and sailed them in the Straits of Malacca.

The only one of Almonds's exploits ever to reach the media was his building of the ketch, the SS *Kumasi*, two hundred miles from the sea in Ghana, launching her at Takoradi and sailing her home to England. He had designed her and memorized the details when under sentence of death in an Italian prisoner of war camp. Years later, he realized his dream and built her without the use of a single power tool. The *Kumasi* had no modern steering aids, no health and safety to speak of and no way of being able to radio for help. A man has to be rather crazy to do that! There was no navigation system either. What comes across is that Almonds had an uncanny sense of direction. He took his ketch out into the wild Atlantic and yet hit the Azores spot on.

This story is also set accurately in the dog days of the Empire. Almonds was doing his duty but his job was sometimes difficult, nearly always dangerous and often unpleasant. He did it nonetheless. Lorna's book is a well-researched and fully sourced account of that fading glory and the contemporary international struggles that were taking place.

You can take a man out of the SAS but you can never take the SAS out of the man. Here is the story of one such.

Ranulph Fiennes

Exmoor.

ACKNOWLEDGEMENTS

I am very grateful to all the people who helped me to research and write this book, the sequel to *Gentleman Jim*. A few must receive special mention: my brother, John Almonds and my sister, Gloria Almonds, who gave unstintingly of their time to find documents and photographs, recall memories and comment on drafts; Ben and Douglas Robson, whose father crewed for my father when he sailed from Africa to England; Alan Cameron – the other member of the all Scots crew who assiduously kept a very detailed log of the voyage; Ann Apthorp; Ann Schlee, daughter of Duncan Cumming; and Barbara Gent of Giggleswick School who provided photographs, memories and other assistance; my dear friend Elizabeth Bradley, who after reading *Gentleman Jim* said she wanted to know what happened next; my dear friend Rosemary Summerfield, who gave great encouragement; Ray Bell; the late Leonard Dickson; Doreen Gander; Edward Horne; Ernest Miller; the late Professor Richard Pankhurst; Stuart Perry; and the late Sir Wilfred Thessiger who all provided expertise, input and wise counsel.

I acknowledge with thanks the assistance of the National Archives – records held by them appear courtesy of Her Majesty's Stationery Office – and the invaluable help of the staff of the British Embassy and British Consulate, Addis Ababa, Ethiopia. My thanks go also to the great team at Troubador Publishing Ltd, to Paul Futcher of Lorraine Inglis Design for the maps and to Philip Field for my photograph.

Lastly, thank you to the many readers of *Gentleman Jim* who kept telling me that they were anticipating the sequel. I'm sorry for having kept you waiting.

AUTHOR'S PREFACE

In 1954, I was nine, a child of the British Empire and a daughter of the SAS Regiment. Life in Singapore was idyllic. School was easy. We went sailing in the Jahore Straits every weekend. I could wear shorts every day. I had numerous pets. And boys were just a nuisance.

I did not realize the dangers through which my father, 'Gentleman Jim' Almonds, 'L' Detachment, 1ˢᵗ SAS had passed in order to give me, and the rest of my family, such a privileged existence. And he had done it in so-called 'peacetime'. His post-war active service, chasing and catching *shifta* bandits in Eritrea and clearing Communist terrorists out of northern Malaya had not been deemed to have taken part in a theatre of war. For political and commercial reasons, the British Government had not dignified these terrorist insurrections with the word 'war'. But British soldiers and police got killed putting them down.

More danger was to come. Almost all of it self-imposed. By some miracle, my father had survived the Second World War unscathed, despite coming close to death nine times in my first book – the prequel to this one: 'Gentleman Jim: The Wartime Story of a Founder of the SAS and Special Forces'. He chose to go to East Africa, then rejoined the SAS in Malaya. When he was not chasing outlaws, he was exploring and hunting alone in some of the most dangerous places on earth. Later, he made good his own POW camp promise to himself to design and build an ocean-going boat and sail her back to England.

The son of a Lincolnshire smallholder, my father had left school at fourteen without any educational qualifications. But there at the small Stixwould Village School, long since closed, he learned how to learn. Self-taught, he made things with his hands: cars, boats and even an aeroplane. And he learned from his mistakes. He also developed a love of adventure. After his death-defying war, he was driven to create his own challenges. And pursue them.

Before my father died in 2005, we got this book 'in the can'. He relived what he had done and I researched the background to his story at the National Archives and in Addis Ababa. More than anything, I hope that this book will encourage people who began life holding very few cards. Anyone can learn new skills and, with determination, escape from a life they feel is ordinary. I hope too that it will reveal more of the enigma that was my father.

For me, life has come full circle. It is again idyllic. I no longer have to go to the office. I can wear shorts every day, weather permitting. I have two highly intelligent cats. And (most) men are just a nuisance.

Lorna Almonds-Windmill
Norton Saint Philip
April, 2020

MAPS

Eritrea and Ethiopia 1950
Eritrea 1950
Singapore 1954
Gold Coast/Ghana 1956–1960
North West Africa in 1960
Atlantic Ocean

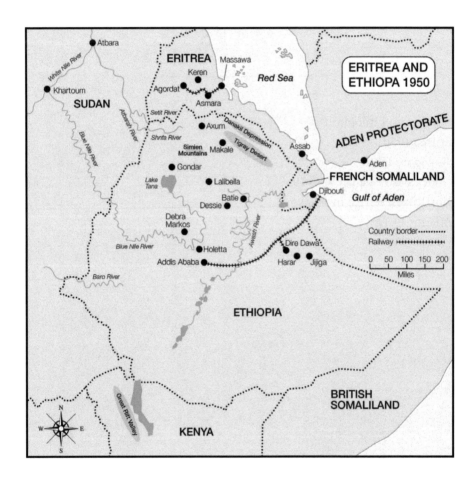

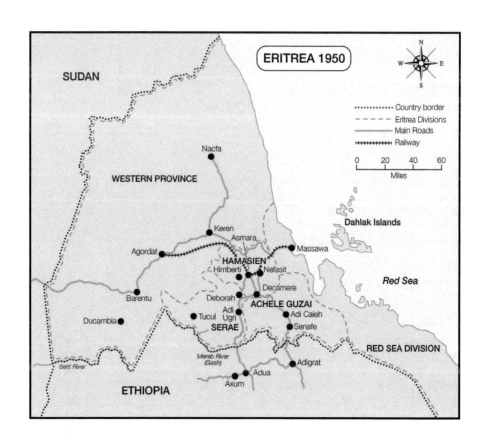

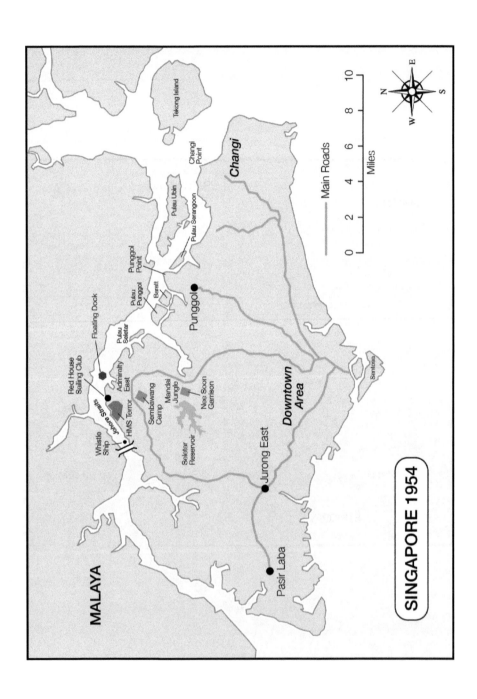

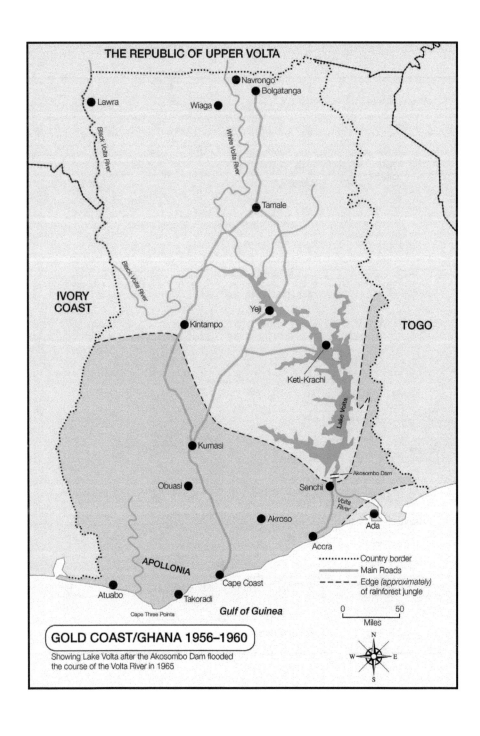

THE REPUBLIC OF UPPER VOLTA

Navrongo

Bolgatanga

Lawra

Wiaga

Black Volta River

White Volta River

Tamale

IVORY COAST

Black Volta River

Yeji

Kintampo

TOGO

Keti-Krachi

Lake Volta

Kumasi

Obuasi

Senchi

Akosombo Dam

Akroso

Ada

Volta River

Accra

APOLLONIA

Cape Coast

Atuabo

Takoradi

Cape Three Points

Gulf of Guinea

············· Country border

Main Roads

– – – – Edge *(approximately)* of rainforest jungle

0   50

Miles

N
W ✦ E
S

GOLD COAST/GHANA 1956–1960

Showing Lake Volta after the Akosombo Dam flooded the course of the Volta River in 1965

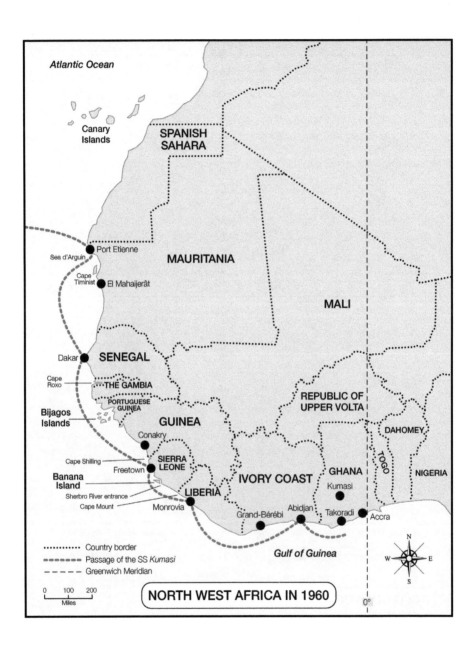

Atlantic Ocean

Canary
Islands

SPANISH
SAHARA

Port Etienne
Sea d'Arguin

MAURITANIA

Cape
Timinist · El Mahaijerât

MALI

Dakar · SENEGAL

Cape
Roxo · THE GAMBIA

PORTUGUESE
GUINEA

Bijagos
Islands

GUINEA

Conakry

REPUBLIC OF
UPPER VOLTA

DAHOMEY

Cape Shilling · SIERRA
Freetown · LEONE

Banana
Island

Sherbro River entrance

Cape Mount · LIBERIA

Monrovia

IVORY COAST · GHANA

Kumasi

TOGO

NIGERIA

Grand-Bérébi · Abidjan · Takoradi
Accra

N
W · E
S

··········· Country border
‑ ‑ ‑ ‑ ‑ ‑ Passage of the SS *Kumasi*
‑ ‑ ‑ ‑ Greenwich Meridian

Gulf of Guinea

0   100   200
Miles

NORTH WEST AFRICA IN 1960

0°

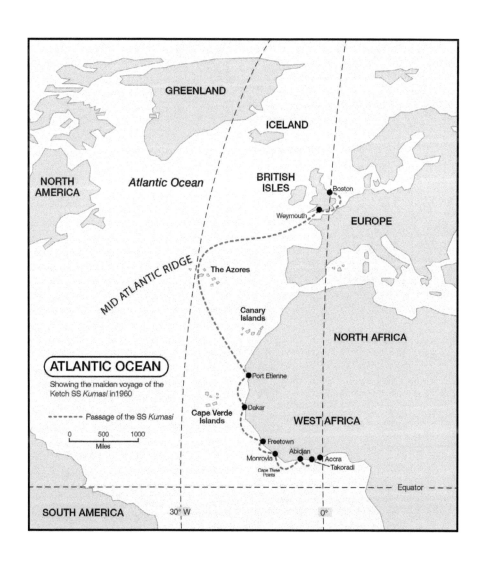

GREENLAND

ICELAND

NORTH
AMERICA

Atlantic Ocean

BRITISH
ISLES

● Boston

Weymouth ●

EUROPE

MID ATLANTIC RIDGE

The Azores

Canary
Islands

NORTH AFRICA

ATLANTIC OCEAN

Showing the maiden voyage of the
Ketch SS *Kumasi* in 1960

- - - - - Passage of the SS *Kumasi*

0   500   1000
       Miles

● Port Etienne

● Dakar

Cape Verde
Islands

WEST AFRICA

● Freetown

Abidjan

Monrovia ●   ● ● Accra
              Takoradi
Cape Three
Points

Equator

SOUTH AMERICA

30° W

0°

PART ONE

October 1945–March 1951

Prologue:

THE PRISONER

The prisoner had not long to live. The fact made him super alert. Every sense was alive. Italian winter, 1943 was bitterly cold. Icy gusts of February wind blew in under the iron door of his makeshift cell (a brick outbuilding in Italian POW Camp PG65 at Gravina). Above his head, a column of cold air funnelled down through the hole made by a brick removed in the wall. Jumping up, he could catch a glimpse of the outside world. Despite his hunger, he had refused to barter his woollen Red Cross vest for a loaf of bread from a visiting Catholic priest.

The floor was not as long as his 6 foot 4 frame. To sleep, he had to lie with his legs bent. A bucket stank at one end of the cell. The melodious singing of the Italian guards came to him on the evening air.

He looked like an Italian himself. Dark brown eyes with thick, black eyelashes gazed calmly out under black, arched eyebrows. Only his skin looked English: clear and pale above dark stubble. His hair, razored by the enemy, was growing again, thick and dark brown.

Yes. He could have been an Italian. But he wasn't. Faded blue wings on the left breast of his tattered tunic meant only one thing: L Detachment, 1st SAS. His captors had recognised the wings after he had leapt from a burning SAS jeep, packed full of explosives, at Benghazi in September 1942 – a third, failed SAS raid attempt. After a manhunt, Italian soldiers had shackled his hands to one foot. They towed him around the town in the back of open truck, while a *Carabinieri* held a loaded pistol to his temple. The prisoner had divulged only his number rank and name: 2655648 Sergeant John Edward Almonds – known in 'L' Detachment, 1st SAS as 'Gentleman Jim'.[1]

An enemy warship had brought him to Italy. A first escape – abandoned when one of the group he was leading got pneumonia after two weeks on the run in the sleeting Italian winter – had led to his solitary confinement.[2] During the breakout, he had overpowered, tied up and gagged an Italian officer, removing the man's teeth in the process. A Court Martial offence under Italian military law. Now, he faced the death sentence.

The thought of execution focused his mind, but not on his past life. He thought only of escape and the future; of his wife and baby son in England; and everything else he wanted to do. In his mind he was planning and memorising a boat. He had built one for David Stirling to return SAS parachute trainees dropped in the desert back across the Great Bitter Lakes to 'L' Detachment's camp at Kabrit.

Almonds had twice gone to sea without knowing where he was going: first from Britain with 8 Guards Commando to the Middle East in early 1941, then on an Italian warship through the Corinth Canal to Taranto.[3] He thought of his recent breakout escape as 'the Italian Picnic'[4]. But now he needed to escape death. If by some miracle he got out of this spot, and if money were no object, one day he would build his own ocean-going yacht and sail it where he wanted to go.

He went back to his mental boat designing – a 32-foot ketch. He loved its lines and the symmetry of its two masts. Each morning, he added to the design in his head and recited it. Hearing it out loud helped him remember it.

Each night, he rehearsed the whole thing, pacing up and down that tiny freezing cell.[5]

Chapter One

MANHUNT

Eritrea, 26 April, 1951. Two o'clock in the morning in desolate rough country, 6000 feet above sea level and 11 miles from the Ethiopian border. Twelve men lay on their stomachs around a camp fire, facing outwards, with their feet towards the glowing embers. Weapons beside them, they watched and waited. After a six-hour forced march and about to mount a raid, they must not sleep now. To stay awake, each man tapped the next on the shoulder, around the circle.[1]

Their leader, Captain Jim Almonds, was thirty-seven. Super fit, with long, strong legs, he had not become heavyset and retained a lean appearance. Despite touches of grey at his temples and tiny lines around the dark eyes, he looked young. The privations of war and a gruelling six-week escape through enemy territory eight years earlier had not marked him – at least, not on the outside. He was a quiet man and spoke sparingly. Taciturn, it was difficult for others to get to the man himself. He did not help them to fathom him. This reserve and ability to retreat inside himself had saved his life when in enemy hands.

Next to him lay Alf Gould, one of the toughest men Almonds had ever known. A genial bruiser, Gould, a 6-footer, was built like an ox, with a broad face and massive jaw. His light brown hair, receding slightly at the temples, framed a habitual wide grin that revealed big, strong teeth. A born fighter and survivor, he could take care of himself. An ex-Palestine policeman, Gould came with a reputation for total fearlessness.[2]

Before first light, Almonds got his men up. They wore bush shorts and shirts and on their shoulders was a leaping green *dik dik*, the insignia of their outfit, the Eritrea Police Field Force – a British armed paramilitary organisation. The Field Force (EPFF) did not carry out police duties, but instead hunted outlaws – the *shifta* bandits of the region.[3] Almonds was after an armed and dangerous *shifta* gang, wanted for murder with bounties on their heads. Earlier that day, he had agreed with Duncan Cumming, Britain's Chief Administrator running Eritrea, to catch the *shifta* and retrieve fifty stolen cattle. He and Gould had tracked the animals almost to the Setit River, which formed the border with Ethiopia.

Almonds could cover 50 miles on foot in twenty-four hours. But the *shifta* could do seventy. The only way to hunt them down was to chase and catch up with them, then mount an early morning raid before they could move off at daybreak. Almonds shouldered his light, semi-automatic .22 Savage rifle. His choice of weapon had been influenced by the lightweight M. 30 Carbine he had carried with 1st SAS in France. Both weapons were American: lightweight, semi-automatic forerunners of what today might be called an assault rifle. Critics say that both lack killing power. The short barrels and small calibre might support such a notion, but success depended on an accurate hit – and Almonds was a marksman. Leaving three soldiers with their mules and provisions, the remaining twelve Field Force men ran the last 10 miles to their target. On open ground, bone hard and rough, each footfall was a potential ankle-breaker. A dull glow of sky to the east was their only light.[4]

They timed it just right. Near the river, in a small settlement, the *shifta* had commandeered a couple of thatched huts and lain up for the night. Almonds could see the round grass roofs outlined against the sky. He had the huts encircled. Dawn came. The adrenalin started pumping. After a spell in Ethiopia training the emperor's army, it felt good to be back in action, to smell cordite and hear the crack of rifles.

Realising they were surrounded, the *shifta* made a run for it. The Field Force shot dead the first one who came through the door. Cleverly, he came out at an oblique angle, running fast and almost making it between two men, one posted opposite the door and one further round to the side of the hut. A Field Force *askari* screamed at him in their common language, Tigrinya, to stop. But the desperate, fleeing man ignored the shouts. He dropped like a stone. The *askari* turned the *shifta* over. He was very young. That was why he had been made to go first. He carried only an antiquated rifle. Almonds (my father) once told me,

'I've never seen the face of any man I've killed'. Therefore, since he saw the dead man's face, I know that he did not shoot him.[5] Five more *shifta* emerged, throwing their arms on the ground in front of them – handguns, a sword and even a spear.

On the way back to the Field Force makeshift fort, another *shifta* tried to escape. An EPFF man shot him through the calf. With the mules, who also carried their own fodder, it was slow going back to Keren, the headquarters of Almonds's command, the Western Province of Eritrea. He shot fresh meat for the party and his soldiers raced for it. Sometimes, one of the NCOs got the men into extended order and they all fired at once to see if they could catch their supper.

They got the prisoners back and handed them over to the civil Eritrean Police. With Almonds went the *shifta* sword. Its blade was of old railway line steel, but it was exquisitely made, with a handle of rhinoceros horn. Dating from before the turn of the last century, the sword pommel was a Maria Theresa silver dollar, while the cross-piece was a crusader's rectangle. An artisan himself, Almonds could not help but admire the design and skill behind its creation. The weapon had probably been passed down through several generations.

Unorthodox, Almonds was an innovative soldier. It was being unorthodox that made him innovative. The Savage had a fifteen-round tube magazine. Since 0.22 is a small calibre round, he used high velocity hollow point (dum dum) bullets to improve its lethality. Otherwise, it would not usually be a 'man stopper'. The army was not allowed to use dum dum ammunition because it contravened the Geneva Convention. But police and law enforcement officers could. Almonds's secondment to the Eritrean Police Field Force justified its use. He was ahead of the trend in using the Savage rather than the standard 0.303 rifle. The Savage round was smaller, so many more could be carried for the same weight. The rifle itself was also lighter and more rounds fitted in a magazine. It was easily adapted to automatic rather than bolt operation use.[6]

Almonds was well armed, but his men lacked munitions and equipment. The Field Force had recently complained to the War Office, 'You may have noticed that we are still, on paper, short of seventy-six NCOs... deficiencies in personal clothing and equipment have been shown at 75 per cent for many months past. The Crown agents have apparently allotted us a very low priority for supply... Urge most strongly that supply be expedited.'[7]

Shifta attacks were vicious. A few days later, twenty *shifta* fired on five unarmed American soldiers at Donnollo Basso on the Asmara to Massawa road. The attackers wore quasi-military uniforms with the Ethiopian national colours on their shoulders. The US had a radio relay station, Radio Marina (later Kagnew Station), a captured Italian facility, on the outskirts of Asmara, at 7,000 feet above sea level. It employed many American servicemen stationed in Eritrea, gathering and beaming information into the Pentagon. Its altitude and position, 15 degrees north of the equator, made it an ideal site for Cold War listening. Almonds knew a few Americans. They said Radio Marina was a telephone exchange, but, like most hilltop listening stations, everybody knew its real role.

One of the severely wounded Americans had two broken legs. The *shifta* burned his motorbike and robbed the other soldiers. The terrorists beat the American soldiers with the flats of their swords.[8] *Shifta* also killed seven villagers at Beni Amer, the home of the shock-headed Beni Amer tribe.

Back in Keren, Almonds received a report that *shifta* had wounded five people and rustled herds of goats and donkeys near Ducambia in the Western Province. He raced to his Auster light aircraft with his dedicated pilot. They took off and headed southwest, towards Ducambia and the Ethiopian border beyond. In the late afternoon sunshine, halfway between the town and the Setit River, the rustled animals threw up a dust cloud over the bare, dry land. The *shifta* were making for the border. But Almonds had one of his platoons deployed not far away. He radioed them with instructions and directions. They just had time, he said, if they 'moved themselves', to head off the *shifta* before they crossed into Ethiopia. The platoon did a forced march and engaged the *shifta*, killing four, wounding six and recovering the stolen animals.[9]

The attack on the Americans could not have come at worse time. Cumming was planning to offer a general amnesty to all *shifta*, even those wanted for murder.[10]

The Foreign Office asked Cumming for more details of the attack. The American Consul-General in Asmara also demanded to be told 'when a person... of this band is taken into custody'.

British discomfort increased. At a press conference on 1 May, the United Nations (UN) Commissioner, a Bolivian called Matienzo, who was in

Eritrea to implement a recent UN Declaration on the Federation of Eritrea with Ethiopia, announced that he must suspend his formal consultations with the Eritrean people. The territory-wide banditry meant that he did not think it right to travel around the country with an armed escort while the inhabitants ran the risk of being killed.[11] This was all very embarrassing for Britain, responsible for keeping order.

On the way back from Ducambia, Almonds flew over several of his outposts, which he had built for his platoons. On naturally defensible high points, with good all-round visibility, he had shown the men how to construct low-walled sangers of stone and wood (like those he had built during the Siege of Tobruk) with outer barbed wire defences. At each fort, he built at least one hut and a flagstaff, from which the Field Force flag – the leaping green dik-dik on a white background – fluttered in the breeze. Almonds had with him several bag drops for his deployed men. They were sometimes away from Keren for weeks, so their mail and rations, plus leaflets about not helping the *shifta* and little bags of sweets for distribution to the local people, were dropped by air.

Almonds shared his Auster, 'the eyes of the army', with another Field Force officer covering the Serae Province. It was an Auster Autocrat 5J1 built in 1946, perfect for light observation reconnaissance, mail delivery, VIP transport – and joyrides. All good *Beau Geste* stuff. His was a dun-coloured, three-seater monoplane, twenty-three feet long, with a maximum speed of 120 miles per hour and a range of 320 miles. When combined with the rapid use of fresh intelligence it gave him the edge on the *shifta*. Flying was a bit nerve-racking whenever they crossed a length of saw-toothed mountains, knowing that an engine failure meant curtains. Where possible, they followed *wadis* to have a good chance of a forced landing. The Auster's wide undercarriage meant it could land on rough terrain. Its high wings made it easier to see the ground, while a fairly low stalling speed allowed for short landing strips and enough power to get them out of trouble.

After dropping mail and rations to each Field Force outpost, Almonds circled, ready to approach again to pick up reports, messages and mail to take back to Keren. The pick-up system had been quite well developed during the war using Dakotas in Burma, but the EPFF had adapted it for their own purposes. The Auster flew in again, low. Two long poles on the riverbanks across a dried-up ravine had a rope stretched between them, decorated with bunting to make it visible. The rope had a bag tied to it. As the Auster swooped, a hook beneath the aircraft caught the whole string and retrieved it. They had to be strict about the weight. On one occasion, a well-meaning young officer, who had bagged some guinea fowl, put one in the bag tied to the rope for Almonds to take back to the mess for dinner. It nearly pulled the Auster out of the sky.[12]

Catching *shifta* was not going to solve large-scale Eritrean unrest. Cumming wanted a general amnesty for all *shifta*, regardless of their crimes (an existing one excluded murderers, but had not worked.) He did not like it and could not guarantee its success. But it was the only chance of bringing the disorder under control. No more than twenty-five *shifta* leaders were expected to give themselves up. But if they did, their gangs would probably do the same. The EPFF could then concentrate on 'hunting down' those who remained in the field. Otherwise, the Administration faced either the continued embarrassment of a British-administered territory unable to maintain law and order or the expense of a large increase in British security forces and a major military operation to do it.[13]

Shifta outrages continued. In the Western Province, Almonds and a Field Force platoon went after a thirty-strong gang. Almonds and Gould tracked all day, arriving in the target area with the *shifta*, they hoped, just ahead of them. Almonds settled down to lay an ambush in a *wadi*. Just after last light, the large *shifta* force came up the middle of the *wadi*.

Gould, in the lead this time, was heavily outnumbered. He knew he needed to put them to flight early on. He was carrying a Verey flare pistol. He lay down in the *wadi* unseen as the group came towards him. Waiting until the last possible moment, he fired the Verey at one of the *shifta* at close range. It hit the man in the stomach. Because of the time delay, it exploded inside him, lighting him up like a candle. For a moment, he was a walking, screaming firework as flames spurted from his body. He died quickly. The others, totally unnerved, turned tail and ran. Gould and his men pursued the gang and shot seven dead.[14] In the darkness, lit only by flashes of gunfire, ten wounded *shifta* fled, abandoning their arms.

Two days later, thirty *shifta*, under a young leader called Tecle Asfaha, held up the Keren cattle train and stole 100 cattle. Asfaha, of Corranacudo, was wanted for murder and had a price of £20 (the equivalent of £400 Sterling in 2016) on his head. In his mid-twenties, Asfah had a high forehead with a shock of hair, stubbly side whiskers and a thin moustache. Three weeks earlier, the Field Force had killed his brother, Grazmac Ilfai Asfah, with a price of £35 on his head (the equivalent of just over £700 in 2016). Tecle Asfaha had taken over as gang leader. He got clean away.

Nine Coptic *shifta* also held up the Asmara to Keren steam train and stole food from the passengers. When Almonds got there, the *shifta* had placed large boulders across the track, rifled the train and scattered all the passengers' belongings along the bank. The son of a District Chief in the Western Province then turned *shifta* (this was not unsual: some Eritrean politicians had previous *shifta* careers). Unidentified *shifta* also raided a Kunama village near Barentu, wounding two villagers and stealing 100 head of cattle. The one saving grace at the end of these calamities was that the UN Commissioner supported a general amnesty.[15]

Almonds sometimes spent the whole day flying around in the Auster. Then it was joyride time. His pilot tended to cut it a bit fine clearing things. When empty, they would dive down and fly along river valleys, following their courses to the sea. Once, after visiting some platoons, they headed southeast towards a 10,000-feet mountain, Emba Soira, in the Eritrean highlands, not far from the Red Sea. The pilot wanted to see if he could fly over it. Each time he flew round the mountain, he got about a foot higher (the ceiling of the Auster was 14,000 feet). Finally, he skimmed over the top. Below lay nothing but jagged mountains. It was with some relief that Almonds regained his quarters in Keren.[16]

Almonds mounted another raid. Gould knew of a *shifta* band in their patch. With a few fit men, they did a high-speed forced march. After tracking the *shifta* and gaining on them, the Field Force located the gang. Gould did not mess about. He went ahead, still tracking them. At last light, the *shifta* stopped. Gould stopped. He waited until he saw their firelight. He did not risk taking his men with him. Alone, he took a Bren gun and some hand grenades. Keeping very low and downwind, he crawled towards them. When very close, he lobbed a couple of grenades, then Bren-gunned the survivors.[17] It was kill or be killed where the *shifta* were concerned.

Extramural activities were equally dangerous. Where the Setit River went over a waterfall, was a large pool where a crocodile lived. Almonds had often seen it sunbathing on the bank. He and Gould tried to tempt the creature out. It didn't rise to the human bait. But boys will be boys, so they tossed in a hand grenade. Still nothing came to the surface. They lived off the land, cooking an 'all in' stew at the end of the day. Just after dark, Gould put a hare in a pot over their fire.

'What are these crispy things?' said Almonds, as they munched.

'Onions,' Gould replied.

In the morning, the pan was covered in winged flying ants.

The lower Awash valley abounded with wildlife: wild African ass, oryx, gazelle and zebra. Alone on foot, Almonds followed the river downstream. Gradually, the bank on one side became higher than on the other and ceased to have exposed rocks. On the low rocky side, dead crocodiles had been shot and lay drying in the sun. Around the back of them crawled their live kindred.

Almonds noticed the glittering eyes of the crocodiles, brilliant and sharp. The Nile crocodile is the most dangerous. And so quick that he knew they could get him before he could get them. But he tried. Mud had settled between crevices in the rocks. He lay in a channel, perpendicular to the river. Flat out, he crawled along it until he was in a good position. But then, abruptly, the crocodiles shot off into the water: a great slithering mass, their claws rasping on the rock before they plunged into the river. On land, at least, perhaps they felt that Almonds had the advantage.

Shifta attacks increased. The EPFF engaged a *shifta* gang on 18 and 19 May, led by Hamid Idris Awati, the most notorious *shifta* leader, with a bounty of £300 on his head. Almonds caught them red-handed rustling cattle from the Beni Amer. Awati lost, with five Kunama *shifta* killed and three wounded. In Hamasien, rural police arrested Coptic *shifta* in possession of hand-grenades and ammunition. Thirty unknown *shifta* attacked the Embatkalla police station, but were driven off without casualties on either side. At Adi Caieh, nine of a gang led by Ali Schum surrendered to the SDO. Four Coptic peasants then turned *shifta*. A few days later, more Coptic *shifta* attacked two Italian concessions (land with a Government licence) in the Dorfu Valley and stole livestock. In the Serae, forty-eight Coptic *shifta* raided another concession and stole two water pumps. But the Field Force engaged six *shifta*, capturing one and wounding the leader, who escaped. The *shifta* were raiding with impunity.

Sometimes, the *shifta* fought each other. In the Western Province, on 20 May, Hadendowa *shifta* killed two Beni Amer *shifta* and stole 500 cattle, 640 goats, eight sheep and some money. Unknown *shifta* also attacked two local employees of an Italian-owned goldmine near Ducambia. They looted the mine, killed one man and wounded another. But a police patrol engaged seven Muslim *shifta* and captured two without suffering any casualties. On

23 May, twenty-three *shifta* held up a steam passenger train from Massawa at Mai Altal in the Red Sea Division. Five Coptic *shifta* attacked a native-driven truck near Adi Quala in the Serae, but a police patrol drove them off. Police then shot dead a minor *shifta* leader attempting to escape from the central police station.[18]

On 26 May 1951, Almonds wrote home to say that he was now a (military) Superintendent of Police in the EPFF:

'I dislike police forces intensely but this one has its compensations as it is almost military. I have just finished a period of active warfare against the *shifta* in the Western Province and had quite good results in the various engagements. We have killed quite a few of them, with personal losses of five wounded only, which is better than anyone else has done to date.

I have now been pulled back into Asmara, against my will in charge of 'A' Company and the Depot, presumably to see if I am any good at Administration. This is quite against the grain as far as I am concerned but I am far too old and experienced now to worry over things of this nature so I just carry on. I am very fit and tanned dark brown through long hours out in the hot sun of the Red Sea lowlands, which now come under my command and am quite contented. In my spare time I am building myself a car and a canoe for a trip to explore the Jikawo[19], the Setit and Atbarah rivers from Ethiopia next month, through Eritrea and the Sudan to Khartoum, which should be a good trip.[20]

He had not been pulled back to do administration – perish the thought – but to use his experience to help other provinces to get the same successful results in tackling the *shifta*.

At the SAS disbandment parade in November 1945, he had thought he would never see active service again.

Chapter Two

ESCAPING THE ORDINARY

In 1945, Colonel Paddy Mayne[1] had striven to keep the SAS in existence.[2] In the latter stages of the war, he even deployed 1st SAS at the Battle of the Bulge in the Ardennes. Albert Youngman, 1st SAS, remembered the bitter cold: Mayne had them all kitted out in navy blue uniforms. It was the only warm kit available, though not the best camouflage in the snowy woods.[3]

Almonds was deployed on SAS operations in Belgium, Holland and Norway. The SAS made a triumphant entry into Bergen in flower-laden jeeps. Almonds, a captain, was driven by another 'L' Detachment original, Bob Bennett. In a contemporary photograph, all their SAS comrades look euphoric, while Almonds retains his usual calm gaze.[4] I asked him what the fracas known as 'the battle for Bergen' was all about. 'It was all about women,' came the surprising reply. The local Norwegian girls were attracted to the SAS men. Bergen's men attempted to fight for their own and a punch-up ensued.

While rounding up stray Nazis in Norway, a chance came in May 1945 for the SAS to help hasten the end of the war. Sven Heden, the great Swedish explorer, geographer and photographer, had written about getting through 'the back route' into Japan. Mayne was interested. So Almonds got hold of the books and talked to Mike Sadler (Stirling's fabled wartime navigator) about the possibility of attacking the Japanese in a surprise rear action. With a new set of jeeps, the SAS could travel down through Asia to Lake Lop Nor,[5] known as the 'Wandering Lake' because the Tarim River feeding the lake kept changing its course.[6]

Almonds jumped at the chance. The route was a long, straight run, littered with bodies and skulls, which ended at Mastagata. But while plans were in the making, the US dropped atom bombs on Hiroshima and Nagasaki, rendering an SAS operation unnecessary. On 6 August 1945, Almonds's 31st birthday, he heard the Hiroshima announcement as he was sitting down at a reception in the *Mairie* at Nancray-sur-Rimarde held in honour of 1st SAS's wartime exploits there.[7]

Other options for adventure also arose. The post-war land grab left Antarctica the only remaining unappropriated continent. The Americans flew over the South Pole, dropping leaflets in an attempt to claim it. But this did not assert ownership rights. Getting a man to the Pole on land was more difficult than parachuting one in from a B-29 Super-fortress, who could then walk out, SAS-style. David Stirling, fresh from his time 'in the bag' at Colditz POW camp, thought the idea a goer. At the SAS base at Chelmsford, he and Almonds drew up some plans for 'boys dropping by parachute'. Stirling asked Almonds and Sadler if they were up for it. They were certainly were.

However, even Stirling and Mayne could not keep the Regiment in existence. It was disbanded in November. Then came a final adventure proposition so extraordinary that it was only ever known as 'the thing'. A mysterious American intelligence officer, possibly of the OSS, the forerunner of the CIA, wrote several times to Almonds and then visited him. The officer wanted Almonds to mount a private, SAS-style operation to recover Nazi gold bullion. But in a post-war context, this seemed like a raid too far.

Almonds returned to England in September 1945. After their wartime separation, he owed it to his wife Lockie (my mother) to settle down. And he felt a sense of loyalty to the Bristol Police.[8] He resigned his Commission. Until his demobilisation, he was posted to Bristol to assist the County Welfare Officer at 2 Beaufort Road, Clifton. He left the army (for the second time) on 20 January 1946, medical category 'A1'. The now family of five (my sister Gloria and I had arrived as surprise twins in May) bought a house in Bristol for £700 (this was after house prices had shot up at the end of the war).

Back in the police, Almonds's collar number was '112', followed by 'A', the divisional prefix for 'A' Division of the Bristol Constabulary. From time immemorial, the division had been centred on the Central Police Station at Nelson Street, commonly referred to as 'the Bridewell'. Helmet plates (badges) and closed-neck collars carried each officer's divisional number and letter. Sergeants referred to the officers by their number, but not the letter:

'Late on parade 43' or 'Dirty boots 112!'

Almonds worked from Trinity Road Police Station near Lawford's Gate, St Jude's. Foot-beats operated from there, which included those to St Werburgh's and York Street, where Almonds had first seen Lockie at '3 beat on the 4th Section'.[9]

Always attracted to water, Almonds tried, but failed, to get into the River Police. According to Ernie Miller, a later senior Bristol police officer and ex-Grenadier Guards, my father probably experienced discrimination. Wartime decorated returnees were resented, even if, like Almonds, they did not hail from Bristol. Police who had been in reserved occupations, said things like,

'You don't know what it was like here in the blitz!' The culture and discipline were Dickensian, rather than that of the Guards, apart from an emphasis on turnout.[10] Almonds did not notice any discrimination. But after the wartime SAS, he did find being a bobby on the beat rather dull. To lighten the tedium, he resorted to the 'shoe box affair'. Armouries were sometimes broken into, so the police had to be on their guard. The IRA also posed a threat. The sergeant in charge of Almonds kept saying, 'Don't forget the IRA!' And just as Almonds and a colleague were setting off on their beat, the sergeant added, 'And suspicious parcels, as well'. So Almonds put a loudly ticking alarm clock into a shoe box and placed it outside the Bristol City Police Headquarters. Twenty-four hours later, it was still there ticking away.[11]

The transition was too great. Almonds found his bosses incredibly nit-picking. He sometimes arrived a few minutes late and one morning his inspector gave him a great rocketing. A few weeks later, after a sleepless night with twin babies, he overslept. Lockie awoke to the sound of small stones being thrown at their bedroom window. Looking out, she saw a police car and two policemen. By this time, Almonds had already had three dressings-down. His inspector, chief inspector and chief superintendent had all had their turn. So that morning he went to work with a letter of resignation already written out. This time, he went to see 'Maby', the chief constable. Almonds listened to the tirade for a while and thought, Really, I can't see my face fitting here…, so he said, 'I'll save you the trouble. You're obviously enjoying this, but I'm not. I'll bring my uniform in a box tomorrow.'

'Now, there's no need to be extreme,' said Maby. But with that, Almonds left.

'You've done what?' said Lockie.

Undeterred, Almonds went off to the recruiting office. His mind flashed back to the Lincoln Recruiting Office in 1932. This time, the recruiting officer said,

'Fine. But you won't get your rank back.' Wrong. Within three months, Almonds was back up to captain. He repainted the Bristol house, built a garage beside it and sold it at a profit. His escape from ordinary life was complete.

Almonds had been commissioned into the wartime Army Air Corps, but he had little in common with aviators. The Gloucesters Regiment were in barracks at Horfield not far away. [12] It was a worthy regiment, the old 28th being the only English regiment the Duke of Wellington mentioned by name in his Waterloo Dispatch.[13] When Almonds joined them, the 'Glorious Glosters' had more battle honours on its colours than any other British Army regiment.[14] They immediately posted him to Eaton Hall Officer Cadet Training Unit. On 11 April 1946, he was TOS as an instructor and the MTO, replacing another Gloucesters officer. No army quarter was available so he moved his family to his Lincolnshire home at Stixwould. During the terrible winter of 1947, Almonds commuted or was on leave.

Neither the weather nor the coming and going prevented him from building. From a garage in Lincoln, he bought a war surplus left-hand drive jeep, with very few miles on the clock. He converted it to right hand-drive, extended the chassis and added a supercharger, an oil cooler, big headlights and a fishtail silencer that burnt your hand if you touched it. This hot-rod, called the 'Silver Bullet', was made of aluminium on a wooden frame and had no moving doors, just sills to climb over. He worked on it in the garden, during the worst winter in living memory, wearing his white army PE vest and looking like Bruce Willis in *Die Hard*.[15]

At last, in March 1947, an army 'hiring' became available at Malpas, into which we moved. In this large, old English country house, I mounted my own first 'escape'. In an empty, carpeted room, where my sister Gloria and I played with a few toys, I disappeared up a disused chimney, placing my feet on tiny brick steps either side of the flue. Lockie, at first mystified by my disappearance enlisted help to get me down.

Six months later, a quarter at Eaton Hall finally became available at Poulton. Our house, two joined Nissen huts, was half-cylindrical with corrugated steel roofs, which curved down to the ground as walls. Previously an army dental centre, the signs were still on the doors and John had the stump of a dentist's chair under his bed.

The CO at Eaton Hall, Colonel Darling, was nicknamed 'Crafty Clara'.[16] One day, he came into one of Almonds's lectures on vehicle maintenance. The officer cadets sat in rows at small desks, while Almonds stood in front of them talking. Without saying a word, Crafty Clara came round behind Almonds and lifted his hands out of his pockets. The CO then stood still and silent, at the side of the lecture room, rocking on his heels and putting his tongue on the outside of his upper teeth, so that he was making a grimace. Almonds ignored him and carried on instructing. The man who had saved men and vehicles in the Western Desert by cannibalising spare parts knew how to get his message across.

At Eaton Hall, Almonds met up again with Pat Riley from his 'L' Detachment days. Both found the Glosters not that welcoming to former SAS. Riley went to Belize for two years, even though he wanted to stay with the man he had called 'one of my best pals'.

As David Stirling had said, Almonds could be deadly when necessary. He took the officer cadets to Okehampton, Dartmoor on exercise. One evening, they went to a local dance. Some Irish navvies were spending their wage packets with drunken fervour. Suddenly, fighting erupted on the dance floor between the navvies and the cadets. Almonds immediately strode into the centre, put one hand up, policeman-style, as if directing traffic, and shouted,

'Stop!'

'Says who?' said a big Irishman, before taking a swing at Almonds. He ducked, then landed a huge punch on the navvy, who went down like a sack of potatoes.

'Cadets!' said my father. 'Back to camp!' Turning to the navvies, he said, 'You lot – out!' Then, gesturing towards the horizontal labourer, 'And take this thing with you'.[17]

Our childhood toys were never ordinary. Almonds made my brother John a land yacht. The front wheels were a pair of old pram wheels, while the back pair were of wood, onto which Almonds nailed strips of rubber hose to act as tyres. We took it onto the nearby disused aerodrome, where it went like the wind. My sister lay face down on the front, watching the runway flash past beneath her, while John sat on the back and used what little steering there was to control the schooner. She ran very fast before the wind. There were no brakes to speak of.

Later on, my father made Gloria and me scooters – huge, heavy things. We could be heard thundering along on them from miles away. Lockie was sublimely happy. She had a beautiful singing voice and, like a wartime bird released from its cage, she sang most of the time. I was only three, but I remember that soaring voice as she washed up at the kitchen sink.

Almonds had no formal engineering training, having left school at fourteen. But he was a sound mechanical engineer and continued to mess about with cars. The Silver Bullet was more like a battleship than a car. He raced it in a Welsh hill climb event with the number 63 on the front and my brother hidden below the dashboard in the passenger seat (no seat belts). In June, he entered it in some races near Chester, again with John on board but out of sight. When he parked it outside the officers' mess, Crafty Clara appeared. He said that the car must be parked behind the mess because it was 'not a vehicle suitable for an officer'. When Lockie had had enough of being blown about in the Silver Bullet, Almonds converted it again into a shooting brake. It became our family car. He also bought an old Bugatti and modified it, shaping a fitment inside to hold the weight of a Ford V-8 engine. He didn't race it, but spent many hours roaring around the old airfield. In due course, he sold both of these cars. The Bugatti went to a brother officer, who did race it.

In May 1948, Almonds went home to Lincolnshire for his father's funeral. Richek ('Ricky') Kopyt, of the Polish Army 2nd Armoured Division, was engaged to Almonds's sister, Gwen. Kopyt saw a tall, straight-looking uniformed army officer wearing three pips and an SAS beret walking up the road to Stixwould from Horsington. The Pole had been an officer cadet, but when the Second World War had broken out he had abandoned his training to join up. The two men had a lot in common.[18]

After one golden year of being together as a family, in April, Almonds was posted to Abyssinia to serve in the British Military Mission to Ethiopia (BMME).[19] He thought this would be for about three years and accompanied. But by the time he embarked a month later, permission for accompanied postings had been rescinded so his family could not go. After the wartime three-year separation, this was a bitter blow to my parents. In some haste, they bought a house in Horfield, Bristol. On 8 April 1949, Almonds was SOS Eaton Hall awaiting travel via Massawa, Eritrea, to Ethiopia.

Lockie wrote to her mother-in-law:

'… the actual parting we do not mention… it will be awfully hard for us both. I've never seen Jack [my father's family name] hate going away so much before; but I keep cheering him up with the idea that he must make a success of his new post and I must keep the flag flying here with the children until that wonderful day when he'll come back to us.'[20]

It would be more three years before we lived together as a family again.

Chapter Three

ETHIOPIA AND THE BRITISH MILITARY MISSION

O n 15 May 1949, Almonds sailed to Massawa, Eritrea on the *Empire Ken* troopship (formerly the *Ubena Ken*). Unlike his wartime embarkation in January 1941 with 'Layforce', Almonds knew his destination so did not keep a diary.[1] But there was another reason. When life was fresh, straight and honest, the 'knight in armour' wrote diaries. Then, the crusading went out of him. The aftermath of war in Britain had brought disillusionment and even depression at the economic and social injustice he saw.

During the voyage, another officer gave Almonds a copy of *Rudyard Kipling's Verse Definitive Edition* and it became a favourite companion. Another young subaltern had just returned from China. He addressed himself to Almonds, saying that he was full of life, wanted to be a good soldier and do well, including winning plenty of medals. Almonds said that he was not the best person to give advice. Despite having received a Military Medal (then the 'other ranks' equivalent of the Military Cross) and Bar and the French *Croix de Guerre*, he had never set out to win medals, just to do his duty and get back home. But he *was* up for action. If he had to be away, he wanted adventure and to avoid an ordinary job. So he had volunteered for the Guards Commando and accepted David Stirling's invitation to be one of the first men in the SAS. He was the only founder to keep a diary.

Five weeks later, Almonds disembarked at Massawa, Eritrea on the Red Sea coast. In 1941, following the final surrender of the Italians in the mountains near Keren, Britain had been left holding the former Italian colony of Eritrea. Britain ruled it as an Overseas Enemy Territory Administration – known as 'Old Etonians Travelling Africa'. Initially, ten British Army officers and nine Sudanese policemen had run the whole civil administration. Despite some nervousness, Italian civil servants had continued to do their jobs. The new British Administration, with an eye to the pragmatic (low cost) option, let them. They did remove the Royalist *Carabinieri* and the exceptionally fascist *Polizia Africana*.[2] They were replaced by one brand-new police force.[3] However, the Italian Penal Code remained in force. It was easier to use that than to attempt to replace it with a British equivalent.

The future of Eritrea caused intense speculation. The whole world had an interest. The matter had been submitted to the United Nations. Backroom horse-trading was rife. Italy wanted Eritrea (and Somalia) back. The *Ethiopian Herald* published an article about an alleged Italian attempt to barter Ethiopian support in return for 'a particular settlement in Cyrenaica'. The Foreign Office dismissed it:

'The Ethiopian Government have been made very jumpy by rumours… that the Italians have not given up hope of obtaining Eritrea with the support of the Western Powers.'[4]

Almonds took the steam train to the capital, Asmara, 70 miles away. The locomotive engine dated from the 1920s. The Italians had built a very good railway in the late 1890s. It was a feat of structural engineering. The train twisted its way upward, round precipitous mountainside bends towards Asmara, passing through rock-hewn tunnels and over myriad bridges. Halfway there, they stopped briefly at Ghinda. Almonds could see clear to the horizon, past citrus groves and slopes dotted by white houses. The people seemed industrious, digging into the hillsides and moving large rocks to make best use of the available land.

On arrival in Asmara, a stunning art deco city, Almonds took charge of five trucks of armaments and some soldiers, bound for Addis Ababa. Two of the vehicles, full of old Enfield rifles, had yet to arrive. HQ Addis Ababa feared that the rifles might go missing. On no account were they to fall into the hands of the *shifta*. Banditry had been customary in Eritrea and Ethiopia since time immemorial; due to the mountainous and inaccessible country, it was extremely difficult to combat.

While waiting for the trucks, Almonds headed off on foot for the hills. On the high plateau, he was at 7,000 feet. Another thousand feet higher afforded magnificent views all the way east towards the Red Sea and south to the mountains at the Ethiopian border. Fruit and vegetables grew on the upland: a strange mixture of the common and exotic: potatoes, barley and corn alongside cotton, oilseed and coffee. Cattle herds mingled with sheep and goats.

The trucks arrived and Almonds ascertained that each had a box marked as containing 1000 rifles. Travelling via Dessie in Ethiopia, the armed convoy took seven days to reach Addis, staying in Italian rest houses and transit cafés. At night, double sentries kept guard, the soldiers taking turns to catch up on their sleep in the vehicle cabs during the day.[5]

The British Army also had other ways of protecting its property. Stuart Perry, a young subaltern destined for the SAS but commanding an Armoured Car Squadron in the Reserved Areas of Ethiopia and Somaliland, modified his vehicles with an arrangement that gave anyone who touched the metal hull an electric shock. It was simple (the instructions came from East Africa Command in Nairobi) and involved splicing an additional HT (high tension) lead from the existing harness and running that feed through to the outside of the vehicle body. The lead had a six to nine-inch chain attached, which led to the ground. The HT system had enough power to create an electrical field around the vehicle – wet conditions were ideal. Anyone touching it received a shock. It was not life-threatening, but certainly off-putting. The system saved an awful lot of 'aggro'.[6]

Arriving in Addis, Almonds was struck by the pleasant climate: fine, like an English summer day, but with a crispness in the air. He was at 7,600 feet. The sun shone out of a blue sky with small, fluffy white clouds. He got out of the leading truck and crossed the road to an unprepossessing military building with square, yellow-framed windows and a corrugated iron roof. All was quiet. The Guard Room had an air of lassitude. *Not a good sign for a guardroom*, Almonds thought. After some chat with the duty sergeant, the arsenal of arms and ammunition was unloaded, checked, signed for and placed in the BMME Armoury.

He booked into the officers' mess, a grand abode. The BMME was down to thirty-six officers and twenty-six other ranks – more chiefs than Indians. It had begun in 1941 with forty officers and eighty ORs. In the mess, Almonds met Major Harry Hawkes, also new to Ethiopia. He greeted Almonds warmly and was soon joking about life in the BMME. Their job was to train the emperor's army, while a Swedish Mission trained the Imperial Guard. Hailie Selassie preferred bilateral support relationships.

The BMME originated from regiments of Orde Wingate's successful Gideon Force guerrillas, composed of British, Sudanese and Ethiopian soldiers who had defeated Italian occupying forces with the blessing of the emperor.[7] The mission had done a good job in the Tigrai province of northern Ethiopia during autumn 1943. Units of the Imperial Army and British irregular forces had fought alongside each other successfully during active operations.[8] Two BMME officers had been killed. So there had been a common purpose and bond. In 1947, an anonymous local pamphlet, entitled *Background of Ethiopia Today* had even claimed that the BMME had had a positive influence on general progress in the country.

> 'Whatever the future may hold… there stands before the Emperor 'the whole machinery of mischief in good working order'. That this mischief has been restrained is an achievement not to be underestimated. The part played by Britain and the Emperor in maintaining not only order but in starting the machinery of progress should be counted as a notable achievement.'[9]

Britain wanted Ethiopia to have an adequate military force, so that in the event of 'rebellions and border terrorism', British Middle East forces would not be called upon. The British Army would assist the emperor to organise and train his own army. The C-in-C ME, General Wavell, had recommended Brigadier SS Butler, CB, CMG, DSO, as head of the mission with the rank of major-general.[10] But in May 1947, after a BMME WE review, Britain's War Office said it could not justify further support. The Foreign Office protested: BMME officers and NCOs in Ethiopian frontier units reduced border incidents with other territories under British control. Without the Mission, the UK would have to consider increasing the garrisons on the frontiers of the Sudan, Eritrea, the Somalias and Kenya. Army chiefs responded that powerful political arguments for the mission's retention were no reason why British Army funds should foot the bill.[11]

The year before Almonds arrived, it was clear that a new treaty to be negotiated with Ethiopia would not cover the BMME. So would the Ethiopians pay for it? The British Envoy Extraordinary and Minister

Plenipotentiary at the Legation in Addis Ababa, Daniel William Lascelles[12] doubted it. Ethiopian rulers, he said, had long had an all-absorbing interest in the acquisition of arms and a bad record as regards the treatment of foreign advisors. The mission had failed (in Ethiopian eyes) as a supplier of arms. Nor were Ethiopians interested in other people's ideas about military training and efficiency, 'being at once too self-satisfied and too stupid to appreciate them'. Lascelles did not accept non-essential invitations.

'I'm the minister', he was known to say. 'I'm not here to socialise.'[13]

The British Legation had recently been raised to embassy status. Lascelles, now ambassador, aged forty-eight, of medium height with brown hair and eyes, was the grandson of Henry Lascelles, 4th Earl of Harewood. Educated first at the Royal Naval College, Osborne, Isle of Wight and the Royal Naval College, Dartmouth, Lascelles had not distinguished himself in the St Vincent Gunroom. He kept so low a profile that hardly a trace of him remains.[14] He excelled at *nothing* – his name was not even in the punishment book.[15] So he changed direction, went up to Balliol College Oxford and joined the Diplomatic Service.[16] He was certainly no slouch, presenting his credentials to the emperor in fluent Amharic and writing an English-Amharic grammar and dictionary. But there was another side to him. He would scatter sweets just outside the gates of the legation for the local children. They came to expect it and hung around the gates in anticipation.[17]

The threat of Communism was another BMME funding factor. Standards of living in Ethiopia were very low and economic conditions poor – it was a fertile breeding ground for Marxism. If the British Army pulled out, Czechoslovakia might send a mission there and supply arms. Stable conditions in Ethiopia were also vital until Britain could 'get rid' of its former Italian colonies in the Horn of Africa. The BMME, therefore, still had valuable strategic influence. Britain hoped to extend the mission for five years, with a clause that it could be withdrawn with three months' notice.[18]

The result was cuts. The CIGS ordered the BMME be reduced to just enough resource for it to carry out its five tasks: '(i) to advise on the administration of the Ethiopian Army and to ensure that it got its pay and allowances; (ii) to supervise army training; (iii) to assist in equipping the army; (iv) to supervise the maintenance of army transport; and (v) to ensure that the army could give prompt aid to the civil power when called upon.'[19]

It didn't work. The understanding (the British thought they had) was that the emperor would be bound by British advice in all important matters touching his Government. And he would raise forces and undertake military operations only as agreed by the British Representative on the advice of the Military Mission. In return, the BMME would help establish the Ethiopian Government and army and maintain roads and railways to the extent necessary for these purposes. These proposed fetters on a recently restored emperor were unrealistic. Hailie Selassie was not going to let his people perceive him as being bossed about by the British, especially in military matters. Ethiopian upper-class status did not rely on hereditary aristocracy. It depended on military rank. Their titles of *Ras, Dejazamach, Fitauran, Qenyazamach,* and *Gerazmach* were also military.[20]

Almonds's first job was to play bridge. A leaving party for the head of the BMME was being held at Holetta, the site of the Imperial Military College (the equivalent of Britain's Royal Military Academy Sandhurst and Staff College rolled into one). The party was one person short for 'an important' game of bridge and Almonds was the only other officer who could play. A truck picked him up and drove him to Holetta, about twenty miles northwest of Addis. The camp was laid out on British military lines. White single-story buildings bounded a parade ground with a flag staff.

The officers' mess was an old Ethiopian palace: a square, brick building with imposing front double steps leading up to a spacious balcony with a grand balustrade and drooping magenta bougainvillea. At ground level, curved arches opened into a cool area underneath. Eucalyptus and banana trees grew in the gardens. Holetta was still preparing to receive its first intake of Ethiopian officer cadets. Nonetheless, it was a Staff College in the middle of its working day. British officers, who should have been busy, were playing cards. Almonds dutifully played some good rubbers of bridge, but felt embarrassed at having to collude with this bad behaviour.[21]

At the BMME RHQ, things were no better. Almonds found morale low and a chronic lack of kit and equipment for the soldiers. Off-duty officers (who were actually *on* duty) played cards. Others were absent, playing tennis or riding. Nobody was motivated because they had no clear vision. It was that most soul-destroying of situations, especially for an army, of being forced to fail. Quite often, someone would say, 'To hell with this, let's go and have a drink.' British NCOs who trained Ethiopian soldiers had an easier time of it. Ethiopian officers, it seemed, needed neither training nor advice.

The Ethiopian Army did go on manoeuvres. A 1951 booklet entitled *Britain's Aid to Ethiopia* – optimistically numbered edition Number 1 – shows the BMME in a positive light. Ethiopia was laying 'the foundations of a modern fighting force, comprising Infantry, Artillery, Signals, Engineers and Field works, Ordnance and Service Corps'. A British NCO in tropical dress and a plumed bush hat instructed cadets in white shirts, khaki shorts and white side hats. They cluster round a rifle mounted on a tripod. Other cadets lie on the ground, holding (presumably unloaded) rifles pointing at another British NCO standing in front of them. Training was 'carried out on the lines of the British Army', but, the booklet stated, 'British Officers take strictly the role of advisers'. Ethiopia had a developing Armoured Car Regiment (the vehicles had metal turrets with eye slits) and an Artillery Battery, with captured Italian artillery pieces pulled by mules.[22] But there was only so much time a British officer could spend visiting these activities when he wasn't commanding and his advice wasn't needed.

Emperor Hailie Selassie was back on the throne. But the country was still war-torn and backward. Ethiopia was, nonetheless, unique in Africa. First, it had never been colonised, though it had been invaded by Italy during the Second World War.[23] Second, unlike any other African country, it had got its Christianity direct, rather than from missionaries – and centuries before Europe. Isolated by its high plateau and its faith, Ethiopia remained a Christian country surrounded by pagan African cultures for centuries. Almonds found the people quite different from the North Africans he had known during the war. Ethiopians showed no deference to Europeans (why would they?), but were friendly, efficient and hardworking. Almonds hardly ever saw a fat one. They were tall and slim, with aquiline noses and high cheekbones.

The emperor did things in style. He kept young lions at his palace, as befitting the 'Lion of Judah', a title that recognised Ethiopian emperors' lineage to Solomon and the Queen of Sheba. The palace, made of large blocks of unevenly squared stones and surrounded by gardens and a fountain pool, had a red, corrugated roof and a central balcony jutting out over the main entrance steps. Two carved lions of Judah formed part of the overhead stonework framing the emperor's coat of arms. Either side of the main steps, two covered ways formed by touching arched bougainvillea hedges offered shady alternative entrances. The side windows had brown louvered windows and to the left, another set of graciously wide stone steps led up onto another porch.[24]

In the late afternoons, Almonds saw Hailie Selassie being driven around the capital. Addis had a veneer of modernity. The roads were metalled, but petered out into mud at their edges. Tall palm trees were interspersed among low-growing clumps of squat date palms. Vehicles skidded to a halt to let the emperor's car through. Barefoot Ethiopians in breeches and white cheesecloth *shammas*[25] prostrated themselves to the ground. When at prayer, Hailie Selassie also prostrated himself publicly. Was his faith genuine? Wilfred Thesiger, who was born in the legation and knew the emperor, certainly thought so.[26]

The BMME nicknamed the emperor 'Highly Delighted', because reports said he was pleased with them. In reality, he was just pleased they were there. And perhaps he had some fondness for Britain. During the Italian occupation, he had stayed for a while at the Branksome Towers Hotel in Poole, before spending several years with his family in Bath. However, it is doubtful that he forgave Britain for recognising Italy's annexation of Ethiopia in 1935.[27]

At public appearances, the emperor sat on a portable throne. He stepped out of his car onto a carpet. When he sat down, an embroidered pillow was placed under his feet. This grandeur and facade of civilisation clashed incongruously with other aspects of life in Addis. The country still had public executions and corporal punishment. The Ethiopians made a display of hangings. To his great distaste, Almonds had to witness one. The victim was made very drunk and brought on the back of a truck. The executioners put a noose around his neck and drove the truck away. On Fridays, one would sometimes drive past a body hanging from a gibbet as it twisted and turned in the wind (we still hanged criminals in Britain, of course, but we didn't do it in public.) In market places, criminals were tied down and beaten to death with crocodile hide whips. [28]

In November, Almonds was posted to the headquarters of the 2nd Division of the Ethiopian Army at Dessie, some 300 miles north east of Addis Ababa towards Eritrea. He was to be second-in-command to Major Dudley Apthorp, Royal Norfolk Regiment. Their task was to reform 2 Division and socialise with Emperor Hailie Selassie's second son, the Duke of Harar. Almonds's predecessor was a captain in 'some Midlands regiment'. He wasn't a good communicator so two British officers from Addis went to see him. Finding the said officer staggering about wearing only his shirt, 'as drunk as a newt', they brought him back to Addis Ababa.

The Ethiopians certainly knew how to throw a party.[29] Before Almonds's predecessor left the country, a senior Ethiopian official called Ata Bilai gave a leaving party for him, to which Almonds was also invited. Bilai, a huge, jovial man, was a lavish host. The centrepiece of the supper (a raw meat feast) was a cow carried in on a pole. The midlands officer wandered in, wearing some sort of nightdress. After ambling around good-naturedly for a while, he blessed the house of their host. He blessed the food and blessed the table and then fell under it. He was carried out and put to bed upstairs. The next day, he was loaded onto a plane bound for the UK.

Bilai seated Almonds on his right and offered him a large piece of meat, thick and raw. He, of course, could not refuse. A man sitting on his other side showed him how to bite the meat and then slice a chewable piece off upwards past his nose. Almonds thought he wouldn't be able to eat it, but he did and found it excellent.[30]

The food was terrific. *Injera*, a sort of sourdough pancake made from *tef* flour, was served with meat and vegetable stews called *wat*. It was permissible to wipe the plate so nothing was wasted. They drank *tedj*, which was yellow like a juice. Bilai said they made it in an oil drum by encouraging bees to nest in baskets inserted into hollowed-out trees. The beekeepers collected the baskets at night, dropped them into the drum, along with some gesho leaves, covered them with a cloth and left them to ferment. *Tedj* was collected from the first and subsequent takings, while the final taking (handled with great secrecy) was the primer for the next batch. That night, at the party, they drank a next-to-last taking, which looked clear and harmless but could knock your teeth out. Almonds did not remember going home that night. Ata Bilai threw another equally good party for some of the British soldiers. They simply weren't up to it and asked Almonds,

'How on earth do you cope with all this?'[31]

As soon as he could, Almonds and his driver, Private Tebede Teferi, left Addis for Dessie. The roads were appalling. Surfaces were rapidly crumbling away; sections of road on the edges of precipices had fallen into the valleys below. The truck jolted up and down abominably all the way to Debra Berhan, where undulating grazing land stretched for miles. Early next morning, they climbed up to the Mussolini Pass. Through a tunnel at 10,000 feet, they emerged to find a stupendous view down to the plain at 3,000 feet. Gazing across the expanse, Almonds saw villages on hillsides. Vegetation covered the mountains right up to their summits. Dropping down to the

Great Rift Valley, full of acacia, grasslands and thick creepers, they drove along it for about 100 miles, before making a steep climb up again to Dessie. It was only about 4 miles as the crow flies, but the twisting, winding road and hairpin bends made it 15 miles.

Dessie, the capital of Wollo region, looked rather dingy, spread out along the valley with high mountains on either side. Through misty fog, the damage done by the Italians during the war was still clearly visible. Strewn along either side of the road lay smashed, upside down vehicles and gun carriages with two sets of wheels that turned in any direction. The BMME Officers' Mess turned out to be a bungalow on a hillside, surrounded by eucalyptus trees. Just below the mess, destroyed Italian vehicles covered a flat green area the size of two football pitches. They had clearly been bombed. Almonds was met by Challa, the Ethiopian soldier who would look after him. The other officer there, Dudley Apthorp had his own man, but they shared a cook. [32]

Every morning in Dessie, the two British Army officers, smartly turned out in full uniform, canes under their arms, went down to the military lines of the Ethiopian Army. They knocked at the first door of the Ethiopian officers' houses – rows of *tukuls*: round, thick-walled, grass-roofed buildings that were very cool inside. When the first door was opened by the freshly got up Ethiopian, Apthorp would say,

'Good morning Ata (whatever the man's name was). 'May we help you with anything today?'[33] Apthorp was tall and slim, with a keen, finely boned face and light, sand-coloured hair. He wore the uniform of the Royal Norfolk Regiment. Almonds wore the collar dogs and cap badges of the 'Glorious Glosters'. Usually, the Ethiopian officers said they did not need any help and always refused any unsolicited advice. They would not even say what their plans were for the day. At the time, accepting advice was seen as weakness in Ethiopian culture. But Apthorp and Almonds were courteous men and would linger, chatting and exchanging pleasantries, so as to smooth over any sense of any rebuff having been given or received.

The men they were trying to advise were the officers (said to be the best). Almonds was concerned that these leaders of the Ethiopian Army were unable to learn anything. And all the time they stood there, their conversation was punctuated by the screams of some poor bastard being flogged in the courtyard just behind them. The unfortunate man lay face down on the ground, while three other soldiers held the ends of ropes tied to his hands and feet, and a fourth stood just in front of his head and thrashed his back with a huge stick.[34] Almonds imagined it was the sort of punishment that would have been regarded as normal in the British Army some 150 years earlier. But the floggings were probably a soft option. At 10,000 feet, Dessie was above the tree line and there was nowhere convenient from which to hang anybody.[35]

After completing their tour of the lines, Apthorp usually rode for the rest of the morning. Almonds would make his way towards their small office. With the altitude, it was cool and Almonds often went down the mountain to get logs for the hearth and to heat water for their baths. One morning, he met a young Ethiopian officer staggering up the road wearing a leather flying hat, with flaps dangling in true Biggles fashion. In response to Almonds's greeting, the Ethiopian replied, 'I'm a pilot now. I fly planes.' He got Almonds into conversation and said 'And I'd also like to be able to…' Then he stopped and asked if he could sit in the driving seat of Almonds's jeep.

'Can I just try it and see if I can drive it a bit?' he said, as if driving were some innate natural gift. Almonds was not keen, but in the interests of good relations, he demurred.

'I shall be with you,' he said, adding half under his breath. 'I'm not sure that you know very much about driving.' They went off together at great speed and Almonds had to remove the ignition key.[36]

Almonds was aware of the *shifta* bandits across the border in Eritrea. In December 1949, following a spate of serious attacks, Whitehall decided to send military reinforcement to Eritrea.[37] This would take time; so something else had to be done in the meantime to prevent the *shifta* problem getting even worse. Bounty hunting was the answer. The Eritreans did not allow the *shifta* to push them around, especially when tribal issues were at stake. On New Year's Eve, Berhe Mosasghi, a notorious *shifta* leader with a price of £200 on his head, and eight of his gang attacked the village of Adi Quitta (about 500 people), including the house of a prominent Sheik, near the Asmara to Adi Caieh road. They cut the one phone line and told the villagers that they had come to kill the DC (District Chief), an old personal enemy of the Mosasghis. But the DC was away. Fifteen armed village tribesmen opened fire on the *shifta*, who threw two grenades, one of which a villager picked up and threw back. The second bomb exploded, seriously wounding one tribesman and seven others.'[38]

As the new decade of the 1950s began, the world did not envy the lot of the British trying to keep order in Eritrea. On 6 January 1950, an American newspaper piece entitled *The British Tommy in the Middle Again* compared the Eritrean situation to that of British troops in Palestine. Caught in the crossfire of bitterness between Jews and Arabs, the British were targets for both sides. The Italians wanted Eritrea back under a trusteeship. The Ethiopians claimed that Eritrea belonged to them. Moreover, they thought they deserved it as payment for the unwarranted 1935 Italian invasion. It was difficult for the British to quell disorders without being accused of taking sides.

'That is the situation that the home-loving British Tommy is called upon to face once again', said the article, 'and nobody can envy him the job.'[39] Thus, Britain faced a slow war in Eritrea with its Administration being systematically undermined by both Ethiopia and Italy. Meanwhile, the UN Commission was expected to arrive in Asmara by mid-January. Something had to be done to control the *shifta*.

Wild West outlaw hunting was the answer. On 7 January 1950, the Commissioner of Police and Prisons for Eritrea, T W Fitzpatrick, published a large, petrol blue, public Police Notice in Asmara in English, Italian and Amharic script. This 'Wanted' poster listed fifty-one *shifta*, together with rewards that would be paid 'for information leading to their arrest or to the person producing their bodies, *dead or alive*.' [My italics][40] The awards varied from £300 for Hamid Idris Awati (about £6,000 in 2016), down to Chelete Gheresghir with £20 (£400) on his head.[41] All were wanted for murder. In parallel, Fitzpatrick announced a partial amnesty for other *shifta*: a free pardon provided they had not been involved in murder or action against the forces of the Administration. All they had to do was surrender themselves and their arms to the nearest police post and disclose their association with the *shifta* bands. Helping *shifta* was also punishable under the law.

The Foreign Office sniffed.

'These measures have given rise to some criticism from Miss Pankhurst's paper (Sylvia Pankhurst of the Suffrage Movement was Editor of the *New Times and Ethiopia News: The paper for all interested in international justice*) that we are reverting to Fascist practices by subsidising the murder of natives by Europeans. I imagine they are fully backed by legislation?'[42] The bit about 'bodies, dead or alive', they said, was 'objectionable and unnecessary'. The officials were, of course, sitting in Whitehall – not in Asmara dealing with the *shifta*.[43]

Neither measure worked. On 11 January, two Eritreans on bicycles threw a Mills[44] bomb into a bar in Asmara. A third Eritrean, standing near the bar, opened fire with a pistol. A few days later, *shifta* threw two unexploded Mills bombs into the house of Brigadier Grenville Drew, Eritrea's Chief Administrator. In Asmara, a middle-aged Italian woman was shot twice and died on the way to hospital. The police then mistook as *shifta* and shot a police constable in plain clothes who had turned out with a gun. A night curfew was imposed, except for British and US troops in uniform, police on duty and those with permits. The UN Commission duly arrived. Unhelpfully, on 24 January, bomb incidents were reported at the political Unionist Party HQ, at Adi Ugri, halfway between Asmara and the Ethiopian frontier on the 'Coptic' plateau.[45]

Murder was self-avowed. A group calling themselves 'Eritrean Patriots' wrote to Peter Freeman, MP at Britain's House of Commons (care of Miss Pankhurst). The Patriots said that although Italy had renounced claims to Eritrea at the end of the war, employer members of the Italian *Blocco di Indepenza*[46] would not employ anyone not belonging to it. This meant unemployment, misery and crime.

'We do not desire the return of Italy...' they claimed. 'It is our fervent desire to be incorporated within our Motherland, Ethiopia. Italians in Eritrea suspect that Ethiopia directs Eritrean *shifta* to murder Italians but that is untrue. *The idea came from our own mind.*' [My italics] [47] On 7 February, six *shifta* ambushed a military jeep, wounded one British officer and got away with 300 cattle. Fifty *shifta* attacked two Italian farm workers, killing one, escorted by four armed constables on a concession[48] between Asmara and Adi Ugri. The *shifta* were after arms and it was probably easier to get them by attacking Italians.

In Dessie, Almonds built, with Apthorp's help, a large double garage and workshop. Together, they renovated a Humber four-by-four car, putting a Range Rover type body onto its one-ton Humber chassis. The two British officers played cards and tennis, swam, went shooting, read books and talked. It was hardly a punishment posting. But they were isolated. For the rest of his time in Ethiopia, Almonds knew only Apthorp. But he did not mind. They had much in common, not least the war and having been POWs. The only danger was the demon drink. Officers without interests became prey to it.

From outside their house-cum-mess, it was a two or three hour walk, around the mountain, to the summit. Almonds did it regularly and would come down scree-running. On the other side of the road, beside the Ciao Hotel, a track lead into Dessie. The British had repaired the bombed Addis road with filled steel oil drums in tiers. The road was never flat; it turned perpetually up, down and from side to side. Almonds always imagined himself chariot racing along that murderous road. At one narrow point, the only ground under the vehicle was the width of his jeep and he could look down on clouds on either side. Ahead lay 50 miles of twists and loops. He got out frequently to move boulders out of the way.

Almonds admired the Ethiopian soldiers. He introduced them to the good old British Army assault course, with poles, cross bars and ropes to climb on. Being extremely fit and athletic, they scrambled across in half the time it would have taken the average British soldier. They were also tough, going to war with just handfuls of maize, barley, chickpeas, sunflower seeds and dried meat in their pockets. But they were there one day and gone the next, so planning their training was complicated. Almonds also had responsibility for anti-terrorism. But that was difficult, too, as some of the emperor's own generals had been subverted. The tricky part was working out which ones.

Almonds tried his soldiers at river crossing. They were terrific athletes. Over a dried-up riverbed, too wide to jump but not very deep, he set up a pole with a rope for them to swing across, Tarzan-style. The first soldier came up, gave a cursory glance at the riverbed and a disdainful look at the rope and walked away. Almonds was wondering what was going on when, to his astonishment, the man turned, ran forward and jumped the expanse completely unaided. The world had yet to witness Ethiopia's outstanding middle and long-distance runners.[49]

Ethiopia is vast; five times the size of the UK but, at the time, had one of the poorest road networks in the world. Almonds explored this overwhelmingly beautiful land of extremes: dry and barren country intersected by lush river valleys, majestic mountains, leaps, waterfalls and endless rolling countryside. He also hunted. Wearing a bandolier and carrying water but no rations, he supported himself out in the wild. He brought back game for the mess: wild pig, waterbuck and bustards. He was a dead shot with his Savage rifle. He could shoot a running hare in the half-light and kill it outright. He also carried his Colt 45 pistol against big animals at close quarters, a USMC Camillus fighting knife issued to the SAS while behind enemy lines in wartime France and a Commando Sykes-Fairbairn fighting knife. He made a fishing rod from a copper vehicle antenna.

The Great Rift Valley teemed with unique wildlife. In the Ethiopian highlands, he stalked, but did not kill, the unique gelada baboon, the highest living baboon on earth. In the same area, he stalked red and white furred Ethiopian foxes, with long, thin skulls, which lived only on mole rats. He encountered strange alpine plants, at which he could only marvel. The skies and valleys were home to the black-bellied bustard, the Ethiopian snipe, the secretary bird and innumerable waterfowl and wading birds. Still a Lincolnshire country boy at heart, he revelled in exploring miles of country alone with its wildlife: bush pigs, hogs, wild ostrich, hartebeest, gazelles, kudu, zebra, dik-dik and the mountain reedbuck.[50] In the extreme north of the Danakil Depression, in the bad land desert area spanning the border with Eritrea, he investigated Erta Ale, a continuously active volcano with the world's only molten lake in its crater. The rock-hewn churches of Lalibella awed him. He imagined the years of work it had taken to create the hand-carved basilicas.

Hunting was not without risk. As he sat fishing alone at the Borchenna River, a troop of olive baboons suddenly attacked. They charged straight at him. Scrambling to his feet and turning to face them, Almonds had to shoot one after another with his Savage rifle. Fortunately, they broke and loped away before the magazine ran out. Being a tube magazine, he had to refill it, not just change it. Had the weapon not re-cocked automatically, he would have been dead. One day while fishing up on the high plateau, his rifle just out of reach, a black-maned mountain lion padded into view a couple of yards away. Almonds sat stock still. Man and animal locked eyes. After a long moment, the big cat dropped its gaze, swung away and moved off. When interviewing him, I asked if he was not afraid. He was. But by sheer force of will, he refused to allow his instinct to reach for the rifle to override what his brain was telling him – like all cats, the lion would pounce on anything that moved suddenly. It would have been on him before he could get to his weapon. [51]

As foreseen, the Duke of Harar, Prince Mekonnen Haile Selassie, the second son of the emperor, invited Almonds and Apthorp to tea. The two British officers, wearing their Sam Browne belts, called on the prince at the appointed hour. He lived in a large house in Harar, within driving distance from Dessie. The duke was not very forthcoming. Almonds got the impression that he had been told to issue the invitation. He did not look very athletic. He and his aide wore British Army style service dress uniform. Servants served the tea and remained hovering in the background. Apthorp made small talk. During long silences, the duke seemed ill at ease. At the first indication by the British officers that they would take their leave, Mekonnen Haile Selassie was all too ready to let them go.

Almonds did try to socialise with Ethiopian officers. Not all of them had uniforms. Being in and out of the Ethiopian Army was a casual business. It was necessary to get used to this odd (to British eyes) peculiarity. Almonds took one young lieutenant who had a uniform (but no duties) into the Asmara Officers Club. Conversations died. Everyone frowned. Nobody spoke to them. They stood at the bar and had a drink. Despite the cold-shouldering, the Ethiopian, who spoke good English, was delighted. They went shooting together. [52]

Occasionally, the Ethiopians did seek advice. They asked Almonds to go and look at a bushfire 'that would not stop burning'. After two or three days' bumping up and down hills in his jeep, a large group of excited villagers met him. He was armed and felt the need to keep his eye on them all. The chief came to talk to him, leading a tethered sheep. The villagers watched their guest closely to see what he would do. Almonds gave the animal a pat, thereby sealing its fate. It was taken away and a man reappeared with its liver on a stick. They then went to a blazing mountainside; huge flames and black smoke whirled up into the air. On closer inspection, it was a coal seam. The villagers thought it a potent omen: 'The rock that burns!' But Almonds reassured them that it was just natural fuel that somebody's fire had ignited by accident.

Despite the acrimony about BMME withdrawal, the usual diplomatic and social niceties continued. Lascelles held cocktail parties at the British Embassy: a typical Palladian-style building on land that Ethiopia had given to Britain, with pillars, corridors, huge rooms and ceilings that went way up.[53] At polo matches, Emperor Hailie Selassie presented the winners with their cups. At gymkhanas, he presented rosettes – handed to him by Dudley Apthorp.

But while Addis fiddled, the British Empire was burning.

PART TWO

April 1951–December 1952

Chapter Four

RISE OF THE *SHIFTA* BANDITS

May 1950. British fears about Communism crystalised. The Ethiopians wanted to buy twenty Czech tanks at around $US 627,000 (equivalent to $US 6,160,000 in 2016).[1] The BMME advised against it. The Ethiopian Army lacked the technical skills to maintain such armour. It really needed such unassuming items as ammunition, uniforms and trucks. The Foreign Office noted, 'The Ethiopian Army must be a fantastic affair: it does not seem worthwhile keeping the BMME there to train it".[2] Direct Soviet influence was also growing. A report filched from the Soviet Legation revealed that this Communist sway was, 'controlled by the Soviet Legation, staffed by a variety of rascals, both black and white, charged with the task of fomenting trouble in outlying territories, including in particular British and Italian Somaliland.'[3]

September. The situation was critical. The BMME, not a priority for the UK, was costing around £100,000 a year (equivalent to £2,044,000 in 2016). Whitehall cut it by one third. By some alchemy this saved 50 per cent of the budget.[4] Lascelles suggested the BMME be withdrawn. To avoid the risk of the Ethiopians publicly asking for withdrawal, the War Office wanted to pre-empt. 'Since we have left Italian Somaliland and are shortly to leave Eritrea, there seems little military advantage in retaining a Mission in Ethiopia.'[5]

Sure enough, in October, the BMME spotted signs of Ethiopian Government intentions of withdrawal. General Dothée (an Ethiopian) went to Belgium on a secret mission on behalf of the emperor. He then accompanied the Ethiopian Minister for War on a tour of Ogaden – notwithstanding that a similar tour had been made a few weeks before by General Turnbull, the BMME commander. (He and the Minister for War had originally been scheduled to make the Ogaden tour together.) In the towns, rumours of imminent BMME withdrawal were rife. One local trader even approached a Royal Army Service Corps officer to ask for British Army supply in future. Almonds heard that the Glosters 1st Battalion was on its way to Korea. They were setting up some sort of SAS-style unit. He felt a pang; he could have fitted right in.[6]

General Dothée proposed a new 4th Division of the Ethiopian Army. This idea cut right across the reorganisation of the army recommended by the BMME. The clash resulted in a general deterioration in relations and respect shown by Ethiopian officers to their British counterparts. The advice of the Mission, even on the rare occasions it was sought, was ignored. All this was very damaging to British prestige. The War Office urged General Turnbull to threaten withdrawal unless there was a rapid and marked improvement in the attitude of Ethiopian Army Officers.[7]

Meanwhile, the *shifta* caused disruption in unimaginable ways. On 19 October, Sir Frederick Pearce, Chief Secretary in Asmara (and second-in-command to the Chief Administrator), reported to Lascelles a 'somewhat embarrassing and unfortunate incident'. The senior administrative officer for the Akele Guzai province, Peacock, had visited Makalle on 12 October. On return, he submitted a report, a copy of which he sent with a covering letter to Martin, SDO (Senior Divisional Officer) for Serae. A special 'Banda' took it by bus via Adi Ugri. *Shifta* then held up the bus. Usually when *shifta* stole mail, the letters were found torn open all over the surrounding countryside. But this letter was missing. It mentioned Peacock's impressions of the difficult Ethiopian personalities he had met and was couched in rather undiplomatic, language. It would certainly give offence to the personalities concerned if it ever came to their knowledge. Lascelles was furious.[8]

The *shifta* became even more militant. A well-known gang operating between Obel and Tucul in Serae province engaged twenty members of the nascent Eritrea Police Field Force[9] led by a Lieutenant Chambers, 'a young man with a blond beard, who would have fitted into a Victorian exploratory expedition without causing comment'.[10] After two hours, the *shifta* surrendered.[11] In a politically motivated murder, twenty *shifta* opened fire on Ghido Railway Station, killing the Italian Station Master and ticket collector. Italy immediately demanded the presence in Eritrea of a UN Observer and UN police forces.[12]

The *shifta* also increased their strengths. An EPFF platoon, escorting SDO Martin, engaged a *shifta* force estimated at about 150 strong led by Asserassie Embae, with a price of £100 (just over £2,000 in 2016) on his head, at Adi Laghan. The fight lasted until dusk, when the *shifta* leader withdrew. He had a trumpeter whom he used to call up reinforcements. Martin had run out of ammunition, but, courageously, went on foot to parley with Embae – such was the power of this particular *shifta* gang. The Eritrean EPFF men had only just left training school and lacked their full scale of equipment and clothing. Moreover, as a subsequent report made clear,

'Had the platoon been in possession of a wireless set, they would have been able to summon to their assistance men of the 1st Royal Berkshire Regiment who were in the vicinity.' Despite the eventual truce, the Field Force lost two men, with two wounded, but they killed eight *shifta* and wounded four.[13] On 6 November, *shifta* threw two hand grenades at the house of Dedjatch Abraha Tesemma, advisor to the British Administration on Eritrean Affairs.[14]

The fighting also got personal. Twice in November, in the Serae Division, EPFF platoons commanded by British officers went into action against *shifta* estimated at about 120 strong. Embae paid Lieutenant Chambers the compliment of sending him a message that he would make every effort to ensure his death. Chambers returned the compliment and this second action resulted in *shifta* casualties and damage to Embae's prestige. He withdrew rapidly to the Tigrai carrying his wounded.[15]

In Ethiopia, it was showdown time. On 7 November, General Robertson, C-in-C, HQ MELF,[16] HM Ambassador Lascelles, the fluent Amharic speaker, and the head of the BMME, Major-General Turnbull, went to see His Imperial Majesty. A local British coffee merchant, Geoffrey Wetherall, used to meet Turnbull playing cricket and found him amiable, doing what he liked doing, but was unsure of his attitude to Ethiopians.[17] BMME officers thought Turnbull a 'bit of a screwball'. Almonds had the distinct impression that locals disliked Turnbull.

At the meeting, Robertson was first off the mark, telling the emperor that his army was short of mechanical and animal transport. Ethiopia might well have budgetary constraints, but these military needs were fundamental. He then set out the economic reasons for the BMME's withdrawal. The emperor accepted the arguments, but hinted at the possibility of a fresh agreement. He had, after all, lent a contingent from his own army to Britain for the war in Korea. The BMME should continue, although (as translated from the Amharic in which the emperor spoke) Hailie Selassie also hinted that British officers did not appreciate that they were advisors, not military commanders.[18] He seemed upset about the possible impact that an announcement about withdrawal might have on discussions at Lake Success (the talks taking place in Canada in connection with UN Resolution 390A concerning the future of Eritrea). Above all, Ethiopia needed a port, preferably Massawa to the north, if not, Assab at the southern end of the barren Danakil coast. So nothing should jeopardise the talks.

Robertson stuck to his guns, pointing out that the Ethiopian Minister of War had remained absent throughout his visit, despite constant promises to return. British officers had been placed in an undignified and thankless position. The condition of the Ethiopian Army had to be seen to be believed. Through corruption, inefficiency and parsimony, it was starved of everything, including food. The emperor, Robertson implied, was perhaps focusing too much on Lake Success.[19]

In Eritrea, politically motivated personal vendettas increased. On 12 November, twenty-seven Coptic *shifta* entered Mahado and cut off the ears of eight Muslims. In response, four days later, a gang of fifteen *shifta* under Techeste Haile entered Embei village, about 20 kilometres from the Asmara to Decamere road. They cut off a hand and a foot of a Coptic villager. Two days later, *shifta* fired on a jeepload of three EPFF officers and two constables from Keren, about 35 kilometres from Asmara. A police patrol from Asmara then attacked the *shifta* and shot dead their leader, Zaggai Hadgu. He had murdered two Italians near the Adi Nefas goldmine on 2 May.[20]

At Lake Success, on 2 December 1950, the United Nations General Assembly adopted a resolution that Eritrea should 'constitute an autonomous unit federated with Ethiopia under the sovereignty of the Ethiopian Crown'.[21] It prescribed an Eritrean Representative Assembly, with an expectation of Federation by September 1952. This compromise between the two extremes of complete union with Ethiopia and total Eritrean independence pleased nobody.[22] Italy did not want Ethiopia to have any control over Eritrea. From that moment, *shifta* violence increased, polarising along religious and political lines. And catching the ethnic and religious *shifta* who carried it out got harder.

The fates of Ethiopia and Eritrea were now entwined. Robertson wrote in blunt terms, to the CIGS. 'The Foreign Office have a tender spot in their heart for this country and its Emperor. I have none.' The emperor was not the great pioneer of freedom and social advance that he was said to be. He was only in effective control of a small part of his country and he governed that part very inefficiently and despotically. In his dealings with foreigners, he was 'sly and self-seeking'. If Eritrea was added to his dominion, Robertson prophesied that Eritrea and Tigre would one day 'form together a powerful, dissident mass and either overthrow the emperor or secede from him.' Strong words indeed from a serving British General.

He went on that in Eritrea, Brigadier Drew had improved relations between the civilian administration and his troops. But, Robertson emphasised, 'the important thing today is to get the so-called Field Force built up rapidly so that it can assume responsibility for anti-*shifta* operations. The provision of British officers for the Field Force continues to cause difficulty. This is a pity. It is a splendid job for a young fellow and one which would give him an element of experience and make him much more valuable to his regiment when he returns to it.'[23] The War Office was doing its best to provide British officers for the Field Force. But because of the danger, they all had to be *volunteers*.[24]

The Eritrean Commissioner of Police thought that *shifta* activity was being coordinated from across the border with Ethiopia.[25] Drew agreed. The Nebrid of Axum, a senior cleric of the Ethiopian Orthodox Church, paid and harboured *shifta* gangs in Tigrai. The men of Asserassie Embaie's gang, wounded in the recent action with the Field Force, were believed to be in Adowa Hospital. The Governor of Adowa stated categorically that there were no *shifta* there, but would not allow Martin and his wife – a doctor with a legitimate professional interest – to visit and see for themselves. This refusal suggested something to hide.

Martin ascertained that the Governor took his orders from the Nebrid and that Amaré Embaie, brother of the wounded Asserassie, was wandering around town in Adowa. The Abuna Marcos, another religious figure, had asked the Governor for help against the *shifta*. But he, too, got the impression that the Governor was succouring them. 'His Majesty Haile Selassie should be induced to deal with the arch mischief-makers of the Nebrid,' said the Abuna.[26] Lascelles also believed that *shifta* were using Ethiopian territory as 'a tom tiddler's ground'.[27] What Lascelles craved was positive, cast-iron proof of the Nebrid's misconduct that he could cast in the teeth of the central authorities. But that was more than he was ever likely to get.[28]

In Dessie, Almonds was aware of increased *shifta* activity. If there wasn't a real job to do in the BMME, there certainly was on the other side of the border. As part of his expeditions and getting stores for his Ethiopians from Asmara, he 'wandered about a bit' in Eritrea. The *shifta* varied their tactics and deployed methods of sabotage, of which Almonds would have been proud during his wartime SAS days, such as blowing up tracks and derailing French trains. On 22 November, *shifta* successfully derailed the Littorina train from Keren to Asmara at kilometre 71 by removing a rail – the first time they had tampered with a permanent way. They then attacked the train with grenades and rifle fire, but were beaten off by the Field Force escort and six men of the 1st Royal Berkshire Regiment. The *shifta* had cut the telephone wires, so as to isolate their points of attack.

On 10 December, an Eritrean constable absconded from Embatkalla police station with sixteen .303 rifles and 1,280 rounds, which he handed out to accomplices. The next day, fifteen Muslim *shifta* shot up a goods train, travelling from Massawa to Asmara, about 2 kilometres from Mai Atal on the Asmara side. They wounded the fireman, but did not succeed in stealing the American stores and equipment on board. However, three Americans riding shotgun were relieved of their carbines and sixty rounds.[29] So much for US military superiority.

Towards Christmas, Apthorp went on leave and Almonds was alone in the mess. He heard that a young RAF pilot officer, Leonard Dickson, would be booking in. Dickson, of No 8 Squadron at Royal Air Force Khormaksar, had left Aden to play in a polo match in Addis Ababa with the Ethiopians. The British team had their pick of some excellent polo ponies, but the Ethiopians were very much better players, despite not playing textbook polo. As one British wag said,

'They've just swapped their swords for polo sticks and hitting a ball instead of lopping off people's heads'. One Ethiopian rider, Ras Makonnen Tedessa, ADC to the emperor, was huge, weighing 18 stone on a massive horse (not polo pony). Haile Selassi presented the cups, including one to Dickson.

Dickson had some leave, so when the polo team left, he stayed on. An Aden contact had arranged a truck for him up to Dessie. The BMME booked him a room in their Dessie Officers' Mess.[30] Dickson felt like the greenest of airmen, never having heard a shot fired in anger, while he knew that his host was an experienced wartime soldier. But Almonds welcomed him warmly.

When Dickson had settled in, Almonds drove him up to a high vantage point, Bora's Leap, to view the immense drop into the valley below. During the war, the Italians had thrown Ethiopians from this height to their deaths. Later, Almonds and Dickson went in the Land Rover with one of the Desert Locust Survey team, Ken Scott, to see hordes of duck at Lake Haik. They returned to an impromptu drinking party until 1am. Next morning, Almonds had them up at 4am. With Scott and Dickson in the Land Rover and Almonds with his driver in the jeep, all with 0.22 rifles, they left Dessie by bitterly cold moonlight. At daybreak, they shot guinea fowl before going on to the Borchenna River, which was fed from a hot spring. It was full of huge catfish. Baboon were also all around them and Almonds warned Dickson that the animals sometimes pelted perceived invaders with small rocks.

Almonds was first to cast a line, warning others to hold onto him if he shouted. At first, Dickson did not understand, but within a few seconds, Almonds was bellowing to grab him as he was dragged rapidly towards the river. Eventually, three of them heaved out an extremely ugly monster of about 40 pounds. Their presence soon attracted locals, carrying immensely long spears. Almonds spoke to them and, since the catch was more than enough for the planned Christmas party, gave the rest to the local men. Threading the huge fish through the mouth and gills onto their spears, they disappeared into the undergrowth.

Moving along the dusty road, the hunters came to a vast plain. In the distance, Almonds spotted a white-headed eagle high in an acacia tree. Scott wondered if he could hit it and took a pot shot. To their amazement, it fluttered down with a broken wing. Since it could not survive, they had no option but to kill it. Rather sobered, they drove on to a wild savannah area, where Almonds took his .303. He wanted to shoot wild pig while they were still out of the thickets, where they lay in the heat all day. Even after a long wait, they saw only one tusker. Almonds fired but missed. It would have been very difficult to get it back to the mess.[31]

Ten days before Christmas the *shifta* gained the upper hand. They ambushed an EPFF platoon near Maadi Grundi, killed one Eritrean sergeant and three police constables, wounded another and captured one Sten gun and three rifles. On 16 December, a British police officer reported the area to be 'infested' with Coptic *shifta*, led by Ethiopians. The chief of Lij was telling villagers not to resist the *shifta* since the UN had 'awarded the area to Ethiopia'. On 18 December, Asmara's report to the War Office began, 'Herewith our tale of woe over the weekend: seven *shifta* incidents, six of which are favourable to the *shifta*.'[32] The *shifta* were winning.

As the Christmas holiday approached, Whitehall confirmed the BMME withdrawal date as 1 March 1951. The Ethiopians asked for an extension of the deadline and that the 'most valuable service now being rendered by the Mission at the Staff school in Holetta should not be lost'. GHQ MELF swiftly poured cold water on that idea.[33] Lascelles sent the final letter of refusal to His Excellency Ato Saude Gabre-Heywot, Ethiopian Vice-Minister for Foreign Affairs.[34]

On 23 December, Almonds and Dickson found a suitable Christmas tree from lower down the valley, brought it back to the mess and put up some decorations. Most of the few Europeans in Dessie came to their party: a family of Greek bankers called Moriatis; Willie Merson, the manager of the local *Besse & Co* outlet; an ex-Canadian Air Force pilot and his American wife (Dana and Vernon Mullins), who ran the local school; Pierre, a Swiss road engineer, whose thankless task was to try and keep 250 miles of the Dessie to Assab road open; and a man who founded *The Daily Herald* and became a naturalised American.

On Christmas Eve, in several vehicles, Almonds and Dickson drove with others, including two former Nazi SS officers, fifty miles along the (really bad) Gondar road. After a picnic at the pretty Kus-Kus River and a swim, they returned to the Mess. On Christmas Day, Almonds presented Dickson with a beautiful Ethiopian fly whisk made from the tail of a colobus monkey.[35] They all set out again for Batie Market, 50 miles to the east. Taking the road to Assay, past the lone telegraph post used occasionally for public hangings, they dropped over 4,000 feet from the escarpment until they came to Batie. Here, a huge market was used by the famed and feared Danakil nomads. They brought salt from the desert below to trade for items made by the Galla people from the top of the plateau. The hilltop above the market had a gallows, used frequently.

Later, when they were all having a drink, one of the ex-SS officers mentioned that he was employed using his medical skills. He asked Dickson if there was any chance of getting hold of some antibiotics. Dickson couldn't help him. The conversation then drifted to the SS doctor's wartime medical work and he said,

'We did some operations with patients trying to exchange their blood with transfusions.'

'Wasn't that dangerous?' someone said. 'What happened to them?' Back came the very open answer, 'Well, they died.'[36]

On 28 December, Dickson needed to get back to Aden. At 6am, Almonds took him in the jeep towards Assab on the Red Sea coast. At the customs barrier, an officious immigration officer delayed them. Dickson tried telling him that he was in the country as a guest of the emperor. They were soon through. The barrier was 300 miles inside the border. The Ethiopians were afraid of the Danakil living in between; they had nasty habits if they caught people they didn't like. Only a few years before, during the war, they had castrated every Italian they caught. Whenever an army uses a superior technology, as the Italians did by bombing from the air, its POWs suffer.

In the middle of the Danakil desert, the jeep front right spring snapped. For four hours, on that totally desolate road, not a single vehicle passed while Almonds constructed a makeshift repair. His temporary job done, they crawled slowly back towards Batie. Just below the massif, a large Italian transport lorry agreed to take Dickson. It had delivered oil from the coast up to Addis and was on its way back with sacks of oil seed. From Assab, Dickson got a ride on an Aden Airways Dakota back to Aden. But his contact with Almonds and his family was not to be his last.[37]

The Eritrean police had an impossible job. On 30 December, a dirty white local bus from Himberti bumped its way along the all-weather gravel track towards the main Asmara to Adi Ugri road. Like a Wild West stagecoach, the bus was under heavy escort. Three Eritrea police constables rode shotgun on the roof and three sat inside. After 10 kilometres, the bus picked up six more passengers. When it was halfway between Himberti and the main road, it met a roadblock of large stones. Suddenly, a large gang of about thirty *shifta* appeared. As the police constables prepared to engage them, the six new 'passengers' attacked the three constables inside. Taken completely by surprise, one was shot dead and two seriously wounded. Two constables on top were wounded, while the other escaped after abandoning his weapon. The *shifta* carefully robbed the travellers. Four rifles were lost in this new kind of hold-up.[38]

Like their unofficial vehicle protection method, the British Army also had informal ways of dealing with unrest in East Africa. At HQ British

Somaliland, Perry received a signal that the 'natives were restless' over some waterholes at Awareh. Perry agreed to help since he had 37mm cannon and Brownings and the natives did not. He departed with four armoured cars and two soft vehicles. On arrival, Perry reported to the Officer Commanding, the Colonel of the Somaliland Scouts. Ensconced in a deckchair drinking gin with cocktail onions, the officer introduced himself as Oliver Brooke: a very charming, rubicund-complexioned colonel, also destined for the SAS. He offered Perry a glass, which he accepted. Brooke said that the *matata* (trouble) concerned clan disputes about watering rights, but all it needed was a display of force. Perry suggested firing off some spare canister shot and a belt or two of Brownings for about twenty minutes. He duly set up his four cars, made sure nobody was in the beaten zone and opened up, noting as he did so that a canister would make a marvellous gardening aid. It completely shredded small thorn bushes and lopped off all the medium-sized branches.[39]

The slow failure of the BMME was a sad finale to a successful past. Not funding it properly had been a waste of the resources expended. To Almonds, it seemed that Britain was appeasing Ethiopia, while standing up to Ethiopia. He certainly thought that Ethiopia and the emperor were not as stable as the western powers who had decided their future seemed to think.[40] Despite these nagging issues, in January 1951, he wrote home:

'Things in Ethiopia are not so bad; soon I shall have completed my first year… The duration of stay has been cut down to two years, which is rather a pity. It is such an interesting country and the wild and woolly people are so full of surprises that they are really delightful. Time passes very quickly as there is always something to do and see. Life has certainly been varied since my days at Stixwould School and seems partially to have fulfilled some of the desires which possessed me at that time. If the world should again be plunged into war I might fulfil the remainder; otherwise there is little more to be expected from the army. This will be my last tour abroad; further promotion is most unlikely as there are so many senior officers without adequate employment.'[41]

He was quite wrong about the last tour abroad – and the promotion. And, of course, the active service.

Chapter Five

ERITREA POLICE FIELD FORCE

Policing Eritrea by consent was a nonsense. The security situation was akin to that of the British Palestine Police in 1948. House-to-house searching of 300,000 people in Tel Aviv, the biggest search in military history, had been a policing disaster. It did not catch the terrorists and it destroyed community relations.[1]

The answer was the EPFF – an armed paramilitary force of policemen and soldiers. Its constitution declared, with a delightful intermingling of military and police nomenclature, 'The Field Force shall consist of such superior Field Force officers, Inspectors, NCOs and constables as the Chief Administrator may from time to time direct and shall be under the command of the Commissioner of Police and Prisons appointed by the Chief Administrator.'[2]

The Field Force had two main functions: to prevent crime against the person or property; and crime involving disturbance of the public peace or security and *the apprehension of offenders*. This last phrase made it unique: even the police in mainland Britain had not originally had catching criminals as an objective. Service was certainly full-on, 365 days a year: 'Every member of the Field Force shall be considered to be always on duty.' All members carried military rank, even the police.[3] Every EPFF member of the rank of inspector or above also had the powers of an officer of the judiciary. To Almonds's joy, EPFF members had no ordinary policing duties. [4]

The Field Force was also unique because it had ex-Palestine police. Their flair for 'up and away' immediate action added to the military muscle. The army came to admire that, because however good they are policemen and soldiers do things differently. Powers of arrest, entry, search of the person and use of force were taken from the earlier Proclamation of the Eritrea Police Force. Some offences related specifically to the Field Force: 'Aiding, abetting, or being an accessory to sedition or maliciously endeavouring to seduce any member of the Field Force from his allegiance or duty shall on conviction by a British Court be liable to be punished *by death* or imprisonment.'[5]

The EPFF hunted three kinds of *shifta*: men who ran away for personal or tribal reasons and engaged in feuds; men originating from Ethiopia's Tigrai province, motivated by easy robbing of Eritreans and their livestock; and men who wanted to free Eritrea from Italian rule and influence and unite (or, as they maintained, reunite) Eritrea with Ethiopia. The latter supported the Eritrean political Unionist Party. Religion also played a part: Coptic Eritrean *shifta* professed a longing for union with Christian Coptic Ethiopia, while the Muslim, largely coastal, *shifta* wanted complete independence. Thesiger thought the Eritrean Copts got their Christian faith from their Ethiopian counterparts, helped by the railway from the late 1890s.[6]

The *shifta* lived by stealing and looting, holding up trains and rustling cattle. Both sides carried out sectarian killings. Sometimes they murdered their former Italian masters. The robbing and rustling led to reprisals and blood feuds, which were protracted, bitter and almost impossible for the authorities, even the local *Residenti* 'native' courts, to resolve. *Shifta* were numerous, operated in organised bands several hundred strong and attacked the authorities without compunction. Their leaders were young and bold. They did not live long enough to become old.

Outbreaks of violence around Asmara at the end of 1950 started small. In one early attack, two *shifta* were two killed, three captured, one wounded and captured; and six wounded and escaped. The Field Force recovered four German rifles and an Italian one with 179 rounds of ammunition. *Shifta* held up and robbed two civilian buses and assaulted one local civilian. They held up a civilian lorry, killed the Italian driver and one 'native', wounded two others and helped themselves to an Italian rifle and fifty rounds of ammunition.

They then moved up a gear. After several large-scale cattle thefts, in which one local was killed, they burned down fifty houses in one village and killed six Copts. An ensuing battle between Muslim and Coptic *shifta* resulted in three *shifta* surrendering in Asmara and two hand grenades being recovered. More *shifta* bands operated on the Eritrean plateau than ever before and they were better organised.[7] In Whitehall, FOAAT, the division responsible for running Britain's African territories, could not wait to get Eritrea off its hands.

Matters escalated internationally. From being a matter of local policing, the extraordinary war on the *shifta* waged by Britain, Italy, and indirectly by the US became of interest worldwide. The battle for public opinion became intense. People in Britain and Italy were disturbed by a faceless terrorism, which, if left uncontrolled, threatened their own lives.[8] It got into the British newspapers. These included one produced in the UK by Miss Sylvia Pankhurst of the suffrage movement: *The New Times and Ethiopian News*. She also published *The Voice of Eritrea* in Tigrinya in Ethiopia.

In Asmara, Drew tried to lower the political temperature. He prosecuted the editor of *Eritrea Nuova* for publishing an article calculated to cause alarm and suspended him from the Asmara press. In Italy, the press responded by suggesting that 'muzzling the Eritrean press constitutes a complete victory for Unionist terrorism, which thus secures the effective stifling of all propaganda in favour of Independence'.[9] *London Reuters* put out an article entitled 'Press Restrictions in Eritrea – Action by British' and *The Times* carried an article referring to the British Administration 'crushing pro-Ethiopian terrorist activities'.[10] In January, 1951, the Administration renewed the partial amnesty to the *shifta*, but still excluded those guilty of murder.

It made little difference. On 10 February 1951, 'a hard core of political *shifta*, up to 300 in number' encamped in the vicinity of Makalle. The leaders, Voldegabriel Mosasghi, Asserassie Embae, Teccheste Haile and Halie Abbai were waiting there while their wounded *shifta* were treated in Adowa hospital. A British NCO, Corporal Haynes, was murdered. Another *shifta*, Haile Cashi, and his gang of seventeen, together with Hailie Abbai and his gang, were responsible.[11]

On 14 February 1951, the name of Captain John Edward Almonds appeared on the EPFF Establishment Register.[12] He was to fill one of two SO III grade posts as a senior assistant superintendent reporting to the SO II superintendent of police heading up the EPFF, Paddy McGill.[13] Also on the list were Alf Gould and T S Baxendale. Both had served in the

Palestine police.[14] Brigadier Drew left and handed over to a non-combatant replacement.

This first (and last) civilian British Chief Administrator for Eritrea, Duncan Cumming, seemed right for the job: Chief Civil Affairs Officer, Middle East, 1945–1948; Governor of Kordofan Province, Sudan, 1949; and Deputy Civil Civilian Secretary, Sudan Government since 1950. Cumming had also been a wartime major-general. He was powerfully built, with an open, pleasant face and had great faith in East Africans' 'grasp of the democratic process'.[15] At Giggleswick School, it had been said of him, 'Cumming is one of those who… makes a success of whatever he does… a good leader who keeps his forwards going hard until the finish'.[16] He would need those skills in Eritrea.

The British had their hands full. Handicaps were many: difficult country, skilful opponents, uncooperative people living in inaccessible places and British officers' almost total ignorance of local languages and habits. Cumming wanted an end to the dysfunctional partial amnesty. The Tigrai *shifta*, having been told that they would get no more Ethiopian money, had even reverted to non-political brigandage.[17]

Cumming did a recce, visiting remote outposts of the EPFF by air. He landed first on the plain, west of the higher ranges. A Field Force platoon, commanded by a former Benin Amer officer of the Sudan Defence Force, paraded alongside the landing strip. There were no settled villages, just various nomad herdsmen wandering through the area. Cumming harangued the Field Force on the importance of appropriate techniques for 'tracking down *and killing*' any *shifta* from the hills. The platoon officer blamed the Copts of the plateau for the raiding but Cumming doubted whether the young man's battle training was any better than that of the *shifta*.[18]

Their next hop was southwest for half an hour, flying to the Gash (Mareb) River. Lieutenant Chambers of the blond beard awaited them. He ran for a quarter of a mile in front of their little Auster aircraft, leading them along a track from the landing strip to his camp. With him stumbled a black school pupil, carrying on his back a blackboard with 'FOLLOW ME' chalked on it.

Chambers, who commanded this remote platoon and another one 10 miles away to the west, said he liked the life, spoke some Arabic and was just the man for this kind of work. But he had been at it for three years and was about to return to his regiment. While the visitors shared a mug of tea in his tent on a hill within a strong point designed for defence by two men, Chambers told Cumming about another action in which he had been ambushed in the hills south of the Gash in December. His two best Eritrean NCOs had been killed. He had not been able to take suitable revenge and had suggested another Royal Berkshires officer to replace him. Unfortunately, only yesterday, that officer had also been killed in a brush with *shifta* south of the plateau. It was active service in so-called peacetime.

Next, Cumming went across to the Ethiopian frontier further south and then along the Gash River to the west. This rough, hilly country had been the scene of inter-tribal raiding throughout recorded history. As they left the frontier, they flew over another Field Force platoon, which presented arms to the Auster at long range. On they flew, over the camp of another platoon out on patrol and then north to Barentu. There, the Kunama tribe were cultivating crops. Herdsmen from the north bullied these villagers, but they invited trouble by their own cattle thefts and by burning much of the grazing to smoke bees from the trees while collecting their honey. Vivid evidence was visible from the air.'[19]

At Barentu, the district officer and tribal leaders were holding meetings with *shifta* bands to persuade them to surrender. Meeting papers were distributed. At the right point the literate members turned the page. After a pause, the illiterate members also turned the page. The visitors took off for Tarkina where three more Field Force platoons were shadowing the largest of the *shifta* gang meetings at long range. They flew over the remains of four Kunama villages burned by the *shifta* six weeks before – a sorry spectacle. The gang leader was a dangerous killer with a large and well-armed band, capable of dealing with an EPFF platoon if it came to a stand-up fight.[20]

Cumming then flew to the broad fertile plain of Cofit, where tribesmen and *shifta* were assembled. [21] They did not find Cofit, but shot up several villages – with a roaring engine, not guns – before carrying on to Agordat, passing over a goldmine still operated by Italians. The Agordat district officer was absent at a tribal meeting, so they flew on to Keren. The local platoon was on patrol in pursuit of animals stolen from an Italian concession. The bumpy flight back to Asmara over inhospitable scenery of bare granite crags was alarming in the light plane. They had covered about 330 miles, nearly all of it just mountains, rocks and scrub. Seven platoons of half-trained levies simply could not cover it closely. [22]

A few days later, Cumming went by road to HQ Serae District at Adi Ugri, a market town of about 5,000 local inhabitants and 400 Italians, 40 miles west of Asmara. The area was so disturbed that anti-*shifta* operations were under the military control of a British company and nine Field Force platoons. In a former Italian fort on top of a hill, their commander, a major in the Royal Berkshire Regiment, briefed Cumming on his elaborate patrol system. It seemed rather rigid. Cumming stressed the importance of dogging the *shifta* relentlessly by intelligent field craft, so that they could be brought to action. While they were talking, news arrived that shots had been exchanged with an eighty-strong *shifta* gang at Obel north of Adi Ugri. A full engagement ensued. British platoons were running short of ammunition and food, so an aircraft resupplied them by bag drop. Other platoons were directed to the spot during the night. The action lasted two days, with only two dead *shifta* to show for it.

Cumming decided to fly to Obel. On the way to the aerodrome, he passed twenty police who guarded the Italian market gardeners. *Shifta* had destroyed their houses outside Adi Ugri. The *shifta* made a habit of wrecking water pumps. All this was going on within a mile of Adi Ugri. They flew over the usual tortured country to Obel and landed in a deep valley. To reach the Field Force post, Cumming and his aide walked about a mile along the valley before Field Force mules carried them up the precipitous hill to a stone fort on its crest. All around were high hills with Coptic villages on top of them – heavy work for the British officer who patrolled them. It was not clear whether the *shifta* or the Field Force were in control.

Aircraft engine trouble prevented Cumming from flying over the Hazimo plain further east, where Coptic *shifta* had driven out all the Muslims who had been farming near the Ethiopian frontier for forty years. Both sides were raiding and village burning. Several hundred Muslims were gathering, ready to take their revenge, while various Coptic leaders were mustering a force across the frontier. The *shifta* were also clever enough to engage in disinformation. The apparent impending clash was probably a rumour to cover a plan for quite a different operation, but a patrol had gone out to investigate.[23]

In Ethiopia, as the end of the BMME approached, the *Ethiopian Herald* headline on 10 March 1951 read, 'BMM is leaving Ethiopia. Has been here since 1942.' Commenting on the platitudes at the end of the article, Lascelles wrote to the Minister, Ernest Bevin: 'The last paragraph [talk of harmony and deep appreciation] by the Ethiopian Government is of course not a true statement. But its untruthfulness is in keeping with the official pretence, which we ourselves have encouraged in the interests of preserving good relations.'[24] Typical *Yes Minister* speak. The strength of the mission at the time of its disbandment in March 1951 was still twenty-six officers and twenty-three NCOs.[25] The closure characterised gradual British withdrawal all over the world. Ethiopia and Eritrea were not even part of the empire, but were tying up resources.

Meanwhile, the *shifta* redoubled their attacks. On 28 March, a gang of forty ambushed eleven Field Force personnel, killing five and wounding six. Reinforcements captured one *shifta* and found the body of his dead leader near the scene. On the same day, *shifta* murdered two herdsmen and stole 200 goats and electric cable from the Italian goldmine. The local people did their bit, capturing two *shifta* – one being the son of the President of the Asmara native court. But *shifta* stole goats, six donkeys and 950 cattle in two incidents, killing two local men. On 4 April, the Field Force in Hamasien engaged two *shifta* gangs 17 miles south west of Keren. They killed one *shifta* leader, Grazmac Ilfai Asfaha – the brother of Tecle Asfaha – and captured the other.

It was time for Almonds to leave Ethiopia. Along with spears, Maria Theresa dollars and other gifts, one chief gave him a beautiful ebony walking stick. Haile Selassie presented Almonds with an Ethiopian medal. It depicts two angels guarding the Ark of the Covenant and the Lion of Judah in front, carrying a mace in its paws, the whole surmounted by a Star of David.[26]

Almonds, who, according to George, Second Earl Jellicoe, always ran *to* the battle[27], immediately volunteered to join the Eritrean Police Field Force.

Chapter Six

NEW 'WILD WEST'

Almonds arrived in Asmara on 31 March 1951, the same day as a special Peace Mission delegation from Haile Selassie. This time, Almonds was the gamekeeper, not the poacher. And his quarry was men – men he understood. Six weeks on the run in wartime Italy had taught him what it takes to survive as an outlaw.

The EPFF was based in the main HQ buildings at Battalion HQ, Eritrea District, Asmara. The new force was officered by the army, but commanded by the Superintendent of Police, Paddy MGill – Almonds's new boss. (Eritrea was not officially at war, so a policeman had to be on top.) McGill had a British Empire Medal for gallantry after extricating a convoy from ambush by an armed gang on the Jerusalem to Jaffa road on 25 March 1937.[1] He welcomed Almonds warmly. Not only was his new officer a captain in the army, he was an *ex*-policeman. McGill had the perfect hybrid.

The HQ team consisted of McGill (SO II level) and Lorimer (also SO II, whom Almonds remembered as part of 'Layforce' on board HMS *Glenroy* eight years before). Almonds, Head and Allen (all SO III) made up the rest of the team. There were eight SO IV level lieutenants (with three vacancies). Since British Army officers had to volunteer, some were only available for short secondments, got wounded or left on resignation. So keeping vacancies filled was a constant struggle. About half of these SO IV grade posts were taken by the Eritrea police, so the unit was an odd mixture of soldiers and policemen.[2] The Eritrean uniformed police included armourers, drivers, farriers, WT operators, clerks and interpreters. British Army support was distributed around Eritrea. 'A', 'B' and 'C' companies of the resident battalion had their HQs at Sembel Camp, The Fort at Adi Ugri and Keren respectively. The officers messed either at the central mess Penzione Belvedere, or at the 'A', 'B', or 'C' company messes.[3]

The Field Force ethos was redolent of the Palestine police. Almonds found McGill likeable, but 'an old rogue'. Short, round-ish and not very soldierly-looking, he was mainly office-bound – and there was not a lot to do in the office. But he did give parties. He never made demands workwise, but if he was about to have a party he would be on the phone asking Almonds to shoot him half a dozen birds, including some turkey bustards. The birds were already becoming scarcer. McGill also emulated Almonds in the firearms department, noticing that he had an American Remington .22 rifle. Almonds had bought it at the 'PX' store at the US information centre in Asmara. McGill went to get one for himself.

McGill was always coming forward as the boss, but didn't quite know what to do when he got there. He held no meetings with his subordinates. It was up to everyone to make it their business to find out what was going on. Perhaps because of the prevailing police culture, there was no battle plan either. From top to bottom, nobody really knew what they were doing other than to 'stop the *shifta*'. This suited Almonds well. He was happy to have a hands-off boss and be left to develop his own strategy. He intended to 'live the job' for a while, develop his tactics and see what worked. One thing he acquired very quickly was respect for his opponents. Despite their atrocities, he admired the *shifta* for their resourcefulness, determination and resilience – all qualities he valued.[4]

Haile Selassie's Peace Delegation wanted to persuade the British authorities to provide for an amnesty offering a *general* pardon. The delegates: Ato Asfaha Woldmikael, Kifleghi Yedhego, Haggai Abdalla, Mohammed Mederic and Azimatch Ahmed Mohammed were a mix of Coptic Ethiopians and Muslim former Eritreans, reflecting the ethnic and religious mix in the population. A communiqué publicised their arrival. But this was by British standards a very informal mission. There were no papers to establish its position *vis-à-vis* the chief administrator.[5]

The delegation highlighted the fact that any member of a *shifta* band taking part in a fight in which somebody had been killed was outside the present amnesty. The custom of Ethiopia, they said, was for a pardon to be complete and unqualified. The emperor should receive full credit for this act of mercy and political wisdom. They would even try to contact the *shifta* leaders – once a general amnesty was announced.[6] For all this, Almonds found Eritrea more advanced technologically and politically than Ethiopia. Italian colonisation had given them more than just roads and railways.

Before taking up post, Almonds took some leave, flying back to the UK on a *Constellation*. As per his usual style, he just turned up, bringing gifts: silver coins, a big Danakil knife, basket work from Harar and exotic threaded shells. He met my brother, John, from school one afternoon. The next morning, he walked with me to mine, holding my hand as I looked up at the suntanned father I hardly remembered. While at home, he redecorated the house, rebuilt a fallen wall, planted a row of trees, made two new garage doors and erected a flagstaff. Then he ruined this homely image by going round to *The Fellowship* pub for a drink. Nonetheless, as Lockie wrote to his mother, her joy was not just about having him home again.

> 'The depression he has felt these past few years has practically gone. The strain of his war ordeals, as you know, made him strange – hard – anything but himself. Now he is conscious of things neglected... He is once again himself and full of plans for the future. He suggested that we should go to church together on the first Sunday we could, deeming it a thanksgiving for his restoration to life and love, gentleness and simplicity... His ways now are more different than I have ever known; habits have changed too – he smokes, but limits himself. This is all very surprising to me... his one longing is to be in his home, to plan it and to spend his time with his dear ones.'[7]

She might have been wrong about that last bit.

Almonds met Cumming on one of his trips to admonish local chiefs about supporting the *shifta*. For recce purposes, Almonds went with him. During a pause in the meeting, both went outside for a break. Almonds was exploring a patch of rough ground, as was his wont. Cumming asked him what he was looking for. Almonds had picked up a half-buried human skull.

'Are you sure it's not an ape's?' asked Cumming.

'Quite sure,' Almonds said, pointing out the small jawbone. Cumming then asked what Almonds thought of the local people (a docile tribe) and how he got on with them. They discussed the *shifta* problem and Cumming asked Almonds how it could be managed and what he thought of the *shifta*. How could the Administration pre-empt *shifta* attacks or failing that retrieve stolen goods? Almonds said both things could be achieved simultaneously, by catching the *shifta* and recovering whatever had been taken. The next thing he knew, he was on his way to run the Western Province.[8]

In Keren, Almonds met Stan Baxendale, ex-Palestine police and a chum of Gould, now carrying the rank of captain. Six feet tall, well built and sandy-haired, Baxendale had a firm-featured face and an alert air. An excellent horseman in the mounted section, he had been a lieutenant in the Tripolitania Police before joining the Field Force as assistant superintendent. He was casual about weapons. While visiting colleague Ted Horne at home in England, he said, 'Just a minute while I get rid of this', took out his pistol and plonked it on the mantelpiece.[9]

With Gould and Baxendale, Almonds set about gathering intelligence on the *shifta* and sizing up their capability. He had a strategy – to pursue and take them by surprise – but needed to develop it. He settled on quick reaction to intelligence and raid information, fast follow-up, pursuit, and then – by the aid of the Auster observation on where the *shifta* were going next – putting a blocking force in place ahead to ambush them. So the men he used had to be fit and tough.

Baxendale could be difficult. He was still fighting the Second World War; so contacts with Italians in Eritrea were problematic. Almonds had to rescue him when he got into trouble with one of the Italian police. Baxendale also revered his mother. So jokes about mothers were out. He introduced Almonds to an Eritrean family, who provided an alternative to Mess food: roast goat featured on the menu. The house was within walking distance and even had running water and a bathroom. In Keren, as in Asmara, 'the sanitation… suffered from the fact that the Italian genius for engineering comes to a sudden stop at plumbing.'[10]

British officers played hard. Keren had a CIAO holiday hotel. There, Almonds saw General Turnbull sitting in the swimming pool skimming dinner plates across it. That night he gave a farewell party, at which the revellers did far more than just throw crockery. They smashed it to pieces – together with the windows and much of the furniture. When Almonds called in the next day, the leavers had substantially trashed the place.[11]

The country was like the Wild West and the *shifta* lived a very unsettled life. Consequently, they had some very dirty habits. They favoured hold-ups. One Sunday morning, Almonds was called out when *shifta* held up the train between Keren and Asmara. They blocked the line with boulders and trees. After getting the passengers out, they searched them thoroughly, scattering their belongings along the railway banks before making off with the valuables. Another emergency call came when *shifta* held up a train between Baraka and Keren. When Almonds arrived, the train was gone but the passengers' rifled possessions were littered along the railway track.

Sometimes, there was no call out. One day, Almonds was driving the ninety-one kilometres from Asmara to Keren, snaking along the coil of road beneath frowning black peaks. He looked below past several winding bends and caught sight of a hijacked bus being ransacked by several *shifta*. He had only his pistol, but was ready to use it. He cut across on foot, but as soon as the *shifta* spotted him, they ran off. The *shifta* had done a 'your money or your life job'. The passengers' belongings were strewn all over the road, but they gave Almonds a spontaneous round of applause. When the *shifta* stopped a train near the Highland Light Infantry badge, they knew that the Field Force would be quickly on the scene, so they worked fast.[12]

Almonds's usual response to nearby sea or rivers was to build a boat. He designed and made a canoe, covered its framework with canvas sheeting, caulked it with bitumen and made two paddles. After launching it onto the Setit River, he hunted and fished. Suddenly, after shooting some large rapids, which turned into a big waterfall, the river disappeared underground, vanishing down what looked like a giant plughole. Whole tree trunks were swirling round the spinning, wandering vortex of water, in the middle of which was a huge gaping empty hole. Having managed to stay upright, Almonds had only a few minutes' reaction time. He threw a rope around a leafless tree branch on the riverbank. It was at just the right angle to get a good hold and pull himself and his flimsy craft to the side.

The near miss did not stop him exploring. Dan Calvert from British Administration, Asmara (the brother of Mike Calvert of later SAS fame), was up for expeditions. They put the canoe on the Shinfa River and paddled off downstream to where it ran into the River Atbarah. Occasionally having to carry the craft around rapids, they lay up at night and had fun during the day, living off game. Almonds shot some big rapids while Calvert, being a heavy chap, rounded them on foot via the riverbank. The rapids became a steep cascade and Almonds found himself hurtling forward, leaving

Calvert behind. The canoe capsized and Almonds lost his gear. Thoughts of crocodiles came quickly to mind.

After relaunching the boat, they tried more rapids, but the river became increasingly difficult with almost continuous big cascades and Calvert having to get out. Finally, they tied the canoe on top of a rock near some small waterfalls and left it for the *shifta*. Nearby, on a large flat rock sloping down into the water, lay a dead man, arms and legs splayed, alive with maggots. He had probably fallen and hit his head.

The Western Province was a vast command. The biggest of the five EPFF divisions, it stretched along the Sudan border from where it meets the Red Sea in the north, down to the Setit River, which formed the southern border with Ethiopia. Keren, Almonds's HQ, high on the Eritrean plateau, was the site of the 1941 battle that had finally given Mussolini's Fascists a bloody nose. Communications were a major problem – how to keep roads and railways open? Even when open, drivers could not be in a hurry. Often the jeep had to squeeze through the rock-cut roads. Almonds often wished the engineers had spent a bit longer chiselling out the edges. The railway from Massawa up to Asmara, with a branch line down to Diredawa, was particularly vulnerable. *Shifta* who just wanted to thieve took every opportunity to pillage the trains with various modern and old-fashioned weapons.[13]

There had never been a constructive programme for overcoming the *shifta* problem. It was ignored because it only affected the rural parts of Eritrea. But since the beginning 1951, fifty-three trains and eighty-three vehicles had been held up and robbed. One hundred and sixty-eight engagements with the *shifta* had led to twenty-one members of the security forces and ninety-eight civilians being killed, with forty-eight wounded. Over 10,000 cattle had also been stolen.

There was a mismatch. The security forces' methods against the *shifta* were designed for police operations against criminals of the more orthodox European kind. The situation was almost farcical. Police went to the scenes of crimes to investigate and make arrests. Locals then denied knowledge of the bandits' whereabouts. Where contact was made in the field, the *shifta* were too fast over the rough country for the security forces to catch them. There was also fear of reprisals and even sympathy for the *shifta* in Coptic areas.[14]

And there were security problems. The *shifta* leaders featured in the 'Wild West' Wanted posters were killers and therefore not eligible for the amnesty. Second, the security forces could not stop rural people from aiding the bandits. Third, active operations often led to the *shifta* withdrawing across the Ethiopian frontier until the next time they came back to raid.

The Administration was also hampered by a dysfunctional Fascist law for suppressing banditry that had been kept in force. There was reluctance to use it so many years after the collapse of the Fascist regime. But the legal advice was that it was unjust to deprive a man of his liberty without giving him an opportunity to defend himself. If the Administration could not prove a case, it could not convict. Yet with so many political murders and atrocities, people could reasonably expect the protection of the British Administration.[15]

As Head of the Western Province, Almonds commanded 1,100 native troops, five British subalterns, three British NCOs and thirteen *askaris*. He had the Auster aircraft and a pilot. But mules and donkeys were the only way to supply his platoons in the field. Watching them winding across dried-up riverbeds was like scenes straight out of a spaghetti Western. Once he saw the remarkable power of water. His Field Force platoons were crossing a wide, flat expanse of dried-up riverbed with a 6-ton truck. The truck set off, with its British driver and some local soldiers, while Almonds brought up the rear in his jeep. Without warning, a high wall of water came around the bend in the river. They heard nothing but the new river hit the truck, rolling it over and over like a dinky toy.

Almonds used his forces strategically. Like the early SAS days in the Western Desert, it was more effective to deploy platoons out in the field, closer to likely targets, than to keep taking them in and out. He maintained radio contact with all his commanders, usually a British subaltern or senior NCO. His Eritrea Police opposite number was Jim Gander, the Western Area Chief of Police.

Almonds had a colourful set of colleagues. In the Officers' Club, he sometimes ran into Timber (Edward Joshua) Wood, a wild character, seldom separated from a Melotti beer. An ex-Grenadier, he had transferred from the Dodecanese Administration when the British withdrew. As each bit of British Administration in which he was serving closed down, he jumped to another bit. During the war, he had served in China and tried to shock with tales of his exploits, 'You get hold of them and test their weight before you hang them...' But he was quick-thinking and quick-acting. The previous year, he had saved the life of a severely injured notable, Sheik Milli Ingide, after a car accident.

Wood was always with 'Titch' (William) Bitmead, a true cockney who was the exact opposite of Wood in every way. He was small, nearly square and neat compared to Wood's large disarray, but always an amusing character. Wood embellished most of his extravagant stories with, 'And Bitmead was with me.'[16] Bill Shevlin and John Doody were the Field Force ports and harbour men in Eritrea. Almonds befriended them with a slightly ulterior motive. He contemplated building a boat and putting it out onto the Red Sea. Another avuncular character, 'Burglar' Williams, specialised in getting the *shifta* to give themselves up and retire from their skulduggery. If they did, and weren't wanted for an offence, he didn't bring them in. A big, heavy Englishman called Brans completed this group. He also talked to the *shifta*, but in a different way. He got them to trust him. Then he shopped them.[17]

At Christmas, Almonds invited this motley crew to the Officers' Mess party. Wood, Baxendale and some of their men brought with them a live pig to make the celebrations more festive. They tied it up outside. What to do with it? They could not agree. While they were arguing, one of them got fed up, went outside and shot it. They all heard the bang. A long silence followed. Since there were no freezers in the Mess, they now had a different problem about what to do with the unfortunate animal. Baxendale to the rescue. He soon had it upside down and gave a complete demo, cutting off its head, cleaning and quartering it. Having reserved enough for the party, Baxendale's men went off to give away fresh pork to their local (non-Muslim) employees.[18]

Cumming had inherited another problem: the impending executions of convicted *shifta*. Of seven condemned men, six had been found guilty of 'bearing arms against the authorities of the Administration'. The hangings could be completed in four days and he had asked for authorisation. They would not be secret, but since they could not be concealed, a press notice, giving the names of the executed men and their offences, would be circulated in the areas from which they came.[19] However, it could not be fair for them to hang, without having killed anyone, while others who had murdered could be pardoned under a general amnesty. The executions would therefore be stayed, but a new Emergency Proclamation would provide for repressive powers and swifter justice.[20]

His political problem was more public. *Shifta* terrorism was having a serious impact on the implementation of the December 1950 UN Resolution. Even more embarrassment for Britain. The UN Commissioner in Eritrea,

Edouard Anze Matienzo, said the unrest was having a detrimental effect on public opinion at the very time when confidence in security needed to be assured. This instability was impeding the formation of a Representative Assembly of Eritrea as foreseen by the UN Resolution. He could not consult the inhabitants of the territory, which under his terms of reference he must, since the elections had to be preceded by a period of peaceful preparations. This was impossible in the present atmosphere of insecurity and fear.[21] The *Ethiopian Herald* quoted a Reuters reported statement by the UN Commissioner: 'It is impossible to transfer power to the Eritreans as long as the pro-Ethiopian *shifta* have not been eliminated.' The article continued that the Imperial Ethiopian Government and the majority of the Eritrean people wanted 'peaceful reunion' of Eritrea with Ethiopia. The emperor had now sent a special mission to Eritrea to help.[22]

How to solve the *shifta* problem? Thirty-six *shifta* leaders for whom surrender or pardon was not a possibility had to remain in the field or seek refuge in Ethiopia. In the field, they had to keep gangs and stay alive by robbing and intimidating the local populace, leading to continued blood feuds and disorder. Lack of employment, land or animal property led other men, many of them disadvantaged soldiers, to join the gangs. Most did a stint, went home or surrendered to the Administration and then rejoined. Some thought that if they stayed in the field until the Federation of Ethiopia and Eritrea, they would be pardoned and win favour from the new regime. These regarded 'Italophobia' as particularly useful. Many leaders simply took the law into their own hands for communal or family feuds or made a living by robbery while winning a reputation for bravado. *Shifta* activity also disrupted civil administration, making it difficult to sort out settlements for land disputes and compensation for previous losses. The bandits also took revenge on informers to the police, and villagers who did not become *shifta* were penalised by both sides for not supporting the other.[23]

The January 1950 partial amnesty was useless. The previous year, about 2,000 bandits had been in action, with only 131 *shifta* casualties, including seventy-one killed. Only 519 had surrendered. So either the *shifta* had to be caught or there should an amnesty for *all* bandits and more repressive action. Moreover, if the emperor got his general amnesty, the British would be in a stronger position to demand that *shifta* who took refuge in Ethiopia should be prevented from re-entering Eritrea.[24] But Cumming was determined not to agree to the Ethiopians' wish for a general amnesty until the Ethiopian

Government agreed to 'remove to a remote place all *shifta* now harboured across the frontier and all who cross in future'.[25]

Meanwhile, the *shifta* had not suspended their operations. On 9 April, three *shifta* abducted an Italian, Della Sante Atillo, and his locally employed assistant 3 miles from Adi Quala, where they were repairing a *shifta*-damaged water pump. The gang leader demanded £100 ransom, but then released the captives for £50. On 25 April, seven Coptic *shifta* raided a Beni Amer village in the Western Province and stole seventeen cattle. Thirty Muslim *shifta* held up a truck on the Agordat to Keren road and stole clothes and money. They attacked and robbed a train in the same area. Another *shifta* band attacked a party of Italians 23 kilometres east of Om Hager, wounded a forestry officer in the leg and shot his Arab driver in the arm. They also shot and killed Adolfo Melotti, the brother-in-law of Signora Melotti, who owned the Asmara brewery.[26]

The state of unrest in Eritrea continued to impede progress towards implementing the UN Resolution. Britain looked increasingly incompetent. Whitehall wanted to get on with implementation, since it was in Britain's economic interests to hand over Eritrea as soon as possible. Ethiopian hostility towards Italians did not help. Intense discussion (mostly disagreement) continued between the UN (Matienzo) and Ethiopia (Aklilou, the Foreign Minister) over the new draft Constitution. If they could agree, it might ease its passage through the new Assembly. But it would mean persuading a number of Muslims to vote with the Christians. That wasn't realistic. The Muslims were very isolated and were unlikely to make martyrs of themselves over the constitution. In addition, there were plenty of other pitfalls into which Eritrea could plunge before 15 September 1952.[27]

The *shifta* had the British on the run.

Chapter Seven

THE EMPIRE STRIKES BACK

Britain *had* to grip the *shifta* problem in time for Federation. Cumming wanted to get on with the general amnesty – his first step in decreasing the present activities of the *shifta*.[1] But first Britain had to choose between accepting the erratic, inefficient cooperation of the Ethiopians or reject it and be seen as rebuffing their gesture of goodwill. Six Ethiopian *shifta* leaders (as distinct from twenty-seven Eritrean *shifta* leaders) were taking refuge in Ethiopia whenever it suited them. Would Ethiopia agree to remove both from the frontier area in return for making their peace mission a success? While the Foreign Office dragged their heels, the peace mission's three weeks' wait in a local hotel had not improved Cumming's chances of success.[2]

Lascelles was all for the general amnesty. After a hard struggle, he had, at last, begun to get Ethiopian cooperation – 300 'hard core' *shifta* had been held at Makalle, greatly improving the Eritrean situation. Ethiopian authorities would never admit responsibility for the Eritrean *shifta*, but approached *informally*, they might retain in Ethiopia *shifta* already there and any who went there in future.[3]

The Administration also needed some way of stopping surrendered Eritrean *shifta* from returning to the field. Cumming appointed local commissions to settle feuds and disputes and give ex-*shifta* employment, either by raising a military unit on the Ethiopian plateau for embodiment in the Ethiopian Army in the future, or by using them on public projects. They would be resettled in remote villages – with police stations and telegraphic communications – and receive two shillings and six pence per diem for subsistence until suitable work could be found. Families would be allowed to join them, but, like their head of family, they would report daily to the police. If the resettled *shifta* left their place of enforced residence without permission, immediate action would be taken against their wives and families. [4]

Shifta attacks intensified. Daily hold-ups and robberies on trains meant escorts. Without enough police to do it, surplus goods traffic would have to move by road, with corresponding loss of revenue, until the requested increases in the police establishment were approved.[5] Before the change could be implemented, unknown *shifta* held up the unescorted Massawa to Asmara steam train near Damas and ransacked it.

Almonds was back in Asmara, the 'forest of flowers'. He replaced a friend of McGill's, who would never catch anyone the way he went about it. Almonds now knew what worked. He still ran the Western Province, but he also took the lead on *shifta* strategy elsewhere, keeping an intelligence overview and holding men at 'ready to move'. Every so often, an area would 'light up' and he would swing into action.[6]

On 5 June 1951, the Ethiopian Government agreed to take and retain nineteen *shifta* leaders, but refused to be held responsible if the brigands returned to Eritrea. In particular, the Ethiopian Government resisted any suggestion of any past connection with *shifta* crimes. [7]

As if in a last burst of activity before the new amnesty announcement, the *shifta* stepped up their raiding. On 10 June, a 100-strong gang stole cattle from an Italian concession, wounding a civilian driver. They rustled cattle, held up a goods train, burned seven loaded wagons, wounded five police riding escort and abducted two herdsmen. On 14 June, ten *shifta* stole more cattle and abducted the owner. The next day, they snatched another villager and held up a steam train.

In response, EPFF platoons surrounded the village and captured a number of *shifta*. The scale of the incidents escalated. Four Field Force platoons engaged two *shifta* gangs, involving about 500 *shifta* who attacked a village. Twenty inhabitants and fifteen *shifta* were killed.[8] On 15 June, Asserassie Embaie (now out of hospital) mounted a vicious attack, wounding three villagers, stealing cattle and destroying two houses. Then, sixty *shifta* attacked a Field Force platoon.

Three new policies aimed to stop this mayhem. First, the general amnesty itself; second, the agreement with the Ethiopian Government on cooperation; and third, new more repressive measures to replace the former Fascist law. On 16 June, the administration published a new Public Security Proclamation, 'Eritrean Public Security and Special Courts', in Italian and English as a 'Special Gazette' insert to *Il Quotidiano*, which was quickly translated into Arabic and Tigrinya. It would be enacted when the general amnesty and its accompanying notice were published.[9]

Justice would be swift. Cumming created special courts with appropriate procedures for expediting the trial of *shifta* offences. He would confirm all sentences, including death sentences. Public opinion, particularly Italian, demanded swifter justice for *shifta* atrocities. The new legislation provided that 'there shall be no preliminary or committal proceedings prior to a trial in a special court'. Convicted men would have right of appeal to the president of the British General Court, not later than seven days from the date of sentencing. No sentence of death would be carried out unless confirmed by the chief administrator or the Court of Appeal.[10]

The *general* amnesty to *all shifta* was linked to the UN Resolution concerning the Federation of Ethiopia and Eritrea. It made clear that 'HM Government have approved the granting of a General Amnesty in the following terms to all *shifta* irrespective of their past activities as *shifta*'. *Shifta* had to present themselves to a competent official of the administration within one month of the date of the public notice, must not have committed any further offences after the terms of the amnesty were published and would hand over their arms. A month would allow time for the news of the amnesty to reach *shifta* in remote places and for them to come in and surrender.

The notice also warned of more rigorous action against *shifta* who did not respond or who committed more offences. If the general amnesty was successful, the sentences for the condemned *shifta* would be reviewed. Disputes and feuds created during the period of *shifta* activities would be settled as far as possible by the customary methods of conciliation and compensation.[11] Politically, this approach ensured 'buy in' from both the Ethiopians and the Italians – and some potential for spreading the blame if things went wrong. The general amnesty was the emperor's idea, while the Italians had suggested the more repressive measures for those *shifta* who did not turn over a new leaf.[12]

The Administration proclaimed the general amnesty on Tuesday 19 June. Almonds had copies flown to his divisional officers in the Western Province, with instructions about what to say to local chiefs. The SDOs for Ackele Guzai and Serae arranged for copies to be delivered across the border into the Tigrai. Cumming met local religious leaders to enlist their support for the general amnesty through their congregations. Separately he saw the political party leaders.[13] Other provisions also had teeth. 'Community bonds' would require the chief, headman or other principal representative of a community to enter into a bond of good behaviour and to keep the peace for up to six months.[14]

All Field Force platoons returned to their bases. Action in the event of communal or *shifta* raids was as per normal. SDOs would publicise places of surrender, which might be moved as requested, and arrange reception centres, where DOs would direct the *shifta* to return home. DOs would also act as 'buffers' between the *shifta* and local chiefs. Each surrendered man would be given a copy of a form with his particulars as evidence that he had surrendered. Tools were to be made available to SDOs so that the ex-*shifta* could even be employed at the reception centres.

'Unacceptable' *shifta* were a problem. They could not surrender if they could not return home – for reason of vendettas or other feuds. So SDOs would arrange via HQ 'for disposing of them elsewhere'. An annotated list of the nineteen not-wanted-in-Eritrea' *shifta* leaders was circulated to SDOs. Minor *shifta* who were inhabitants of the Tigrai would be officially deported to Ethiopia. All surrendered *shifta* would then be resettled. Blood money would be paid for deaths caused by them. This would be announced at meetings with the chiefs about the general amnesty. Cumming himself would take up the question of balancing the blood money payments as between Muslims and Copts. Compensation would also be paid for the destruction of property according to the assessments of the courts. Transit camps were organised to receive surrendered Ethiopian *shifta* and those who needed temporary or enforced prolonged residence. Clothing would be issued when essential.[15]

Still not everyone was happy. The Italian Government had expected the proclamation to be more repressive than it was. The Foreign Office hoped snootily that Cumming had chosen the right degree of repression to deter the *shifta* and yet obtain cooperation from the people. They thought Parts I and II of the proclamation (Offences and Criminal Responsibility) gave too much power to the Administration. The only step beyond that would be the imposition of martial law, which they did not want.[16]

Then began a race against time to win the war on the *shifta* so that the UN Resolution could come into effect. Every interested party came at it from a different perspective. Britain sought to keep the lid on tensions between the Ethiopians and the Italian population in Eritrea. Lascelles was caught between remonstrations from Washington and Rome and Ethiopia's denial of succour for *shifta* who committed atrocities in Eritrea. Publicly, Ethiopia distanced herself from the pro-independence activities of the Eritrean Unionist *shifta* and the Unionist Party. The emperor resented the fact that Britain had kept Italian laws and institutions intact. Italy feared an Ethiopian backlash for the unspeakable things done to Ethiopians during the war.

News of the general amnesty was slow to reach the *shifta*. On 20 June, 100 Assaorta *shifta* attacked a train police escort. They killed one police constable and five others, wounded the train crew and stole five rifles. A Sudanese Defence Force patrol engaged about 100 *shifta* who attacked a village near Sabderat in the Sudan and stole a number of cattle. Three *shifta* were killed and one wounded.

Just when things could not get worse, they did. *Shifta* started hiring themselves out as mercenaries in tribal feuds. Now they had another reason not to take advantage of the amnesty. Muslim tribes of the plains to the east and west of the Asmara plateau and the Coptic villages on each side of the plateau fought each other. The Copts enlisted bandits from Ethiopia and the Muslims attacked police escorts on trains and road convoys to seize rifles to attack their opponents.[17]

Since mid-June, Cumming had also been under pressure from the Yemen to stop the *shifta* from attacking its subjects. 'If the Yemeni Minister raises the question again,' said the Foreign Office, 'he may be told that the amnesty was declared on 19 June and we hope soon to have information about the degree of its success. He need *not* be told the unfortunate fact that we have some doubts of its success because inter-tribal fighting has broken out in an area south of Massawa and may influence the willingness of armed bands to surrender.'[18]

The new public security measure was meant to back up the general amnesty and stop the tribal feuds. But first it distracted *shifta* from the amnesty while 'highly excited tribesmen' dissuaded them from surrendering.

Second, the injection of tribal and communal passions into what had been ordinary banditry for gain meant that tribesmen from both sides joined in. They swelled the numbers of the *shifta* so that bands over a 100-strong became common. It was quite daunting to be attacked by one of these huge mobs. Third, far from being feared, police escorts became targets of attack by the large armed gangs. Several escorts were overrun, severely denting police morale.

Large Muslim bands then started operating in the foothills inland from Massawa. Cumming closed the railway between Asmara and the port and declared a local state of emergency. The following day, the police threatened to go on strike. He had to restore their morale and show the Italian community that threats of serious action against the *shifta* were not empty. And he had to suppress the *shifta* trouble itself so that the amnesty could go ahead in time for the UN to implement their resolution.[19] The Public Security Proclamation took the administration about as far as it could go under normal emergency law. The next step would be martial law, or no law but the orders of a military commander.

Things got worse. One ugly development was that a gang of Tigrean *shifta* burnt a train, attacked the police and were caught while waiting to ambush a road convoy from Massawa. They were taken unawares by being attacked from three sides. The EPFF had mortars and five Bren guns and yet the bulk of the *shifta* still escaped. The battleground was in a deep valley where the railway and road ran together on the hillside, after descending from the zigzag road to Nefasit. It was just as hard for the Field Force to hit the *shifta* as it had been for the Italians to hit British troops at Keren when they were dodging about among the rocks on similar terrain. From the captured *shifta*, Cumming hoped to get some incriminating evidence against the Ethiopians.

Cumming went twice in one week to the Sageneti area, in the Akele Guzai province towards Senafe, to deal with the problem of *shifta* enlisting in inter-tribal raids. The second time, he took Almonds with him. Although not in Almond's geographical area of responsibility, his wider strategic role and operational insight were needed. Cumming gave the local people something to think about. If anything further went wrong, he warned them, he would revisit the area with fire and sword. Almonds standing beside him was the menacing presence of the Field Force who would visit this wrath upon them.[20]

Coptic–Beni Amer trouble continued in the remote valleys at the headwater of the Baraka River. The problem had begun with the black Kunama south of Barentu, who burne the grazing usually used by the Copts from both the Hamasien and the Serae. The Coptic herdsmen then muscled into the Beni Amer area. As a result, the Beni Amer stole a large number of the Copts' cattle, who retaliated by butchering Beni Amer people living in isolated grazing camps. All these people were on the move while various *shifta* bands, which ought to be surrendering, were moving to the same spot. British troops and Field Force were in the area, but Cumming asked the Air Officer Commanding Aden to send over a flight of fighters to make a noisy demonstration. Just to make sure, the Administration seized 350 Beni Amer camels and took bonds from all concerned to keep the peace.

Cumming reported to London in positive terms about the amnesty. 'The General Amnesty has strong public support and the *shifta* leaders are known to be considering whether they will surrender and how they can do so with the minimum loss of face. Informed opinion is that they will surrender...' But other things got in the way and took up time. Several hysterical Italians woke up Capomazza, the new Italian representative, at midnight on his first night in Asmara, demanding that he produce £25,000 as a ransom for Tagliero, a kidnapped grocer. Tagliero got away unharmed without paying the ransom. But Capomazza was not at his best when he went to see Cumming the following morning. [21]

Another disturbing development – as if they needed any more – was evidence of Communist influences in Asmara. It was traceable to a Jewish-Italian lawyer who ran courses for Eritrean law students. They were getting at the police with the cry: 'Is it worth losing your lives for two bob a day?' The Asmara police said they would go on strike over their low pay, losses suffered at the hands of the *shifta* and the high cost of living.[22] A somewhat impotent Foreign Office sent a limp telegram of the 'You're on your own with this one' kind: 'We consider it essential to avoid a police strike and we are confident that you will take all possible measures to achieve this.'[23]

Meanwhile, Matienzo wanted a formal consultation on the draft Constitution. Cumming stalled for time, saying he needed to study it. The longer the Administration had to deal with the *shifta* before startling the Ethiopians with democratic consultations, the better. A Frenchman from UNESCO, said to represent 'Technical Aid for Mass Education and Public Enlightenment' was visiting Ethiopia. 'Apparently,' reported Cumming, 'he makes a living by distributing records and arranging radio programmes for backward peoples or some such conceit... I shouldn't be surprised if he suggested a television course in good citizenship for surrendered *shifta*.'[24]

Within a few days, the police and Field Force combined could no longer contain the blood feuding. Cumming placed the area bounded on the east by the Red Sea, by the road running from Massawa to Nefasit, through Decamere to Saganeiti, Catch and Senafe to the Ethiopian frontier and then east along the frontier to the boundary between the Akele Guzai and Red Sea administrative divisions under martial law. He excluded the roads and towns along it and the areas not recognised as territories of the Assarota and Miniferi tribes. Alarmed, the Foreign Office sent a strong telegram asking how the military commander was going to use his authority and pointing out that 'the object is not, repeat not, punitive but the restoration of order.'[25] Cumming agreed, but said it was time to apply 'primitive measures to this end'. The *shifta* were reluctant to surrender because both sides pretended they were letting down their respective communities if one side surrendered before the other side.

Unless the communal trouble was stopped, the whole amnesty was threatened.

Chapter Eight

OPERATION ROUNDUP

I t was time for a showdown. Almonds attended a conference of police, Field Force, SDOs and local leaders at Decamere to agree strategy. After the meeting, the district commander issued an instruction. It bore even more of a resemblance to the Wild West than the 'Wanted' poster. 'The Object of OPERATION ROUNDUP', it said, was '(1) to effect the arrest of named *Shifta* leaders; (2) to arrest any other unlawfully armed person; and (3) by punitive action against the Teroa Beit Sareh or any other of the tribes or sub-tribes of Assaorta or Miniferi groups, to restore law and order and to prevent inter-tribal warfare'. A composite military force would carry out a punitive raid against the Teroa Beit Sareh, using force as necessary. An 'unlawfully armed person' was anyone in possession of any recognised weapon: a firearm, spear, sword, dagger or [even] a club '. The *shifta* certainly used all of the above.[1]

By this time, Muslim and Coptic *shifta* were collecting arms for an inter-communal battle and both sides were planning to use *shifta* as mercenaries in a conflict between the Tzenadegle and Teroa tribes. On 26 June, Cumming issued a proclamation amending Proclamation 104. It enabled him to delegate powers to the district commander and Lieutenant Colonel Cox of the South Wales Borderers (who had replaced the Royal Berkshires).[2]

Cumming then delivered a pep talk about the *shifta* to the representatives of the political parties in Asmara. The principle of the 'clean slate' was a genuine offer, but under the new Public Security Proclamation he said that he would act without compunction against all who refused the clemency offered. He drew attention to the stringency of the measures, particularly those placing responsibility on communities, the quartering of police in the disaffected areas at the expense of the inhabitants, the preventive detention of suspects and the penalties for withholding information about the activities and movements of the *shifta*.

After outlining his arrangements for the reception of *shifta*, the settlement of feuds, blood money, compensation, subsistence and employment, Cumming asked the political leaders to tell everyone *why* there was a new policy to deal with the 'running sore of *shifta* outrages'. No measures could be effective unless there was a widespread change of heart towards the *shifta*, who were a disgrace to the country and to their communities. He had heard people's appeals for a merciful policy. He now asked them to help the Administration by persuading the *shifta* to surrender. The *shifta* were not moving about the country unobserved. Villagers and herdsmen saw them daily and provided food and shelter. The Administration's aim was to make villagers fear the actions of its forces more than they feared the *shifta*. Large *shifta* bands had mounted vicious attacks upon the Eritrea police, killing and wounding several. Strong military action in disaffected areas and the punitive powers of the Public Security Proclamation were at the ready. The British Administration maintained it had no purpose other than to bring peace to the territory, in order that the UN Resolution for the Federation of Eritrea with Ethiopia might be carried through without interruption in an atmosphere of security and understanding.[3]

On 29 June, Cumming visited the area under martial law. Units of the South Wales Borderers (whom Almonds found not very tough, moving slowly and needing half the *askaris* to carry their water for them) and the EPFF searched the hills occupied by the Teroa and kindred tribes. The Field Force then flushed out a *shifta* gang led by Abdulla Barati from a temporary grazing village, but they escaped into the rough and wooded valley below.[4]

Cumming was as good as his word. Having interrogated witnesses who admitted giving shelter and aid to the gang, he had them arrested under the Public Security Proclamation and seized animals to defray a communal fine on the tribe.[5] He then met the leaders of both sides at Beit Gherghis and addressed them in the presence of units of the British Garrison and the Field Force. Both sides agreed to arbitrate and the Copts of Hamasien paid a debt, outstanding since a 1949 Keren court of conciliation judgment. To prevent further bloodshed and thefts, Cumming seized Beni Amer camels and told the leaders that they would be sold daily until the cattle recently stolen by the Beni Amer tribes were returned. He also ordered the seizure of cattle from the Deki Dasheim and Makara people in payment of the debt owed by them as a result of the last conciliation meeting held in Keren.[6]

Cumming then required all the parties to enter into a bond of £1,000 to keep the peace. If the peace was broken, he would fine the aggressors £1,000 and seize from them property equivalent to that sum. Village chiefs said that the *shifta* would not accept the general amnesty until the dispute was settled, to which Cumming responded that the Administration was not going to accept any conditions imposed by the *shifta*. In addition, he proposed to deal with villagers who for so long had been assisting them. The British Administration would remain in Eritrea until September the following year at the latest. There would be no more speeches and exhortations, only action. He concluded, 'I know that you leaders who are listening to me want peace and therefore that I have your agreement and support.'[7]

The *shifta* remained uninterested. On 30 June, police drove off *shifta* who boldly held up camel trains twice – driven by a Field Force platoon with Air Operations flight cover. One gang stole five cattle and demanded money from villagers. On 1 July, the Field Force engaged *shifta* leaders Techeste Haile and Adum Bohame with their gangs, killing two *shifta* and wounding one. A few days later, a Field Force Platoon engaged the gang and captured three, including the leader.

The amnesty figures began to come in. Total *shifta* casualties for the month of June were 26 killed, 27 captured and 33 surrendered, including 24 in the Western Province.[8] One hundred and forty-nine had surrendered in the Hamasien, 39 in Serae, four in Akele Guzai, 13 in the Red Sea Division and 13 in the Western Province, giving a total of 218. Not enough *shifta* were turning themselves in.

Cumming decided that the heads of the districts, tribes and villages were not pulling their weight and issued a British Administration–Eritrea Notice. It began 'TO ALL THE HEADS OF DISTRICTS, TRIBES AND VILLAGES'. It said that half the period of the general amnesty had elapsed and that despite their assurances of supporting his request to end Eritrean banditry, few *shifta* had taken advantage of it. 'IF THE *SHIFTA* DO NOT SURRENDER ON OR BEFORE THE 18TH OF JULY', the notice went on, 'it will be a serious matter for the rural people of Eritrea.'

It was clear that villagers and tribesmen were still helping the *shifta*, feeding them and allowing them water at wells. The Administration had sufficient evidence to punish most villagers and tribes under the new Public Security Proclamation. 'Your duty is clear', the notice said. 'PERSUADE THE *SHIFTA* TO ACCEPT THE AMNESTY; REFUSE FOOD AND SHELTER TO THOSE *SHIFTA* WHO DO NOT ACCEPT THE AMNESTY.' In every case where a whole village community had taken collective action against the *shifta*, the notice maintained, they had been driven off. Opinion had finally turned. The *shifta* were their enemies because they brought disaster upon villages. Now was the time to put an end to the *shifta* who had caused them so much loss and suffering. If they did not want to expose themselves to punishment for assisting the *shifta*, their best defence was to bring the *shifta* back to their homes in peace.'[9] The Administration's notice was signed 4th July 1951 by D C Cumming, Chief Administrator, Eritrea and franked with the purple stamp of the British Administration Eritrea Secretariat. SDOs continued to report the number of surrendered *shifta*, but the authority of the Administration was still being flouted daily.

By 4 July, action to hunt down offenders since the general amnesty resulted in some decrease in cases. Major *shifta* leaders were quiescent, despite their threats to join the tribal disputes. Most had been in contact with the Administration with a view to surrendering. Over 100 had done so and many more were trying various methods for testing the Administration's sincerity before presenting themselves. The confidence of the police and public was recovering. Two villages near Asmara decided to resist *shifta* demands. One village even captured and badly injured three *shifta* and others drove a *shifta* band away.

The pressure on the *shifta* leaders also began to have results. Abdulla Barati asked for terms. On 5 July, the OC Field Force met him at a hideout in the hills south of Ghinda in the northern Red Sea region. Barati offered to surrender on 9 July after collecting the rest of his gang. Previous strong action taken against the whole Assaorta tribe had caused him to capitulate, since those *shifta* had been his gunmen. However, the root of the trouble was their feud with the Tzenadegle tribe. So Cumming signed an order for the detention in Keren of Georgio Habtit, the wealthy and urbanised instigator of the Tzenadegle quarrel, and arranged for both their villages to be searched.[10] But the worst killers remained at large.

On 6 July, Cumming issued a specific notice, stamped in blue, to all named *shifta* wanted for murder. It said that (insert the man's name) had been reported to him for crimes punishable by death. If the man surrendered before 18 July under the general amnesty, his life would be saved and he could resume a peaceful life. If not, the army and police would arrest him and *he would be 'tried and hanged'* [my italics]. Since Cumming was now authorised by HM Government to approve such hangings, he was giving the man his personal warning. Another notice 'To All Eritreans' said that the *shifta* had only twelve days left to surrender. It ended, 'Persuade all *shifta* to surrender and restore peace to this country. THIS IS THEIR LAST CHANCE.'[11]

That day, the latest surrender figure was 192, including 15 Muslims. The Italians were still pushing Whitehall for severe measures for any *shifta* who did not surrender. The Foreign Office pleaded that many areas were very inaccessible and the chief administrator had limited resources. The Italians retorted that if British security forces were inadequate, they could easily be increased by drawing on the large forces that Britain had on the Suez Canal.[12]

In the interests of stiffening tribal chiefs' backbones, Cumming addressed a large meeting of Muslims and Copts in the forest reserve near Decamere. He described his repressive measures to stop further inter-tribal fighting and set up a conciliation court. He gave a firm ruling on the question of Muslim cultivation rights on Coptic lands. As he stood up to leave the meeting, a snake emerged from the ground where he had been sitting. One of the assembly killed it, whereupon hail and rain descended. Such a combination of omens had exactly the right impact. Cumming resolved to cancel the local emergency when Ali Scium surrendered and when operations to relieve the Tzenadegle of their firearms had better results. Entirely missing the point, the Foreign Office noted the surrender figures but asked, 'What about the 19 leaders for export to Ethiopia? These are the people we are most interested to hear about.'[13]

Political wheels turned. On 10 July, the Eritrean Assembly unanimously approved the draft Constitution. The emperor was due to approve it in September, along with the Federal Act, with the date for the transfer of power set for the 15th.

On 12 July, about sixty *shifta*, Tigrinians led by the young Tecle Asfaha (who had got clean away with 100 cattle in May) attacked a police station near Adi Ugri, overpowered the guards and forced an entry. He stole an impressive list of armour including twenty-two rifles, two TSMGs, one 12-bore shotgun, one box of LMG magazines and the remaining ammunition. Cleverly, he had timed the attack to coincide with another assault on the nearby house of two British police officers, who were cut off by heavy rifle fire. There were no serious police or *shifta* casualties, but a joint military and Field Force operation then ensued to surround the *shifta* gang concerned. Again, Asfaha gave them the slip.

On 14 July, Asfaha wrote to the district commissioner to say that he was avenging the death of his brother, Grazmac Ilfai, who had been killed 'in action' by British troops in April. The seizing of weapons two days earlier was, he said, his 'first step'. His second would be the killing of British soldiers. He then ambushed the very Field Force platoon pursuing him. One sergeant was killed and one OR wounded. However, one SMLE rifle, one Italian rifle and a thousand rounds of .303 ammunition were recovered. But Asfaha and his gang were starving. The next day, villagers four miles south west of Adi Ugri fed them. Five Field Force platoons and one company of the South Wales Borderers were now operating in this very mountainous country to intercept the gang before it crossed the frontier. Asfaha and his men were in a tight spot.

On 16 July, a somber communication arrived at the Foreign Office, thought to relate to Techeste Haile and Adum Bohame:

'TELEGRAM 'Asmara: Two *shifta* band members hanged
AAB News Agency Cairo 1774

The death sentence was carried out early this morning on two members of the *shifta* band… arrested at the beginning of July and sentenced to death by a special tribunal. The Governor General [sic] rejected their appeal… the first… *shifta* to be hanged following publication of the Public Order which aims at the arrest of band members.

End BBC Mon 1925 16/7 BG+'[14]

Both gang leaders had only been caught on 1 July. British Justice was indeed swift in Eritrea.

It was not easy for *shifta* wanting to escape their past to go straight. On 22 July, six *shifta*, led by Beine Hagos, an Ethiopian leader, stole sixty cattle east of Asmara and the next day cut off the ears and tongue of a young ex-*shifta* who had surrendered under the general amnesty. The gang stole thirteen cattle from an Italian concession and 400 from villagers, before killing one Muslim, holding up a bus, robbing the passengers, abducting another villager and stealing 200 goats from an Italian concession.[15]

On 25 July, Cumming reported to the Secretary of State on the results of the general amnesty. The numbers had increased from twenty-six in week one to 483 in week four, giving the following picture:

	Coptic	Muslim	Total
Asmara & Hamasien	334	10	344
Red Sea	17	46	63
Akele Guzai	20	97	117
Serae	372	-	372
Western Province	18	247	265
Totals	761	400	1,161

Forty-five of these men were *shifta* leaders. The surrender of firearms was not entirely satisfactory. Apart from knives, spears and swords, the result was 41 .303 rifles; 21 pistols and revolvers; 279 other rifles and guns; and 394 hand grenades. Some leaders had surrendered to the Ethiopian authorities and were handed over to the Governor of Adua. He asked Lascelles for instructions about them. The handover was eventually put into effect with the help of the Ethiopian Mission and the Ethiopian Liaison Officer, Colonel Negga.[16]

Like all police forces, Almonds found the Field Force police occasionally treacherous. Out on a manhunt, he rounded a bend and came face to face with a *shifta*. They were about five yards apart. The outlaw was young, in his late teens or early twenties. Thin and haggard, he looked exhausted. His face, prematurely lined from a hard life on the run, was fixed with a deep, permanent frown. He was near spent and Almonds could see it. It was like looking at the picture of himself taken *six months* after his own escape in Italy. For a few moments, they eyed each other. Then, Almonds said, slowly,

'You, tired? Hungry? Do you know about the amnesty?'

The outlaw had clearly heard about something as he kept pointing east and gesturing, while asking what sounded like a question.

'If you go on, you know you will be shot', Almonds said. He did his best to reassure the *shifta* about the amnesty: 'House; work; no more fighting.'

Still, the young man seemed wary. He was lightly armed with a spear and sword, while Almonds had his rifle slung across his back. Gradually, the *shifta* relaxed. Almonds promised him the terms of the amnesty. He explained them and gave the man his word that he would receive the terms pledged. Finally, the terrorist agreed to come in – he and his small gang. The men came towards him in a group and Almonds and his men walked back with them. On the way, he shot them a hare and sent one to fetch it. Then, keeping them all under scrutiny, he ate a meal with them.

Almonds completed the forms that each man was given as evidence of their surrender. As he completed one for the young *shifta* leader, he looked up in surprise on hearing the name 'Tecle Asfaha'. This was the young man who was avenging the death of his brother, had declared war on the British, eluded capture and ambushed a Field Force platoon. Even he had finally surrendered. Almonds took them to Asmara and handed them over. McGill, full of glee, took charge and said they would be 'okay'.[17]

It was a betrayal. A week later, Almonds discovered that Tecle Asfaha and his gang were being given a rough time. They received the full rigours of the law, some being hanged in a police gaol. In giving his word and personal promise, Almonds had accepted and relied on McGill's word. But that trust had been misplaced. He felt terrible. It had not been his treachery, but he had to live with it. He could not establish whether Tecle Asfaha had been hanged. Almonds hated gratuitous killing. In Norway, on 8 May 1945, he had been observing high on a hill lying next to Paddy Mayne. The end of the war had just been declared. But Mayne was picking off German soldiers below as they loaded trucks at a crossroad. Years later, Almonds told my sister Gloria about it. She asked, 'Didn't you try to stop him?' To which my father replied,

'If *you* were next to Paddy Mayne in killing mode, would *you* try to stop him?'[18]

The general amnesty worked. By the end of July, the surrender total was 1,247, including 353 from the Western Province. By 4 August, it was 1,318 and by 13 August, when no more surrenders were being accepted, it had reached 1,328. Surrenders were later accepted from an additional 43 *shifta*, mostly from the Western Province and other areas where it was difficult for news of the amnesty to reach them, giving a total of 1,371. This total amounted to over 90 per cent of all *shifta*, including 42 recognised leaders.[19]

There was still work for the Special Court. On 23 July, a Field Force platoon searched a village and arrested two villagers in possession of guns and ammunition. The next day, they caught two *shifta* who had surrendered but then rejoined the *shifta* during the amnesty. The EPFF engaged four *shifta* who had assaulted villagers, killing two and capturing two. Military and Field Force patrols then carried out 'punitive action' on the villagers on 30 July.

On 31 July, in yet another variation on the 'inside job', four *shifta* travelling on a train robbed the ticket collector. External *shifta* supporting fire then opened up on the train at a signal given by the four *shifta* as they jumped off. On 1 August, military and Field Force platoons brought about the surrender of a *shifta* leader. The next day, one platoon of the Royal Berkshires, accompanied by a local chief, visited two villages and gave a field firing demonstration to impress the villagers. A company of the South Wales Borderers carried out flag marches through several villages and later gave more field firing demonstrations in the area watched by all the male villagers. The 'natives appeared suitably impressed'. [20]

On 21 August, Cumming reported a general improvement in *shifta* activities. Convoys were no longer in force on any roads. Steam trains were still being escorted, but a reduced military escort travelled on diesel rail cars. Almonds's operations in the Western Province were having satisfactory results. Subsequent sitreps showed a largely reduced level of *shifta* activity.

Almonds had fought in the Second World War for a just cause against the Nazis. In Eritrea, so much pointless killing and maiming had sickened him.

In early August, Almonds wrote to Lockie:

'These words of prayer dear are by St Francis of Assisi. They rather struck me and so I write them for you: – 'Lord, make me an instrument of thy peace. Where there is hatred, let me sow love; where there is injury, pardon; where there is doubt, faith; where there is despair, hope; where there is darkness, light; where there is sadness, joy. O divine master, grant that I may not so much seek to be consoled, as to console; to be understood as to understand; to be loved as to love; for it is in giving that we receive; it is in pardoning that we are pardoned; and it is in dying to self that we are born to eternal life.' I rather like these words Maymie. They are so tender and selfless and so much of the world is given to hatred and greed.'[21]

There was, indeed, a nasty end to it all. On 21 August, Pearce wrote to the Foreign Office that they might be 'interested to know something of the… persons we are now hanging'. The Beine Hagos gang leader was still at large, but attached was a confession by Ghindia Redda, hanged the previous Monday. '[He] gave the prison officials considerable trouble on the morning of his execution. When freed of his handcuffs and manacles, he became very aggressive and had to be forcibly quietened before he was pinioned.'[22] The Special Court had heard evidence from the surrendered ex-*shifta* who had been walking up the road east of Asmara on 23 July when the Beine Hagos gang captured him. They thought him an informer and after some debate (about whether to cut off a hand or a foot) decided to cut off his ears and his tongue. They had tried to pull out his tongue with pincers to keep him quiet while his ears were being removed. But with his tongue hanging by a shred, he walked into Asmara where a doctor was able to save it. Though not very articulate, he had given enough evidence to hang Redda and two gang members. During the period, five *shifta* were arrested, tried and executed for previous crimes.[23]

During September, Cumming reviewed the sentences of *shifta* convicted under the general amnesty and approved the release of 110. The EPFF captured 18 more *shifta*, of whom eight were executed. By 9 October, *shifta* activity had resumed. In an attempt to prevent it from getting out of hand, an air operational flight dropped leaflets throughout Eritrea calling on villagers to resist the *shifta*. Eleven Field Force platoons were deployed to arrest '*or eliminate*' a gang involved in a civilian bus robbery on 5 October. Following the stabbing of a villager by *shifta*, the EPFF caught but did not kill the *shifta* responsible.[24]

On 25 December, a very short priority telegram from 'Eridist' to Lockie in Bristol said, simply, 'Will be together next year. In the meantime am thinking of you, all my love Jim'. It was not unlike the message on a tiny scrap of paper he had written in an Italian hayloft when being hunted by the Nazis in October 1943: 'Shall I make our own lines this time? Yes; I think so. Lockie darling I shall be with you for Christmas'.[25]

In the run up to the end of the British Administration, it remained difficult to keep the lid on the *shifta*. On 12 January 1952, at 1400 hours, Rome Radio announced that after a period of calm, there had been a new outbreak of terrorism in Eritrea. *Shifta* had attacked and robbed Guiseppe Tommassi, an Italian doctor from Asmara, on the Abia road. They also attacked a motorbus, robbing the driver and all passengers. Police combed the area.[26]

In late January, Almonds wrote to Lockie to say that all officers on a three-year posting had had three months added onto it. This would keep him there until the end of the British Administration in September.[27] On 20 March 1952, the vice-chiefs of staff discussed the withdrawal of the British Garrison. The VCIGS said officers and equipment on loan could remain until March 1953, provided that no financial responsibility fell on the War Office – but if they could be released by 15 September 1952, so much the better.[28] The question of additional powers for the chief administrator 'for the suppression of brigands known as *shifta*' arose again. Proclamation 104 was back on the agenda.[29]

The British began to pull out. The District HQ closed on 1 April. The Brigade Commander, Lieutenant Colonel Cox of the South Wales Borderers, took over command of 'Eriforce', together with some services previously in HQ 'Eridist'. All other services moved into the military area under Forte Baldissera. A British officer was wounded in *shifta* trouble on the Ethiopian frontier in a most inaccessible place. Patrols had to cut their way through the bush to get to him.[30]

In June, *shifta* held up an Italian car on the road to Massawa. Then, another gang, in a state of starvation because the EPFF had been chasing it for some time, held up a train. The gang disintegrated and made their way back to the Tigrai. *Shifta* also held up a bus on the Adi Ugri road, but the Field Force caught them. These incidents were not a serious recrudescence of *shifta* activity, but caused comment. Cumming had to pacify Matienzo. The situation was much better than expected, although there were signs of trouble with the Muslims and Christians in the Western Province again.[31]

In Asmara, the EPFF was still dealing with armed terrorism, which was beyond the capacity of an ordinary police force to handle. On 4 August 1952, the Field Force had 1,920 all ranks, including 36 British. But 650 were being transferred to the regular police. The only military backup – one British battalion – was also being withdrawn. As part of the settlement, British arms and equipment would be on loan, on sale or return, decried by Sylvia Pankhurst as an example of British stinginess.

Addis Ababa confirmed that ratification of the constitution would take place on 11 August. They sent a senior officer to Asmara to discuss the number of troops to enter Eritrea before the handover. The Field Force told the British Military Attaché that if the emperor went to Asmara, ten troops would not be enough.[32]

Almonds's British subalterns began to depart and his British NCOs were replaced by locally employed men. The commissioner of police strongly advised *against* disbanding the Field Force for some time to come, since the trained men were likely to go and swell the ranks of the *shifta*! Almonds noticed that the lack of support for the Field Force allowed the Ethiopians to increase their strength on the Ethiopian side of the border. Finally, the Eritrean Police and the EPFF were merged. An ephemeral entity, the Field Force had delivered stability in time for Federation to take place.

Paddy McGill left first. He came to Almonds to say goodbye, adding that he did not know what he would do for a living. On 7 September 1952, Almonds was TOS the Glosters Depot. On 15 September, Duncan Cumming, shining black top hat in hand, watched the Union Flag lowered in Asmara. The UN Resolution notwithstanding, the UK was accused of having 'given' Eritrea to Ethiopia. Almonds thought it a scandalous betrayal of any principle of self-determination. The British Government 'exacted a sum of more than £900,000 from the Ethiopian Government for the stores they had decided to leave in Eritrea.'[33]

As promised, Almonds spent Christmas 1952 with us, his family.[34] Then, he heard that the SAS was reforming in Malaya. Immediately, he volunteered to rejoin them.

And Eritrea went forward – towards thirty years of war.

PART THREE

January 1953–August2005

Chapter Nine

MALAYAN PICNIC

Almonds went to Malaya as OC 'B' Squadron, 22 SAS, known as 'Big-time B'. He arrived just in time to be invited to a farewell party at Kuala Lumpur Railway Station – known as a scene of wide-eyed, sober arrival and drunken departure. The officer from whom he was taking over, Alistair McGregor, and the SSM, Peter Walter, were both leaving. Walter and 'Big Frank' Williams were part of a four-man group departing to attend the coronation.[1] He and Macgregor had heard of Almonds from Bob Bennett and Johnny Cooper. It was quite a send-off. So good, in fact, that the leavers missed their train and departed early the next morning, unwitnessed by anyone.[2]

The reconvened SAS, based at Sungei Besi, was not operating according to the culture and self-discipline Almonds had known at the founding of 'L' Detachment in 1941. David Stirling would never have tolerated such poor performance, excessive drinking and loose talk. Stirling had permitted relaxed standards of turnout and, of necessity, beards during desert raids. But on return to base, he always insisted that men dressed impeccably. As for discipline, Almonds said,

'He held that unit together to a high standard of discipline only by the threat of being RTU'd.' Almonds had never seen anything like it before and he never saw it again.[3] 'B' Squadron had a reputation for a somewhat unruly disposition. Peter de la Billière, then a troop officer in the squadron, certainly found them a challenge to lead and manage.[4] But Almonds was proud to be an SAS squadron commander again, this time as an officer, having taken over D Squadron 1st SAS as SSM when Ian Fenwick was killed in the Forest of Orleans in 1944.

On 19 June, the rest of our family sailed from Southampton for Singapore on the troopship *Empire Windrush*. Our month-long voyage took us through many lands and seas. One beautiful and calm morning, we came up on deck to find the massive Rock of Gibraltar towering over us. Sailing on, close to the North African side of the Mediterranean, we saw little white houses dotted along the shore.

School on the ship was run by two National Service soldiers who were teachers. On a map on the wall I saw the United Kingdom, coloured pink. So was a large part of the rest of the globe, including the country to which we were going, Malaya. I understood that Britain had an empire. The teachers said that the sun never set on the British Empire because some part of it was always in daylight. The school had a small children's library. I soon exhausted that and was allowed, at the age of eight, into the adult library.

The Somerset Light Infantry were on board, mostly young National Servicemen. They did PE on deck, cleaned their kit and attended lectures. Not much had changed in that way since Almonds had been on a troop ship to the Middle East in 1941. Weapon training was limited by being at sea, so the different platoons undertook sessions on weapon care and maintenance. Part of each lesson included dismantling and reassembling the .303 Bren LMG with its curved magazine. The NCO instructor did it first and then each soldier had to follow. After school, I would lie on the deck nearby, hidden under a row of chairs. I watched it so many times that when a soldier hesitated, I could surreptitiously point to the next piece of the weapon that had to be replaced.

On arriving at Port Said, we could not go ashore because of 'local anti-British feeling'. The Suez Canal was narrow, with only a few yards of water on either side of the ship. Small boys swam alongside. Local men pulled up buckets of water for washing. Squatting on the bank, they soaped themselves, deliberately displaying their private parts. Mothers on the British troop ship rushed with white-gloved hands to cover the eyes of their little darlings. One woman, having seen children looking on, said to Lockie, 'How shocking. What are you going to do about it?'

'If you didn't make such a song and dance about it,' retorted my mother, 'the men wouldn't do it. The children are going to see a lot more than that before we go back to England.' But our eyes were fixed on the sands, the great open sky and two little half diamonds in the distance that were the pyramids.

It grew even hotter. We came on deck to find it covered with large red locusts. It was impossible not to step on them and the surface was soon a mass of crushed insects, being swabbed away by the sailors. Not long afterwards, shoals of flying fish landed all over the boat, even coming in through open portholes. The ship's crew, aided and abetted by the Somerset Light Infantry, made quite a thing of crossing the Tropic of Cancer at 23 degrees north. Looking down from a railing onto a lower deck, we watched some tomfoolery with a tin bath and somebody dressed as Neptune with a cloak and trident. Good entertainment in the days before IT and the internet.

There were tragedies, too. The ship's medical officer regularly warned over the loudspeaker about avoiding sunburn. On the ship's side, babies napped in special cots fixed to the ship's rail. These were always on the shady side as the *Windrush* creamed through the ocean. Mothers were warned to keep an eye on them. They were nearby so mothers could hear the babies if they cried. On one occasion, the ship changed course so that the cots were in the sun. One baby did not cry but it suffered sunstroke and died. I watched my first burial at sea.

On reaching Singapore, a British Army band met us on the quayside and played us ashore. At the back of a large welcome party, we spotted my father, standing out head and shoulders above everyone, wearing his red beret.[5] Two jeeps appeared, with two young, good-looking SAS NCOs. The jeeps had no sides. We hung on as they drove us through the new sights and smells of Singapore. Car horns honked, advertising signs in vertical Chinese writing enthralled us and stray dogs were everywhere. In the transit accommodation at the Raffles Hotel, we discovered the delights of the 'gully gully man'.[6] The next day, we caught a train up the Malay Peninsula to Kuala Lumpur. At the back of the caboose, in the breeze of the speeding train, I sat talking to a Malay shoeshine boy who wanted to practise his English. Either side of the track, wide clearings had been made to deter terrorist attacks. Beyond that lay the jungle, broken only by plantations of rubber and palm trees near the towns.

The Malayan situation arose out of the postwar period. Various ethnic groups lived throughout the nine states of what had become in 1948 the Federation of Malaya: Johore, Pahang, Negri, Sembilan, Selangor, Perak, Kedah, Perlis, Trengganu and Kelantan. Muslim Malays, the most numerous ethnic group, were easygoing and tolerated British governance. The Aborigines, a more isolated Malay group, lived in the jungle following their own traditional culture. The Chinese, still culturally and religiously Chinese, supplied most of the economic drive. But many had come to the country as a result of the war and were, in effect, illegal migrants. Indians, mostly Tamils, worked on the rubber plantations, where they were better paid than in India. We saw them chewing and spitting out streams of red betel juice. A mild stimulant, it was their equivalent of the cigarette, the price of which was beyond them. Our *kaboon* (gardener) was a Tamil. We British were less numerous but, because of history, more influential, consisting of the army, the civil service, the police, businessmen and professionals.

We lived in Selangor, in *Jalan Kamuning* (Village Road), not far from the golf club and swimming pool. Slender coconut palms lined our road and nearby grew a sugar cane grove. The cane seller visited it each day and hacked off lengths of cane to sell from his bicycle. He would smash one end of each piece and peel back the hard exterior, so that the sweet pulp could be sucked out. He also passed sticks of cane through the rollers of a mangle and sold the juice. Opposite our house grew *rambutan* trees. Wrapped in a casing of soft prickles, the inside fruit was like a sweet, white grape. A Chinese lady used to hobble out of her house in the mornings on toddler-sized feet, bound from infancy, and clash two coconut shells together for her gods.

22 SAS did not meet on the job. Each morning (except during six-week stints when my father was in the jungle or on two weeks' 'R&R' leave), two young SAS NCOs came to pick him up in a jeep. If he was on jungle training, he wore OGs – fatigues with two thigh pockets and a webbed belt with canteen pockets. Weapons were at HQ, but there was an ammunition pouch on his belt. He wore a jungle bush hat and canvas and rubber jungle boots, which were too hot and had too many laces.[7] If not on jungle training, he wore JGs, a tailor-made starched jungle green uniform with patch pockets, long shorts, metal regimental buttons, long socks, khaki puttees and a webbed belt. On his left breast, above the medal ribbons, were the SAS operational wings won in the Western Desert. His left sleeve displayed the formation sign of HQ Malaya – a yellow *kris*, diagonally, on a green square. This formation sign was everywhere: on camp entrances, buildings, army

information leaflets and all military vehicles, including our school truck. Most of the time, Almonds was deployed in the jungle or training. Hence 22 SAS men had little opportunity to get to know each other.

As in Eritrea, Malaya's government was still trying to restore stability and improve the pace of postwar economic growth. The wartime government had destroyed the plantations and tin mines to avoid them falling into the hands of the Japanese. They fostered discord between Malays and Chinese by persecuting the latter during the occupation. So the returning British found antipathy between these two major ethnic groups. Harmony needed to be re-established. The Malayan Communist Party (MCP) initially tried to gain influence by political means. This failed, so they turned to insurgency. A British Colonel, Spencer Chapman, and his wartime 'Force 136' operated in the jungle against the Japanese and became 'The Malayan Peoples Anti-Japanese Army'. The British swiftly made common cause with these Malayan insurgents. After the war, the good guys became the bad guys: this now rebel force quickly became 'The Malayan peoples Anti–*British* Army'.

The communist terrorists (CTs) were highly organised and carried out surprise attacks, rather like the wartime SAS in the Western Desert and France. CTs worked in tandem with another rebel movement, the Masses Movement (Min Yuen), without uniform or pay, under the aegis of the Communist Party. They infiltrated Malayan society. One target was *The Coliseum*, a seedy bar in Kuala Lumpur occupied by red-eyed Malayan Police and red-faced planters who never went home. So CT intelligence was good. They attacked isolated installations and government offices to create unrest and disrupt normal administration. CTs also terrorised local people, which discouraged enterprise. We saw horrific accounts in local newspapers of terrible atrocities: villagers were tied to trees, tortured and decapitated. Rubber planters were murdered in their plantation offices. British armed forces and police also got killed. The CTs hoped that the British would stop defending these areas so that they could use local people to train their own Min Yuen recruits. They would then attack more ambitious targets like villages, railways and even cities, with the aim of causing economic shocks. Following rebel successes, the police were given additional powers, leading to the ensuing state of emergency.

In Kuala Lumpur, my father reminded us that we children were never to mention the SAS or any connection with it. Even the fact of its existence was not to be acknowledged by us. We did not know that he was risking his life parachuting into jungle treetops, but I was certainly aware of a sense of danger. At night, we heard the boom of mortar attacks on CTs occupying the jungle near Batu Caves. During the day, at school, the explosions of Lincoln bombers dropping shells to flush out the terrorists punctuated our learning. Each morning, an army 3-ton truck picked up John, Gloria and me and took us to HQ Malaya. An armed British soldier with a weapon at the ready sat in the back.. As our truck climbed slowly up the hill, the Malay driver sometimes went perilously near to the edges of the steep, dirt-track road. If we wanted him to slow down, we would shout, *'Nante!'* On the way home, if we wanted him to hurry up, we shouted, *'Jalan!'* School was no more than a series of open-sided huts with roofs thatched with the long, reddish brown leaves of the attap palm. As we sat in lessons, we looked out across our red, laterite playground, shimmering in the heat haze.

In 1950, the arrival of Lieutenant General Sir Harold Briggs, a Burma veteran brought out of retirement as director of operations, had changed everything. Briggs was not going to let the CTs dictate the terms of the conflict. Moreover, he understood that this was also a battle of ideology and 'hearts and minds'. He took steps to settle the many, often destitute, Malay Chinese. Accommodated in *kampongs* (villages) of their own, with good security, they were no longer a recruiting ground or source of sustenance for the CTs. Instead, the new villagers looked to the Malayan government and were less likely to help the communists. Gradually, the *kampongs* displaced the CTs from their hideouts in the jungle. Briggs also introduced war executive committees at various levels of government, to coordinate communications, command and control.[8]

It wasn't enough. Another Field Force outfit was needed. The Federation of Malaya police and the army cooperated with each other, but the situation called for more than ordinary policing. Police jungle squads went on active operations against the CTs. By 1952 some had redeployed as twenty-two jungle companies of the Federation Police Field Force, each with about 180 men.[9] Alf Gould promptly joined it and was appointed District Commissioner for Kalantan. Some of its members were not only ex-Palestine police, but ex-EPFF as well. Whether army or police, the main political aim was to keep the rebels operating as insurgents rather than dignifying their efforts by treating them like an army. For commercial reasons and British prestige, the Government avoided use of the word 'war'. The conflict was another 'war that never was'[10] (but active service, it most definitely was.) Operating from south towards the north reinforced this approach, gradually sweeping the CTs out of Malaya. General Sir Gerald Templer implemented this policy with some gusto, earning him the nickname 'Tiger of Malaya'.[11]

The Malayan Emergency was at its height with the terrorists by no means vanquished. The Chief of Staff at HQ Malaya, Brigadier Rupert Brazier-Creagh, was leading operations to defeat the MCP terrorists. Meanwhile, in Singapore, Lee Kuan Yew, a lawyer who was to become the founder of the modern city state and transform it into a 'Tiger' economy, was championing an end to British Rule altogether. That did not happen until British forces withdrew in 1971, when I was again living there and John was operating in Malaya with the regiment.[12] Lee had experienced the brutal Japanese wartime occupation of Singapore. Many young Chinese were forced to dig their own graves before being shot. He escaped this fate, but a Japanese sentry made him kneel before beating him up. He knew what loss of liberty felt like.

22 SAS were learning on the job. And it was a different task in an unknown theatre. The regiment had only been reformed three years earlier (initially, as the Malayan Scouts).[13] It was a difficult combat action from which to prove that the SAS was worth returning permanently to the order of battle, a position first conferred on it during their founding at Kabrit. The jungle, the enemy and the political environment all offered unique challenges. Moreover, the wartime SAS had operated in semi-terrorist sabotage mode against conventional forces. Now, those roles were reversed: the SAS were fighting the terrorists. And the famous element of surprise was neutralised because both sides had it. The numbers of SAS deployed were also large – not at all the usual style of the regiment. From 1951 to 1953, A, B and D Squadrons were accompanied by C (the then Rhodesian Squadron).

Along with the need to develop their tactics, this large outfit was still implementing new command and control systems. It was vital that these did not hinder men already deployed in the field. Finally, other armed forces units rather resented the presence of the SAS. At first, they did not appear any more effective at defeating terrorists than anyone else. Airborne Forces, in particular, decried the fact that SAS entrants did not undertake parachute training until after they joined. And, due to Stirling's insistence on action not talk, the wartime successes of the SAS were largely unknown, even in the army. For a while, perhaps the most that could be said was that their presence in the jungle at unknown times and places impeded the CT offensive.

British overall strategy had come about via a fortuitous blend of clear ideological thinking and military experience. As far as combatting the CTs was concerned, General Sir John Harding, C-in-C Fareast, decided he needed independent advice from a jungle warfare expert. He called in Major 'Mad' Mike Calvert, an experienced SAS man who had commanded the SAS brigade for its last six months – the cousin of Dan Calvert, Almonds's Eritrea canoeing companion.[14] Calvert and others had tried to preserve the SAS ethic and culture after its disbandment in October 1945.

Calvert's ideas went with the grain of cutting off terrorists from their support and recruitment source. He suggested counterattack in the form of deep-penetration patrol units to locate CT encampments and either destroy them or lead in conventional forces. This strategy would also limit the CTs' ability to operate at will throughout the jungle. Meanwhile, the police would focus on protecting civilians and gathering intelligence. The SAS also collected intelligence while harassing CTs and their communications lines. Resettling itinerant Chinese fitted this approach well. Thus Calvert led the reestablishment of the SAS in Malaya.

He lost no time and was a hard taskmaster, telling the new arrivals that too many officers were afraid to make a decision – 'looking for the bloody rules before they do anything'. An officer who never made a mistake was not doing anything; he was useless (Almonds agreed with him on that). But they shouldn't make the same mistakes twice. Most of all, Calvert pushed the pace on training. 'People want to see results… they put a lot of faith in us. There isn't time to 'do a Monty'. We can't afford to wait until everything is ready before we begin operations.' All well and good, but such operations were dangerous. They cost lives and caused injuries.[15]

In the jungle, it was necessary, even advisable, to grow a beard because it helped with camouflage. Calvert agreed. 'If a man thinks he looks tough, he will often be tough and, more important, act tough.'[16] A beard made no difference to Almonds. He operated the same way whether he had one or not. He was superbly fit and had again returned to parachuting without difficulty, this time after a gap of nine years.[17] As in his desert days, he still 'excelled in the velvet darkness'[18] and was able to blend in with the jungle, just as he had merged into the landscape when an escaping POW in Italy. He still carried the USMC knife, issued to the SAS in the war, and his small axe. Without the latter, he would not have been able to build the log cabin in which he and his men had lived in the Forest of Orleans. But carrying these two items was considered eccentric, even by SAS standards.

In August 1953, Stuart Perry arrived at 22 SAS RHQ. After smartening up and changing into fresh uniform, Perry reported to the adjutant, the very tall Captain Watson, ex-4th/7th Royal Dragoon Guards, who introduced Perry to the CO. The colonel was studying a wall map. When he turned round, he was none other than the rubicund-complexioned officer with the penchant for gin and cocktail onions that Perry had last seen in East Africa. After a suitable moment for a 'double take', Colonel Brooke pointed a finger at Perry, rather like the Lord Kitchener poster and said,

'You again!'

There was only one reply to that: a meek 'Colonel'.[19]

Chapter Ten

DEEP JUNGLE WARFARE

S AS training had progressed, but not much – given that more
sophisticated technology and parachutes were available compared to
the SAS desert days. Aspiring entrants to 22 SAS first underwent a
jungle training operation of three to four weeks to see if they could cope
with the conditions. Almonds was excused this training (he was still very
fit from chasing the *shifta*), but Perry went on his jungle training op in late
September. The officer in charge of this operation was 'Rusty' Westmorland,
whose sobriquet Perry thought entirely appropriate.

After a long approach from Temeloh, Pahang, they 'basha'd' down in
primary jungle. The site was on the fringes of the delineated area for Operation
Boxer, an active 'A' Squadron operation. After the usual meal of curry, they went
through the various SOPs, contact drills and stand-to drills. The next morning,
Westmorland, who had shared Perry's basha, said, 'Did you hear them?'

'Hear what?' replied Perry.

'They were all around us in the night.'

Since the conversation was futile, Perry asked again what had been all
around them.

'Rhinos,' said Westmorland.

Perry knew the Sumatran rhino was extremely rare. It was highly
improbable that it existed in that part of Malaya, if at all. Knowing of
Westmorland's Munchausen proclivities, Perry replied, 'Ah', and then, 'what
an amazing place for epiphytes.' Westmorland shut up.

When it came to parachuting, preparatory 'ground training' was carried out at Nee Soon Garrison in Singapore. They jumped at RAF Changi, using RAF PJIs. Recruit raw material was unprepossessing. Apart from former SAS members like Almonds, others had to be recruited from within theatre. Since they still had to be volunteers, the catchment pool was not large. Although brave, some men were just not up to it. Learning to parachute was not the problem. Many lacked ordinary soldiering experience; some had not learned sufficient survival skills; and a few were simply not intelligent enough to be resourceful or think strategically when required.

Sometimes, they got killed. My mother always welcomed young subalterns to our house for Sunday lunch. We got to know them and then suddenly 'Uncle Guy' or 'Uncle David' were not around anymore. Angus Charrington, whose father was a rubber planter, was among those who joined us for Christmas Day lunch, 1953. Charrington's parents managed to speak to him via British Forces radio that afternoon.

Training focused on jungle warfare, the use of grenades and personal survival. As at Kabrit, the SAS had to make do with suboptimal facilities (only this time, at least, Almonds was not asked to build them). Lectures and exercises took place in large open areas and sports fields around the Sungei Besi base. The SAS established a series of close quarter shooting ranges in the form of lanes through the jungle. As the trainees passed through them, improvised targets sprang up or slid jerkily into temporary view on wires. This was the basis of the 'jungle ranges' (sometimes wrongly called 'Sten gun alleys'). But it was here that the regiment's fearsome reputation for CQB was born. It was further developed, after the regiment returned to the UK, in 'the killing house' at Hereford.

The jungle ranges, and the practice perfected in them, gave the SAS of Malayan days a huge advantage when engaging the enemy, albeit fleetingly, in the jungle. The ability to shoot fast and accurately at short range proved invaluable. But it was a skill that needed constant practice to keep it honed. At the weekends, Almonds took John, aged thirteen, to the jungle ranges. The boy did his best to take on the targets as they appeared suddenly before him with his air rifle – hardly the most suitable weapon for such a task, but he did it. He must have been the youngest SAS recruit ever.

Deployment was even harder and more dangerous than it had been in the Western Desert. One of the main problems with deep penetration patrolling of the jungle hinterland (before the regular availability of troop-carrying helicopters) was the time and energy spent walking into the main operational area. So they would jump in. They faced a new problem. 'How do we break through the trees?' they asked each other. As usual with the SAS, what worked was largely what they invented themselves. They dropped onto the jungle canopy, then abseiled down. They practised on the Sungei Besi Water Tower – known as the 'arm breaker' after one officer failed to hook up and fell to earth. On Almonds's first jungle drop, one trooper screwed himself down into the trees, but then got stuck. As in Western Desert L Detachment days, they had to get themselves down. Nobody could help them. Despite frequent casualties, this practice continued because there was no other way to get to the CTs. Jumping was still just a means to an end. They cleared each area of terrorists as they went.[1]

'B' Squadron parachuted in and walked out. Almonds jumped with his pack slung across his chest beneath a sleeveless jumping smock, wearing two pairs of puttees wrapped around his ankles to reduce the risk of injury as he landed in the treetops.[2] The SAS cherry beret was trapped under his webbing as he hurtled out of the aircraft wearing his paratrooper helmet. His parachute had no reserve. He carried his Browning semi-automatic twelve-gauge, 'useful' for CQB, his Sykes-Fairbairn fighting knife strapped to his thigh, with his USMC and small axe. With him went 240 feet of one-inch webbing, to use for abseiling to the ground (later on, they just used rope). When he finally stopped falling through cracking and breaking branches, he tied one end of the webbing to a stout bough and ran the webbing through the D-rings on his harness. Then, he negotiated a descent, down through the thick jungle forest, vines and creepers, ready to deal with anything deadly he met on the way down.

One directly transferable aptitude from the desert days was endurance. In addition to the danger of sudden attack, the going was exhaustingly tough. Chopping their way through overgrown thick jungle, freeing themselves from swathes of clinging creepers and surmounting obstacles in the terrain was time-consuming and energy-draining. They waded through swamps and rivers like warm, thick soup, at risk of poisonous snakes and inevitable leeches. Men often emerged from the water with dozens of the parasites sucking their blood, but could not stop to remove them. Massive trees and cliff-like ground formations blocked their path and had to be climbed or circumvented. The canopy shut out all light, but the intense, energy-sapping heat was relentless. They gulped dank air, thick with the stench of rotting undergrowth. The weight of their food and water, as well as weapons, ammunition and a bedroll added to the burden. Though sweating profusely, they could not afford to drink much. If suffering from a snake bite or malaria, or debilitated by dysentery, it was hard to remain full of fight for the enemy. Men needed superhuman willpower to stand up again after each rare five-minute break.

My father was sometimes away for about two months in the jungle. He was 'up-country' or out in the *ulu*, looking for terrorists. After the long march out, he came home for a couple of weeks, before returning to daily training at Sungei Besi. He then spent two weeks honing his CQB skills on the jungle ranges before parachuting back into the jungle. Killing the enemy was not an objective and shooting a CT was rare. This was just as well, as the US .30 Carbine used on active service was absolutely useless. Peter Walter fired at a CT and hit him in the back, but he just kept on running.[3] The main aim was to disrupt their attacks and atrocities, while pushing them relentlessly northwards out of Malaya.

First, the CTs had to be found. The combination of civilian and military intelligence, together with evidence from attack victims was used for 'intelligence-led operations'. But the biggest breakthrough in locating the enemy came from befriending the indigenous jungle people, then called the *Sakai*.[4] The ability to live with the *Orang Asli*, as they became known, and win their confidence was vital for the real intelligence it yielded. They lived deep in the jungle and knew most of what passed through their terrain. And they were far better than the CTs at using the jungle to their advantage. The CTs tried to terrorise the *Orang Asli* into submission, but the British charm offensive worked better. Finally, at the end of the Emergency, the *Orang Asli* became a unit of scouts, whose tracking ability was second to none. The Police Field Force and Alf Gould also used them. They were still in existence when John was operating with the SAS in the Malayan jungle in 1970.[5]

As other Commonwealth troop reinforcements arrived, the CTs withdrew deeper into the jungles and were constrained in their choice of operational modes. On both sides of the main roads, rubber and oil palm estates extended outwards for up to three miles before reaching the thick jungle, where the CTs lived and operated. The British Army began to use close air support, though there were few helicopters in those days, forcing the rebels even further into this jungle, away from the villages and plantations.

The British Army also built a series of jungle forts to protect local people, mostly Malays. Involving them in building and running these strongholds denied further support to the CTs, who were mostly of Chinese origin. To make life even more difficult for the insurgents (who were already living very uncomfortably in the jungle), Special Forces would parachute in and pop up where the CTs least expected them. These deployments aimed to clear terrorists northwards, but also to shepherd any local people they found into places protected by the forts.

Gradually, whole areas were designated 'white areas', which were stable, peaceful and normal. Though it would be another seven years before sporadic terrorism ceased, this anti-terrorist approach in Malaya was infinitely more successful than that adopted later in Vietnam. A practical, if costly, hearts and minds and bowl of rice approach, together with improved communications and cooperation, defeated the CTs. Their only means of pursuing their objectives was violence. Together, the villages and the forts made it impossible for the Communists to win.

Steadily, 22 SAS overcame their deficit in training. And they went further. It was in Malaya that the regiment learned the value of language skills, needed to communicate with their trackers or to win local cooperation when on operations. Improved medical skills enabled them to be as self-sufficient as possible and reinforced the hearts and minds approach. And they developed their 'skills to arm' in areas such as signalling and unique contact drills.[6]

During the war, Almonds had never lost a man. Sadly, in Malaya he did. Each time he deployed, he led a party of four into the jungle. They would lie out on used paths to locate or ambush the terrorists. On one occasion, the group included Angus Charrington. The four SAS men had just come through a tricky and dangerous part of the jungle where CTs were known to be operating. It began to get dark. Crawling at night was not on. They stopped. Almonds realised that they were only three. Charrington was missing.

Slowly, they retraced their steps. One of the troopers found the missing man. Instead of following in the footsteps of the others, he had taken a shortcut across a *ladang* (clearing). Perhaps he was lagging behind and wanted to catch up. A bullet through the back of the head had killed him instantly. Death was not new to them, yet they were all shaken. Charrington had been a super young man. Almonds surmised that the terrorists had been there all the time, as the SAS party had passed by, but had not been ready to engage. Nobody had heard the shot. Thick jungle does deaden sound, but not that much. Charrington had been shot at close range by a silenced weapon like a pistol. Certainly there were no snipers in the jungle, where battle ranges rarely went above ten metres.[7]

The terrorists did not have it all their own way. Some counter-terrorists developed a sixth sense about the presence of CTs. Alf Gould had this refined detecting ability. In Kalantan Province, he was sitting in the jungle, motionless and silent. He was fishing and vulnerable. He heard a stick crack. He knew there were at least two enemy near him. He waited, stock-still, which must have taken some nerve since he could have been shot at any moment. When Gould was sure that he knew exactly where the two terrorists were, he stopped fishing, quietly laid down his rod, picked up his loaded rifle and shot them both dead.[8]

Whether dropping in or walking in, the jungle itself was dangerous. When 17 Troop, D Squadron, under command of Stuart Perry, was ordered to move from Iskander jungle fort to a new patrol area in the centre of the Tasek Bera, not far from their LZ, they met a large lake with very swampy edges. The troop made for one of the rivers, which flowed northwards. They planned to use one of the game tracks that ran along the riverbank but realised that was stupid: if anyone was going to mount an ambush, the riverine track was just the place to set it up. This insight was one example of the SAS still learning how to adapt to a jungle setting. Only two months previously, Colin Fotheringham (ex-Artists Rifles) had been killed in an ambush on a river crossing near the Sungei Bertram (Pahang) on his way back to Fort Shean. In addition to clearing CTs, 17 Troop destroyed any *ladangs* under CT cultivation, uprooting tapioca and onions, while arranging for helicopters to spray the areas to prevent replanting.

17 Troop's approach march was through difficult terrain of mostly swamp and very thick bamboo, which was difficult to traverse quietly and was full of ticks. On the first day, they covered about 800 yards. It was hard to reconcile any feature on the ground with the map. These had been made from air photographs and often included large blank areas marked 'cloud cover' – not exactly helpful.[9] As their progress was so slow and unsure of their exact location, Perry decided to get an Auster aircraft fix. This meant putting up a marker balloon. Two men prepared the carbide gas. At the same time, Trooper Ryan managed to get a lump of smouldering carbide down

Perry's boot. He got it off quickly, but declared that he had been marked for life. The trooper smirked in a self-satisfied sort of way. Rank meant very little in the jungle. They did not wear badges of rank, so that, if captured, the enemy would not know who was who. At one point, John Slim joined them from Australia for a couple of weeks. He suggested that officers no longer be called 'sir' but 'boss', which has been regimental practice ever since.[10]

The Auster pilot located the marker and gave a map reference. Perry could not believe it, but the pilot said he was not really surprised as about 9,000 yards of the map were missing. But he gave the group a fix to the river and said they should be able to pick up their bearings in a couple of miles or so. Things looked much easier from the air.

At one of their hourly halts, the patrol chose a tree full of cicadas in full song, which provided an early warning system. If the cicadas suddenly fell silent, it meant something or someone was approaching. 'Jigger' Johnson, a man built like a brick edifice, who carried the Bren gun and whose chest was tattooed with the words 'Mild' and 'Bitter' in apposite locations, sat down on a large tree trunk just off the track. Noticing what appeared to be a spade-shaped rock between his legs, he gave it a whack with his *parang*[11]. The whole trunk and Jigger became airborne. The rock was the head of a large python, more than upset by the interference to its diurnal schedule.

Carrying on up the track, Perry became acutely aware of another beautiful snake. It was a black and yellow banded krait –very poisonous, with a nasty habit of dropping from trees on anything passing underneath. It wound itself down a heavily thorned tree, eying Perry all the time. Eventually, it entered the river and swam off downstream with its head appearing like a periscope, but still giving Perry the eye. They reached their destination, Pulao Benai (an island), about two days later and set up their troop base.[12]

The jungle also played tricks. The usual practice on patrol was to observe individual 'cat sanitation'. They did not want to leave communal latrines – a dead giveaway to the enemy. Lime was also air-dropped as a neutraliser. Perry was out on one such occasion, attending to personal matters, when he noticed, from his squatting position, a yellow-tinged face looking at him. His shotgun with a round in the chamber and safety catch on was within reach, but any sudden movement might result in a reaction. The more he looked at the face, the more its features became obvious: a red star in a discernible khaki hat; two very dark eyes; a mouth; and a sideways movement of the head. Staring at any object in the dark for too long always resulted in it moving.[13]

Unlike a pre-war Welsh or Durham miner, Perry could not remain in a squatting position for ever. Gradually, he stretched out his hand for the shotgun. No reaction. He could not leap to his feet or roll over because his trousers were down by his ankles. Still no reaction. Somehow, Perry made himself mobile, all the while keeping an eye on the head. Gingerly, he went towards it. As he got closer, the face turned into a very long leaf with markings, which his imagination had turned into a human being. He related the experience to his troop sergeant, Paddy Winters, who replied laconically, 'It happens'.

Not everyone got field craft right. On an approach march, again through the Tasek Bera swamp, 17 troop aimed to take over an established operating base from 1 Troop, 'A' Squadron, who were being rotated back to base. After firing the customary recognition three shots and getting a correct reply, 17 Troop pressed on. At about 300 yards out, they became acutely aware of a very human smell. On arrival, Perry asked the outgoing troop commander what system they used for personal needs. He said he had dug and prepared a proper latrine, as taught in officer training. The smell was a dead giveaway. The troop commander, rather miffed, pointed out that he was a regular soldier and knew how to conduct himself in the field – but not, clearly, in the Malayan jungle.

Wherever they are, the British Army socialises. It is practically written into the job description. On Sundays, we went for pre-lunch drinks at 22 SAS Officers' Mess, Ampang Road. We children sat outside on the veranda with glasses of *Green Spot* orange and peanuts, while Almonds was in the bar. The men drank *Tiger Beer*. Despite its advertising slogan 'Time for a Tiger!', Oliver Brooke banned it from the sergeants' mess, as its consumption led to the place being smashed up.

The army catered for children's needs in other ways. Almonds came home one day and announced that my brother was enrolled in the Boy Scouts – the *Ghurkha* boy scouts, where John was the only white face in a troup run by a Ghurkha sergeant major. They taught him how to build *bashas*; jungle survival; enemy tracking; and how to eat curry – all very useful, indeed. But being the only white boy, he was regarded as a 'boss'. The Ghurkha boys therefore deferred to him when really they needed to tell him what to do. The troup leader must have spotted the problem and, no doubt, reported upwards. After a few months, John was removed to a troup of white soldiers' sons, run by a National Service sergeant. After being with the Ghurkhas, John found sitting around campfires listening to Mowgli stories a bit tame. But soon he was thrown out of the Scouts for chasing Girl Guides. He was not a successful Boy Scout, but never forgot his Ghurkha training.

The early to mid-1950s saw the last legs (and dregs) of colonialism. One Sunday, Perry and the RMO decided to pick up on an amorphous suggestion to 'drop in any time if you are passing'. The invitation, to the home of a rubber planter, had come via a man called Shakers in the Malay Police. They were to 'come around *tiffin* time'.[14] The house, on a vast rubber plantation on the coast near Port Dixon, belonged to one of the foremost Malayan rubber planters. Instead of going home from Changi University after the war, he had stayed on and put the plantation back into working order. He was rich from the boom in rubber after the Korean War.

The visitors arrived at about midday, which allowed them time to catch up on *stengahs* (a drink made from a half measure of whisky and soda water served over ice – very much a South East Asian tipple). After greeting them, their host introduced about eight other guests. Never in Perry's short life (he was nearly thirty) had he seen such a dissolute group of people: debauchery and dissipation was etched into every wrinkle of their ravaged faces. Both Hogarth and Gillray would have found it hard to depict the scene. These pillars of the rubber planting world sprawled in their 'Bombay Fornicators' – a term used east of Suez for a grand type of rattan deckchair with an extending, pull-out panel for the feet and strategically located holes for resting a glass. The occupants called constantly in raucous tones for 'Tinker Bell', the *amah* who looked after the house, to top up their *stengahs* in strong 'whisky accents'. The scene not being altogether appealing, the SAS visitors made their excuses and left for a more salubrious stew.[15]

On 6 August 1953, my father came down to breakfast and told me that as he was now thirty-nine, he was 'old'. Sad to think that he himself believed it, though he still had well over half his life left to live (and live it, he did). Shortly afterwards, an inspecting bigwig who visited the SAS seemed to scrutinise Almonds. After the visit, the CO called my father in, told him he was too old to parachute and would have to leave the SAS. He did, indeed, now have all three risk factors for parachuting injuries: he was over six feet tall, over eleven stones in weight and coming up to forty. Almonds was devastated. He had been aged out of the regiment he had helped to found by a date on a piece of paper, rather than by any lack of ability. He felt no sense of entitlement, but, like any unexpected blow, it went deep. Never happier than when on active operations, he was right on top of life at this point only to be dashed so soon. The army can be awfully cruel to good soldiers.

His disappointment was bitter, but he dealt with it in the same way as he faced every challenge. As a boy, he had often been told, 'No, you can't have it.' So he had grown up used to handling disappointment. When training in the pre-war Coldstream Guards, he had seen guardsmen commit suicide because they couldn't take emotional hurt. He had retreated inside himself and stuck it out. When interviewing Almonds for this book, I asked him what happened to the visiting general who tipped him the black spot. He had died sixteen years before at the age of seventy-nine (while my father lived to ninety-one).[16] It is possible that 'sour grapes' had played a part.[17] Almonds still wore his breast wings, earned in the Western Desert and had a chest-full of medals. If discrimination had caused his posting away from the SAS, my father never mentioned it. His character, formed in a tough Lincolnshire childhood, came into play and he just got on with his life. Had he stayed with the regiment, he might have broken his back parachuting into the jungle. As he had said in his wartime diary, 'The turns of fate are past all understanding.'[18]

Other 'L' Detachment originals and wartime SAS who returned to the regiment in Malaya did not have a very good second run either. Mike Calvert, Dare Newell and even Johnny Cooper, who still had age on his side, all did less well than might have been expected. It was a new game and perhaps old players were not wanted. Paddy Mayne, who did not die in a car accident until 1955, was conspicuous by his absence, along with Stirling himself. They had left the army. They, too, might well have been perceived as being too old, from a different war and not compatible with the ex-Para men running the show. Nobody ever wants someone around who says, 'Last time, we did it this way.'

On 10 December, Almonds was SOS 22 SAS and posted to the Malay Basic Training Centre (MBTC), Nee Soon Garrison in Singapore to be a company commander – as he saw it, an ordinary job. We were sorry to leave Kuala Lumpur with its winking, night-time fireflies and huge moths with window panes in their wings. My mother, too, had been happy there. The house was often filled with the sound of her singing a local popular song:

Rose, Rose, I love you with an aching heart.
What is your future, now we have to part?
Standing on the jetty as the steamer moves away,
Flower of Malaya, I cannot stay.

Once again, we took the train down the long Malayan peninsula. By now, the jungle had been cleared for a huge distance on either side of the track. The great, scarred landscape was scoured down to the subsoil in order to delay regrowth, but not only as a terrorist deterrent. We passed a massive, new open cast mine, which my father said was the biggest in the world.

Chapter Eleven

SINGAPORE ISLAND

There was no immediate escape route in Singapore. Almonds was OC, Number 1 Company, MBTC on promotion to major. This meant lectures, parades, training and administration.

We arrived in time for Chinese New Year, January 1954. No army quarter was available for us in Nee Soon Garrison. So we stayed for six weeks at the Cairn Court Hotel, just off Orchard Road. Nearby, a cinema hoarding advertised the film *From Here to Eternity*. A local couple who had been imprisoned in Changi prison during the war offered us chocolate-covered ants, which we declined politely. I saw an elderly Chinese lady with tiny feet, which had been bound when she was a baby. They had grown upwards – seen briefly from underneath her silken trousers, they looked like horses' hooves.

We went to school at Alexandra Service Children's School on the south side of the island, near Gillman Barracks. John was in the senior grammar school. He sat next to a girl called Sandra Paul, who became the wife of Michael Howard, later leader of the Conservative Party. The army truck that took Gloria and me to school stopped to pick up other British children. Every morning, a girl with a long single plait of fair hair got on. It was Joanna Lumley.

In the hotel, I began to hear something of my father's wartime story. Each evening as he dressed for dinner, putting on his mosquito boots and getting into 'planters'[1], he told my brother the story of his two escapes from the Italian POW camp in 1943. Aged nine, I was all ears. Forty years would pass before I heard it from him again as I wrote his wartime story, *Gentleman Jim*. My mother sewed, making shirts, shorts and dresses. Her sewing machine was in transit, so she made them all by hand.

In April, a large colonial house became available at Nee Soon Garrison. We moved in with the help of some soldiers and willing *amahs*. Lower Road was the lowermost of three roads along the side of a hill. Number 3 was the last house in the road, a *cul de sac*, which became a footpath across a small bridge. From our house, we looked across to another hillside and rubber trees. Every day, rubber tappers emptied the small cups of latex sap from freshly made wounds in the bark.

The footbridge also led to the Officers' Mess, a large, white colonial building, directly opposite our house. After regimental dinner nights, young National Service subalterns (in a rather tipsy state) often gravitated towards our house. One Christmas, they arrived after a Mess party, singing 'We wish you a merry Christmas'. Awoken by the noise, I found Lieutenant John Duck flat on his back in the sitting room with a potted palm emptied on top of him by one of his brother officers, Crawford Turner.[2] Turner sometimes sailed with us, but his antics at parties really brought him fame. That night, he posed as an Eskimo with a feather duster wrapped around his face. Lockie asked what he would do after Christmas, to which he replied,

'Get weaned back onto solids'. And so it went on.

The house was built into the hillside, with its front raised on large, white masonry pillars. Cars could drive into the covered porch, from which internal stone stairs led into the house, and then drive out again around an oval lawn with surrounding flowerbeds. Jewel-coloured humming birds hovered over the hibiscus. Pale, sweet-scented frangipani climbed the entrance columns. Crimson bougainvillea nodded against the pillars. In the back garden, we each had a plot where we grew flowers and even a papaya tree. Everything grew at a tremendous rate, so we enjoyed gardening.

The garrison supplied every need. The NAAFI was at the end of Lower Road. We did not keep a car because taxis were cheap and we gave income to the taxi drivers by using them. My father used an old army bike to ride to his office. Gloria did not like that; she thought it undignified. This CO, known as 'Daddy Yates', didn't seem to mind. Our house had no telephone, so to call a taxi we crossed the valley footbridge to a communal outdoor telephone.

Sometimes, we walked as a family to Nee Soon Garrison church. Gloria and I went to Sunday school – she getting top marks for attendance. John hated wearing smart shorts and long socks. Later, I'm afraid we attended only at Christmas and Easter as we were usually away sailing or fishing. One Easter, the padre intoned, 'And he cried from the cross I thirst.' From the row behind us came a muttered 'So do I, so do I' from the 2IC, Major Beattie, desperate to get back to the officers' mess bar.[3]

Almonds could not escape passing out parades at Meerut Square. He walked beside the inspecting general and, back at the saluting base, passed the prizes to the general to give to the deserving Malay recruits. We sat in rows of chairs on a veranda above. The sight of my father saluting always brought a lump to my throat, as the sound of long drawn-out commands and distant regimental band music floated over the glaring, hot barrack square.

Behind the Mess sprawled the Mandai Jungle. Not large but featureless, it was quite possible to get lost in it. Here, my brother would follow my father on the way to a reservoir, learning to navigate by the sun. The boy could only wonder at his father's self-belief and natural understanding of terrain, climate and the outdoors. He had an uncanny sense of direction and location. As John struggled along behind him fiddling with a compass, he would say,

'Put that away; concentrate on the lie and grain of the land and keep direction from the sun and the prevailing wind.'

The valley near our house had large monsoon drains at the sides of the road, which filled rapidly when it rained. When it stopped suddenly, as if someone had turned off a giant tap, we would go exploring. There, we found tiny balls of wriggling red tubiflex worms. Rather gruesomely, we fed them to our tropical fish at home, along with freshly collected tadpoles. We served the worms to the fish in a sort of floating tea strainer. We didn't go to a pet shop to buy the fish; instead, we had hours of fun catching them in the deep channel streams on Nee Soon's Rifle Ranges. In the crystal clear water, we caught guppies, neon light fish, angel fish, tiny ones like miniature swordfish and even Japanese fighting fish. Thereafter, they lived a life of luxury in a large aquarium in our house. All it took to catch freshwater crabs was to insert a stick and gently wiggle it around. The crabs would catch hold of the end and allow themselves to be lifted out. In our aquarium, we also had some bottom feeders, which changed colour to match their background. My father tested this capability by using my mother's nail varnish to paint some shells pink. The fish didn't oblige. When Almonds was asleep, Lockie got her own back by painting his toenails a fetching shade of crimson, after which she hid the nail varnish remover.

We always wanted more animals. In additions to a cat each, I had a large tortoise, which *amah* brought one day. 'Monty' lived happily at 3 Lower Road, occasionally enjoying cool baths in a large washing-up bowl. To keep him from escaping, we tethered him. Being careful not to hurt him, my father drilled a hole through his shell, at the back, through which we threaded a long cord with a shackle on the end. Monty was thus secure wherever he was in our large garden. Gloria and I also kept white mice with red eyes. My father made them a large home of multi-occupation, with stairs leading up to their little cabins with porthole entrances, where they bred happily.

The garrison was quite big and we were free to roam it. As children of the Empire, we always felt totally safe. Nobody would dare do anything to us. But there were other dangers. On one occasion, Gloria, with a couple of children in tow, led the way along the road above our house towards the perimeter fence of the Air Station, HMS *Sembawang*. The road petered out into a scrub track where it was just possible to squeeze through. Soon, they were all inside the fence. At the track edge, soil had slipped away to reveal a piece of metal with two prongs. Across the valley, John was engaged in some piece of stalking with a friend. He saw Gloria and as she bent down towards the object, he shouted,

'Don't touch it, Gloria! It's dangerous'. It was an unexploded landmine: wartime ordnance still lying around. With no thought of reporting the hazardous find, they all carried on with that afternoon's adventures.

Not far from our house was an electricity substation. It was locked but that did not stop me from getting in. By removing a loose flagstone outside, I could come up inside it. I sat among large banks of humming wires and signs warning of imminent death by electrocution, telling myself that as long as I didn't touch anything I was perfectly safe.

Gangs and dens were the order of the day. John spotted some sheets of corrugated iron lying on some rough ground. He got Gloria up early one morning and they set off to collect them. The sheets were large and difficult to carry. With every step, walking through the sleeping Nee Soon Camp, the corrugated iron bounced to its own rhythm like a giant wobble board. After a struggle, during which time Gloria (wisely) obeyed orders, they got the sheets near to the Air Station perimeter fence. After selecting a suitable former training ground trench, the den builders laid the corrugated iron sheets across the top and covered them with earth for camouflage.

Inside the den, we stuck *Players Navy Cut* round cigarette tins into its 'walls'. The screw-top lids meant that we could keep sweets, string, candles, matches and food safe from ants and rain (the tin roof made the den a bit gloomy inside, hence the need for candles.) Four-gallon courier tins and large army biscuit tins were also ideal for the purpose. Empty kerosene cans pushed into the sides created alcoves for storage. We had a superior den and many children wanted to join our gang. To pass 'selection', a would-be entrant had to stand with their back against a well-known red ant tree for five minutes. The red ants or 'fire ants' had a particularly savage bite.

At home, we were looked after by a 'cook *amah*', a 'wash and clean *amah*', sometimes a 'makee-learnee' *amah* and a *kaboon*. A soldier looked after my father's uniforms and kit. On pay day, the staff would line up in the garden in front of the house in a sort of mini pay parade and my father would give each their money for the week. They worked very hard in the unrelentingly humid Singapore heat (which we, as children, didn't seem to notice). The *kaboon*, who was a Tamil, would lift his gnarled fore knuckle to his temple in a kind of salute after accepting his money.

My mother was strict about not letting the servants pick up after us, pointing out that they were there to clean, cook or wash, not to wait on us. The *amahs* brought us moon cakes at Chinese New Year. Sometimes, they took us to their village to an outdoor theatre, lit by Chinese lanterns. We didn't understand the words, but could follow the stories by the actions portrayed with beautiful Chinese costumes and scenery. The wash *amah* used starch for absolutely everything, so handkerchiefs came back like pieces of cardboard and my pyjama trousers could stand up on their own.

The wartime Japanese occupation was still fresh in local minds. In Transit Road, Nee Soon village, shop owners still spoke of the day the Japanese soldiers came. They lined up the village leaders and chopped off their heads. When digging the garden outside my father's office, a *kaboon* came across a splendid Japanese officer's sword. It had probably been buried when the island was falling to the allies. There is nothing like learning history this way. I looked at the sword and thought of the people it had killed.

Nee Soon Garrison had a school for my and Gloria's age group. John continued at Alexandra Grammar School. He was not a model student.

In one English lesson, the teacher asked the class for comments on Shakespeare's *Much Ado About Nothing*. Unfortunately, she overheard John tell his friend, David Fender, that it was 'Sod All About Bugger All'. John was sent to the headmaster, who sent the miscreant home with a letter. When asked what John had said and having got his son's reply, Almonds smirked and eventually said,

'Not good. We'd better go fishing!' It was great to have a father like that. It was the first time the boy was exposed to his humour and how he could be both hard and funny at the same time. This was probably due to his tough Lincolnshire upbringing and his Guards training. If John failed to perform, Almonds would say things like,

'That's about as much use as rearranging the deckchairs on the Titanic' or a parody of the Frank Sinatra number, *Bewitched Bothered and Bewildered*,

'Don't just stand there looking all bewitched and bewildered, do something useful.'4 He was a hard taskmaster and John sometimes felt a bit like the *Boy Named Sue*: 'I grew up quick and I grew up mean...' Today, it might be labelled abuse or bullying, but John did not see it as such.

Gloria and I joined the local Brownies and lined up in uniform in front of my father for inspection. He gave us the Coldstream Guards once-over but, to our dismay, sent us off to improve the spit and polish of our shoes and brass badges. His criticism did make all of us surprisingly resilient and well prepared for the shocks of life. Our parents gave us the 'fair spirit and honest endeavour' gene.

After school, Gloria and I went swimming in the camp pool in the afternoons or roamed the semi-jungle with our friends. We climbed just about every tree in the garrison, visited the Army School of Tropical Medicine to see the large python in a cage, in various stages of post-digestive slumber, and tried to make friends with the many homeless dogs. I found an underground den with a litter of squirming puppies. Naively, I thought that if I told the sentry on duty at the camp gates, then homes would be found for the puppies, but I later discovered that they had all been gassed.

At the southern end of the garrison, a road led to the nearby reservoir. There, we caught small fish in our hands and let them go again. I sometimes paid my pocket money to the Chinese boys who also caught them to let them go. Crossing the reservoir was dangerous. A massive water pipeline, about 20 feet up above the swamp, was wide enough to walk along; so we did. But the pipe had a tarry, sticky surface that melted, liquid and slippery in the hot sunshine. If we had fallen off, there would have been no way to get back up. The smooth pillars supporting the pipe simply vanished down into the depths. It was also miles to the nearest road. At the time, we thought nothing of it. From memory, we omitted to mention it to Almonds and Lockie. Years later, when I was serving in BAOR, I noticed a book, and later a film, called *The Virgin Soldiers*. It was the story of the national service men in Singapore at the time when we were there. The film even included shots of that massive pipeline above the swamp.

We all fished. Gloria and I used hand lines with some success, while John and my father casted in the proper fashion. My father showed us how to fish 'Commando style', which had been his wont in the Middle East. [5] I'm afraid we stunned the fish with depth charges made of *Dutch Baby* condensed milk tins and carbide. John and my father had a running battle with 'something big' in Seletar Reservoir. Their lines kept breaking; they upped the strength, then noted they were being bitten through. So they used a wire trace, made of old signal cable. At last light, John got a bite but could not hold the rod. Almonds took it off him, played the catch and eventually got it into the shallows. After many battles, they finally landed the 'thing' – a freshwater turtle. John dashed in and turned it on its back. It was fairly docile, but getting the hook out of a head that kept going back inside a shell was difficult. He could not put his fingers too close as it had 'one hell of a bite'. Eventually, they pulled its head out of the shell, snapping and biting, and wound some cable around its neck to stop it retreating inside. After a tussle, Almonds managed to disengage the hook from its mouth. He then unwound the cable and turned it over. As it waddled off back to the water, he patted its back and wished it well. Typical Almonds: hard as hell one moment, soft as soap the next.

The next road up above our house was Middle Road, while the last one, Mount Road, crested the summit of the hill behind us. At the top stood a large water tower on stilts. A ladder up its side had been pulled up for the first ten feet to prevent children (like us) from climbing up it. This disincentive proved but a minor hindrance. The larger children got on each other's shoulders, while the others climbed up them onto the ladder, with the last but one child pulling the last up. The top of the water tower was dizzyingly high, but afforded a marvellous view over the whole garrison and the reservoir.

As a company commander, Almonds did not even have any military exercises to provide fresh challenges. But he spotted two opportunities:

the chance to sail and the prospect of building a boat. At this time, John was absolutely Navy mad. He was always spouting chunks of Nicholas Monserrat's *The Cruel Sea*. We all thought he would go on to join the Royal Navy.[6]

My father delegated to John the job of designing the boat we would sail around Singapore.

'Think about how much buoyancy she will need and how much freeboard,' my father said. It never occurred to any of us that the boat couldn't be built. We took that for granted.

The boy set to and designed a craft that began as a Bermuda sloop, but changed to a gaff-rigged vessel with a sail area of 153.5 square feet. Her overall length was 19 feet, while her laden waterline was 16 feet, 4 inches. Her extreme beam was 5 feet, 6 inches. She had a draught of 8 inches when her centreboard was raised and 3 feet when it was lowered. This shallow draught proved advantageous whenever we went aground or had to negotiate the many coral reefs that surrounded Singapore Island. With a displacement of approximately 1 ton, this little craft would be perfect for us.

Boatbuilding began at 3 Lower Road. Almonds began by making two trestles, as he had done when building a boat for David Stirling at Kabrit. The porch and car-parking area of our house became a shady boatbuilding yard, while a small room at lower ground level to the left of the porch became a sawdusty workshop. Each day when my father came home and John returned from school, they worked on the boat together. They had not a single power tool and only five basic hand implements: a plane, a drill, a saw, an axe and the USMC knife. It was just right for certain tasks. They used the axe and knife to cut all the joints and shaped surfaces. The back of the axe served as their hammer, which my father referred to as his 'Birmingham screwdriver'.

We called the unusual craft *Wug*, after a mythical sea monster in some English language version of a local comic – a cross between an eel and a catfish. Lockie dutifully embroidered the image of this beast onto the *Wug* masthead pennant. Three months later, a large army 3-ton lorry arrived. *Wug* was loaded on board and driven to the Royal Naval Base at Sembawang, where we were members of the Red House Sailing Club near HMS *Terror*. Lockie came with us, but was seasick and never tried again. She imposed the wearing of horrid, prickly sunhats on Gloria and me, but not on John, which we thought manifestly unfair. On subsequent excursions, we abandoned the hated sunhats.

The clubhouse was built on stilts over the water with gangways to the jetty. In excited haste, we would leap from the car on arrival and dash along the jetty to the small boy with a rowing boat, who took us out to *Wug*. She did look a little unorthodox. When sailing in the Straits of Jahore, a fellow yachtsman called across the water to us, rather disparagingly,

'What are you?'

'Unique!' my father shouted back.

At weekends we would go sailing for the whole day, taking food, bottles of squash, swimming costumes, charts and fishing tackle. At the age of nine, I was supremely happy: we could sail, swim and explore all we wanted; school was not difficult; boys were just a nuisance and I could wear shorts every day.

We combined sailing with exploring. Singapore is joined to Malaya by a road and rail causeway at Jahore, on the northwest side of the island. So we could not sail right around it. Instead, we first cruised west as far as we could, then turned and sailed eastwards. The Royal Naval Base ran right up to the causeway, where there was a sunken steamship. At low tide, we could see a magnificent and very large brass whistle next to her funnel. We called this vessel the whistle ship. We could only marvel at how much steam it took to blow this massive siren.

Singapore's shores were littered with wrecks, revealed as the tide went out. Some were warships or merchant ships. Not much salvage had been carried out, so we picked up brass or steel to repair *Wug*. Many hulks still had their fittings. We did not know if the whistle ship was naval or merchant, or whether she had been sunk or scuttled. Even at low tide, we could not get close to the funnel to see the whistle while avoiding the wreck's superstructure.

We made many sailing trips to this mystery wreck. On the nearby shore was a very swampy creek opening. On one of our visits, Gloria was holding *Wug* on station when a grey crocodile came slowly out of the vegetation. It slid down the creek bank into the water not far from us. Its very wide head had a 'grin' that ended in an uptick at the corner of its mouth. It was hard to judge its age; from its wide fat belly and slow waddling gait, it was not a pencil-thin youngster. We never found out the name of the vessel. Even in beautiful clear water at low tide, her bow name was a long way down and at the wrong angle to see. We might have found the answer by diving down, but not after seeing that crocodile.[7]

On the way back from the causeway, we passed the clubhouse and sailed east exploring small islands, '*pulaus*' in Malay, deciding on favourites for future reference. Continuing on, past a floating dock, we saw divers working. A shark savaged and killed a professional Navy diver there, about a half mile from the Red House. Next came the gate into the Royal Naval Dockyard, which was followed by the Beaulieu Buoy and some open shore land where John camped with David Fender.

Inside the Naval Base, at its East end, lived Commodore Munn, a fearsomely respected personage who kept a deep-keeled sloop called *Dayang*. As naval base commander and president of our Red House Sailing Club, we held him in great awe. He was always kind to us. Being an experienced naval man, he must have noted our amateurishness and offered regular but un-patronising advice. On one occasion, both *Wug* and *Dayang* were on the water when we were caught in a sudden squall, known locally as a *Sumatra*. We had a hard time staying upright and suffered some sail damage. *Dayang*, being a keel boat, mastered the weather beautifully. As the storm blew itself out, Commander Munn sailed up alongside us with a cheery grin to make sure we were all right.

One of our favourite islands, even further along the Jahore Straits, was uninhabited *Pulau Seletar*, where we would land on the northwest shore. It had a lovely sandbar beach, with a few coconut palms at the western end among prickly mangrove swamp. There was even a central lagoon. It was a classic 'Treasure Island'. We would anchor just off, swim and eat our sandwiches, then dive to see exquisite fish and coral. We could stay down for a while, due to our efforts at swimming underwater in the swimming pool.

When we stepped onto the beach, armies of little red crabs appeared. The plucky little creatures came out of their homes at the pressure of our footfall. As we walked, they raised their pincers to us, with a rippling effect like a pool of red as the little fellows defended their territory. Starfish, sea urchins, sea slugs, a whole host of mud-burying worms and horseshoe crabs with their long, spiky tails made *Pulau Seletar* a tropical playground. In the evening, when we were about to push off, we sometimes witnessed strange mass strandings of large starfish. It was distressing to see them covering the shore. We tried to return them to the sea, but there were just too many.

Next came *Pulau Punggol*, where we once went aground on some coral banks. We jumped overboard wearing plimsolls and pushed *Wug* off. Further on still, *Pulau Ubin* was mountainous and stony so we did not stop there.[8]

Finally came Changi Point, which was the limit of our day's sailing. As John became more proficient, we began to take *Wug* out on our own. John was skipper. Gloria and I were 'able seamen'. However, we were not very 'able'. *Wug's* enormous teak paddles were so heavy that we could not use them. The wind often dropped to a calm and up would go the cry, 'Out paddles'. To begin with, even John could hardly lift one, but he got stronger and fitter, which, of course, was my father's aim. Being left-handed, he paddled on the starboard side while John was a port-side paddler. They would go for hours, while John tried to keep up with the timing. To avoid boredom, my father built another smaller version of *Wug* for David Fender.

Sailing was not risk-free. One day, the four of us were cruising the Straits of Jahore. I was trailing my fingers in the water from a barely moving *Wug*, when a black and yellow sea snake (very poisonous, dead within minutes) surfaced right alongside my hand. Gloria saw it approaching, its image wobbling up through the water as it broke the surface. It saw me and gave a loud hiss. I whipped out my hand and we were all a bit shocked. John asked what we would have done if the snake had bitten me. My father said he would have cut my finger off with his USMC knife – another of its many uses. I had a lucky escape that day. It was the Yellow-Bellied Sea Snake.[9]

Stingrays fascinated us. We often saw them jump and one landed on our baking hot foredeck. Quickly, we baled sea water over it to help it slither a getaway. We even found a dead stingray in *Wug* when we came to set off one morning. It had jumped and landed in the boat. John kept its hard, whippy tail for years. We went looking for them and found some snuggled in the warm sand of the shallows beside the Red House Sailing Club. My father decided we could catch them if we had the right kit. So, he made John an arrow with a big harpoon head and barbs attached to a line, which he could fire from a folding steel bow. He enjoyed many hours gazing into the water, searching for the small swirls of sand that sunken stingrays make and then launching his arrow. He never got one. As well as crocodiles, sea snakes and stingrays, sharks patrolled around us, but we accepted risk as normal.

Alf Gould came on leave from Malaya. He, John and my father went sailing. A Sumatra blew up and Gould was well out of his comfort zone. When the boat heeled over, he asked, 'Is this normal?' Almonds gave him a paddle and told him to go like hell. John later asked my father which of the two, Paddy Mayne or Alf Gould, was the tougher. He said that Mayne was naturally tough, but Gould had trained himself to be. For his leave, Gould had picked up a pretty Chinese girl, but the Japanese had cut out her tongue. Lockie, not understanding the relationship, asked him how they conversed. Gould flashed a grin. 'Easy', he said. 'All she has to do is nod her head.'

Having an ex-SAS father had other benefits. He showed John how to make fuses out of old illuminating cartridges (Verey lights), which John brought back from some of his surreptitious intrusions into RNAS Sinbang – the Navy airfield between Nee Soon and the Naval Base.[10] John learned how to take them apart, lay the cordite sticks end on end and then light them as a long fuse. Joss sticks made even better fuses. My father encouraged us to do such risky things – a far cry from today's Health and Safety culture. However, the risks were always calculated. He encouraged it as part of growing up.

We got into trouble, too. At the end of one day's sailing, John, David Fender and I had gone too far around the island to get back to the Red House Sailing Club by nightfall. So, we moored at the RAF Seletar Sailing Club and went back to Nee Soon by taxi. The next day, we returned and set off again in *Wug* to return her to the Royal Naval Base. My mother was concerned for our safety.

'Do you think they will be all right?' My father replied with something like, 'Well, if they're sensible, they will be fine, but if they're stupid, then it will be their own fault.' My mother was alarmed. For my father, every trip out was a survival or training exercise: just one *Green Spot* bottle of orange drink to last all day, with paddles about twice the size they needed to be, telling us we could do anything if we trained hard enough. He was preparing us for a tough world, but it was always done with a grin.

All went well until we began to have trouble with tides at Punggol Point. At sunset, the wind turned against us. We tacked up and down, but made little headway towards the Point. Singapore had a strict curfew on the water: soon big searchlights were sweeping the darkening sea. *Wug* had no lights, since we were never normally out after dark. Finally, the searchlight picked us up and fixed us with an unrelenting glare. Loud hailer instructions told us to heave to. A small motorboat then made straight for us. The sailors on board were Malaysian Navy. How embarrassing. They took us to a tall tower, up long winding steps, gave us tea and phoned Nee Soon Garrison. Since we had nearly made it home, they towed us and our boat round to the Red House Sailing Club.

While we were sailing up and down the Jahore Straits, Lockie was making our clothes and running baby clinics. In the baby clinic for Malay and Ghurkha mothers, she encouraged attendance at antenatal clinics, regular weighing of babies and good hygiene. The soldiers cooperated for all they were worth. Through an interpreter my mother asked one Ghurkha soldier when his pregnant wife's baby was due. He replied firmly, 'When Mem wants. If Mem wants the baby to come now, my wife will have it now.' Had my mother concurred, one can only imagine by what means he would have effected the instant birth.

One thing happened to spoil the perpetual summer that was Singapore. I contracted Bell's palsy. One morning, I woke up with the left side of my face paralysed. My family noticed something was wrong. They kept asking me why I was making funny faces. I wasn't. My father talked to me, making me laugh and watching my face. The camp MO saw me immediately and admitted me to the BMH, Singapore. There, I was seen by several specialists, including a neurologist. At the time, poliomyelitis was a dreaded illness.

The next morning, my parents and Gloria drove to the BMH. They had an appointment with several specialists, but Gloria was not allowed in and had to stay in the car. She endured a long and anxious wait, wondering what was happening to me. The bond between twins is exceptionally strong, almost telepathic. She waited there, not knowing if I had polio and whether I would end up in a wheelchair.

I escaped being given a lumbar puncture procedure, to extract spinal fluid for sampling. Instead, a female MO examined me. She prodded my face with a pin, asking me which end of the pin was touching me. On the left side of my face, I thought it was the blunt end when, in fact, it was the pointed end. When I closed my eyes, the left one remained open. When I raised my eyebrows, only the right eyebrow moved. When I smiled, only the right side of my mouth moved. She diagnosed Bell's palsy.

Treatment began immediately – and this was still only on the second day after I woke up with Bell's palsy. I wore a black eyepatch, day and night. The left side of my face was strapped up with large plasters. In the Singapore heat, these treatments were uncomfortable, especially when the plaster had to be ripped off. Twice-daily physiotherapy included infrared ray treatment, warm wax treatment and exercises with a physiotherapist in front of a mirror. I had to do the exercises throughout the day. I was told that when I could whistle again, I could go home. This took two weeks. I remained a physiotherapy outpatient for another four weeks, having treatments three times a week and doing facial exercises every day. To this day, I hate the sound of whistling.

I owe my complete recovery to the swift action of my parents and the immediate, excellent and comprehensive care I received from the British Army's medical services. In one way, though, the BMH did not look after me. Due to a lack of beds in the Families Ward, I was admitted to the Babies Ward. Babies cannot talk, so I was vulnerable. The ward was long, with pillared side corridors full of beds under enormously high ceilings, from which slowly turning fans wafted warm, humid air. The QARANC Sister's office was a long way away. In the evenings, a male medical orderly would come to my bedside and attempt to molest me. He didn't succeed. I pretended to vomit, then I went to the bathroom and locked myself in. Finally, I told him he ought to be ashamed of himself and that I would tell my father.[11]

While I was in hospital, Almonds had to quell some riots. He took his company of MBTC soldiers (all Malays) to provide 'Aid to the Civil Power' – always a tricky business. Singaporean students were rioting against Singaporean National Service. My father was away for a few days until the unrest was brought under control. The protests did become violent and, sadly, there were a few deaths. During those days, I had to be taken somewhere else for treatment in a dark green armoured ambulance. There were no windows in the back, but I could hear the crowds shouting as we passed through them.

Just before our tenth birthday, Gloria broke her wrist. She fell as her sweaty hands slipped from a tree branch and landed with her wrist across a hard knoll. For a while, tree climbing was 'out of bounds'. At the camp Medical Centre, Gloria sat beside a soldier with his arm in a sling, stabbed in the shoulder in Nee Soon village during a riot. Eventually, she was taken to the BMH in a military ambulance. Loud bangs reverberated in the confined space of the metal vehicle as rioting crowds threw stones at it.

Back home, I engaged in another 'mini escape' of my own. I had not got my own way over something, so I decided to run away to England. I left a note to my family, bequeathing all my favourite books and toys to various friends. I did not do much packing, though it seemed important to take six clean pairs of knickers and water. I left just after lunch, heading for Seletar Reservoir. By eleven o'clock that night, I was still missing. By this time, my father had half a company of soldiers out looking for me. He was furious; my mother was crying, but breathing out vengeance. I was going to get a smacked bottom when I got home.

The soldiers tried all my usual haunts and came to the jungle near the reservoir. I got right down between some deep tree roots in almost complete darkness. I was not badly bitten by the mosquitoes, but their whining in my ears annoyed me. The soldiers shouted my name, which I thought was stupid. I was not lost; I was running away. I kept quiet. They passed on. Eventually, hunger and thirst drove me back to the camp, where I gave myself up behind the NAAFI (I thought there might be some food there). At the house, Lockie would not let my father smack me. He was furious at this *volte face*. At least I hadn't been caught. I was quite proud of my escape and evasion skills.

On 27 October 1955, another posting sent us back to England, this time on the troopship HMS *Devonshire*. While at anchor, the crew fished for sharks over the stern with a leg of pork. The water foamed with a feeding frenzy. That made us think. We had swum in those waters. The two and a half years in the Far East turned out to be the only time the five of us lived together as a family (when Gloria and I were old enough to remember). It was where we bonded. Separations caused by the army were followed by separations due to educational needs. Henceforth, John would only be with us for the summer holidays.

We boarded the ship a day early because my father had been appointed the ship's Executive Officer for the voyage. This would lumber him with a whole lot of admin. On one of the lower decks, I sat with him in a tiny office with his name on the door. He explained to another senior officer that he really wasn't the best person for the task. He did it so pleasantly that the other chap was almost apologetic. The job done, we went up to the officers' bar and had an ice cream. The next day, a farewell party saw us off. A marching military band played *Auld Lang Syne* as the ship pulled away from the quayside. Its strains carried to us across the widening gap of water until it and the waving handkerchiefs faded away.

Almonds had hated leaving the SAS (just as my brother did later in 1977), but he had found a silver lining in the Singapore posting. He had built the dinghy *Wug*, sailed her in the Straits of Jahore and taught us to sail. He always remembered Singapore with great fondness and would often say in his later years, 'Didn't we have fun in the Jahore Straits?'

More testing times lay ahead.

Chapter Twelve

WHITE MAN'S GRAVE:
THE GOLD COAST/GHANA

H MS *Devonshire* docked a month later in Liverpool. On that chilly November evening, Gloria and I took it in turns to poke our heads out of the cabin porthole. We could not see much, but the smoky, autumn air smelled of England.

On 9 February 1956, Almonds was posted to the Royal West African Frontier Force (RWAFF), Gold Coast Regiment, to command the Boys Company – a unit similar to the British Army's own arrangements for educating and training boy entrants. That year, the Gold Coast assumed control of the RWAFF from Whitehall's War Office. The RWAFF had formerly been deployed to quell internal dissent and occasionally to fight in wars. It fought in the Second World War against the Japanese in India and Burma. Its senior officers were British. Although training of African officers had begun in 1947, only twenty-eight of 212 officers in December 1956 were indigenous. And British officers received salaries, which vastly exceeded those of their Gold Coast counterparts.[1] The Boys Company was based in Kumasi, the chief town in the Ashanti Region of central Gold Coast. This time, we did not join my father until May.

We had more inoculations – essential before going to live in the country still known as 'the white man's grave'. John remained at school in Bristol. It took two days to get to the Gold Coast by air. On 18 May 1956 (the day after our eleventh birthday), we took off from Blackbushe Airport in a British Overseas Airways Corporation (BOAC) Strato-cruiser. That evening, we landed in Tripoli for refuelling. But as we taxied down the runway, something fell off from under the wing. We stayed overnight for repairs.

From our window in the *Del Mahari Hotel*, we watched *gharries* (little ponies and traps) plying up and down the seafront. The next morning, we flew across the Sahara at only 8,000 feet, which was decidedly bumpy. With each air pocket, we dropped about six feet and the arms of passengers holding cups of tea were left up in the air. Around us, people were being sick into bags. We managed not to be. After landing in Kano, Nigeria, we took off again and finally reached Accra, only a few degrees north of the equator. We were reunited with my father and received the usual British Army warm welcome.

The next day, my father drove us to Kumasi: a six-hour journey through dense equatorial jungle on a narrow and winding road. Overladen trucks full of people, goods and assorted animals impeded our journey. The trucks were 'mammy wagons', each adorned with a slogan in English that identified it to passengers and traders wanting to transport their wares up and down the country. 'Say OK boy' and 'Good time one' were typical phrases. Their owners were the enterprising women of the Gold Coast. They began small by taking their fruit, vegetables and crafts to market. Then, they invested in a share in a truck. Then, they owned one outright.

The journey was terrifying. The wagon drivers overtook on narrow bends without much sight of oncoming traffic. When we wanted to overtake them, myriad hand signals waving us on made it impossible to discern which hand belonged to the driver. By some miracle, there was no accident on the way.[2] In places, the potholed bumpy road was too narrow, sometimes crumbling away and especially vertiginous going over a large, bare laterite escarpment as we climbed up from Accra. Large pythons slithered across the road. Despite being run over, with both ends of their bodies extending into the jungle on either side, they glided on without any apparent harm.

During the drive, my father explained how things worked in the Gold Coast. A kind of pidgin English was spoken, which everybody used. One expression was 'fine, fine past Takoradi corned beef'. This was the best expression to use if we wanted to praise somebody or something. It dated from the war when British boats laden with tins of 'bully beef' had come into the port of Takoradi. To those starving stomachs, corned beef was the best food ever. Another important saying was 'left small', which meant 'wait a minute'. It was important to have these words at the ready because the local people were eager to please and sometimes rushed to provide a service that wasn't needed. One British woman found this all too true when using the primitive lavatories at the transit accommodation in Accra. After installing herself early one morning, a trapdoor in the wall behind the lavatory was flung open and the man whose job it was to empty the receptacle attempted to seize it. 'Left small!' the woman cried, with the immediate result that the trapdoor was slammed shut and she was able to continue uninterrupted.[3]

'Dash' meant a bit more than a tip, so that payment was required in advance in order to get something done. 'Dash' was also a verb – 'I go dash you one mango'. Verbs could be used with 'um' at the end for emphasis – 'You no go take-um'. Of other useful expressions, 'humbug' was used frequently, meaning 'to mess somebody about'. 'Palaver' meant 'a rigmarole'. Therefore, the best way to avoid humbug and palaver was to dash!

We arrived just after dark, exhausted, at our new home, a large colonial house at 24 Royal Palm Avenue, Kumasi. Under a slowly turning ceiling fan, we sat down in the sitting room. A house boy appeared from the large, walled veranda that ran all around the house. He bowed to my mother and said, 'You want chop now, madam?' The word 'chop' was pidgin for 'food' or 'a meal' or 'eat'. But Lockie did not yet know this bit of vernacular. She sank back in her armchair, fanning herself, eyelids fluttering faintly and said, 'Oh, I couldn't possibly eat a chop now.' The boy smiled and explained that he had prepared supper. We went to the dining room. There were no potatoes in the Gold Coast, so we ate yam. It tasted good, but was fibrous and difficult to chew. After the main course, the pudding arrived in a pretty, oval glass dish, accompanied by a jug of artificial cream (no cows in the Gold Coast). We eyed the dish speculatively. It contained the contents of a tin of tomatoes, which the boy, not being able to read, had thought were plums.

The Gold Coast was a British colony. Kumasi, in the dense belt of thick jungle, was the commercial centre: gold mining (at Obuasi), cocoa growing and some exceptionally fine timber. The town had a proud history. In the nineteenth century, it had been the site of several battles between the Ashanti people and the British. After an Ashanti revolt in 1900, the region became a protectorate of the British Gold Coast colony in 1902. By 1956, other regions had been subsumed into one colony, known as the Gold Coast.

The Gold Coast was another unique African country. Freedom was coming and the country would be renamed 'Ghana'. On 6 March 1957, it was the first British colony in Africa to gain political independence. At a parade at midnight on 5 March, the Union Flag was lowered in Kumasi and the Ghanaian flag raised. Almonds was responsible for the ceremony, but it was a British NCO, Staff-Sergeant George Hayes, who did the deed. As an eleven year-old, I wondered what we had done wrong for the Union Flag to be replaced by another. I did not realise that the sun was setting on the British Empire.

Ghana is equatorial. Sometimes, the heavens would open. In a second, we would go from bright sunshine to a torrential deluge, which downed butterflies on the wing and made deep holes in the dusty laterite tracks. A strong wind came just before the rain, bringing the smell of hot undergrowth. Stair rods of rain splattered the shutters. Afterwards, when the sun burst forth, everything scorched. Red, trumpet hibiscus flowers steam-dried in seconds. Ants who had hastily rushed their eggs down into their nest to escape the drenching, quickly brought them up again to continue drying in the sun. The soldiers marching past our house as they came back from a route march, my father at their head, sang African songs in a beautiful, slightly discordant harmony. When Almonds got home, he had to wait ten minutes before showering while the sweat made little pools around his elbows.

From November to March, the Harmattan, a dust-laden, northeasterly trade wind, blew from the Sahara Desert. It brought desert-like conditions, creating clouds of fine grit and a haze that blanketed visibility and blocked out the sun. Seasoned wood twisted out of shape; drawers would not open; doorframes buckled so doors would not close; nothing made of wood fitted as it had before. It was maddening not being able to get at the contents of cupboards and drawers. We just had to wait until the Harmattan ceased, humidity increased and everything returned to normal. Patience was a necessity rather than a virtue in Ghana.

Again, we lived near the Officers' Mess, a large, white colonial building with imposing gates and driveways, double flights of steps and a façade of pillars and balconies. We walked across to collect our post via the British Forces post office. Opposite the Mess, during the rainy season, small white egrets picked their way across a verdant sports field. Once a month, an army projectionist came to show a not-too-old film. Halfway through, the reels were changed and we had orange squash and peanuts. Each month, the mess held a regimental dinner night – standard army practice. One evening, the guest of honour was the prime minister, Dr Kwame Nkrumah and my father sat next to him. Almonds found Nkrumah interesting and impressive. He was very ambitious for Ghana, but my father's knowledge of the country made him wonder how long it would take for such lofty aspirations to be achieved.[4]

Almonds wore the uniform of the RWAFF, with a bush hat, folded up on the left side with a red plume. His office was not near so he bought an old black Humber. He drove it with the sunroof open, the plume sticking out of the top, which always made Gloria smile. Commanding a company of boys aged sixteen to eighteen was a new experience but he had a son of the same age. His responsibilities included recruitment, so there was potential for treks to northern Ghana. One frustration of the job was the constant need to replace the kit issued to the boys, which they sold in the Kumasi marketplace. Even though they paid for the replacements, they were obviously making a profit. The Boys Company structure was of a regiment in microcosm so it had all ranks, including an impressive boy RSM, who wore a large wristwatch – remarkable in itself – and exuded self-confidence. Everyone knew that he had Almonds's total support and authority. I once went in an army Land Rover with the boy RSM driving and was conscious of a very powerful presence. I was in awe of him.

Past the edge of our compound, graceful women made their way to market every morning, with baskets balanced on their heads. They sold sweet, white, homemade bread. In Ghana, twins are seen as a great blessing. We used to stand side by side in front of a bread seller, point to ourselves and say 'Atá', which meant 'twins'. At this, the bread seller would take down her basket and give us a small white loaf to eat. Ghanaians believed that not giving to twins would bring bad luck. Later, we felt bad about diminishing the bread seller's income.

While not exactly *Peyton Place*, Kumasi – in particular, the garrison swimming pool – was the scene of occasional *affaires*. QMSI McBain, RAPTC, used the swimming pool to train Ghanaian soldiers and boy soldiers but army wives also swam and sunbathed there. McBain was readily on hand, in his gleaming white PT vest bearing the insignia of the RAPTC, to anoint their backs with suntan oil. He spent a long time applying it to the back of the adjutant's wife – while his own wife, who was one of our schoolteachers, watched through field glasses from their army quarter on the hillside above the pool.[5]

It appeared that Almonds was too far from any water to build a boat. We went to Accra rarely and only for a few days to Labadi Beach. The West African coast has some of the largest surf in the world. We met Californians who came to Labadi for it. The beach sloped very steeply and swimming was dangerous. Apart from ferocious breakers, a powerful undertow constantly changed direction and could take swimmers by surprise.

Almonds had three possible escape routes from his desk-bound job: devise adventure training for the boy soldiers; go on six-week treks to the Northern Territories (the 'NTs') on recruiting drives; and build boats. He did all three. The first meant Almonds taking the boy soldiers, with its permanent cadre of NCOs, on training exercises. With couple of NCOs Almonds first 'recce'd' a possible river trip. He designed and built a 16-foot canoe, using it as a project for the Boys Company and involving the boys in designing and making the craft. They named it *Discovery*. The trip would be a recce for a bigger adventure training trip down the Volta River.

Almonds would also map the river, which had never been done before. Recruiting drives would give an opportunity to see the country and perhaps some big animals. To the north, the land consisted of poor scrub and baobab trees. People laboured to scratch a living. Towns like Tamale, Bolgatanga, Kintampo, Lawra and Wiaga had little or no commerce or jobs. Hence, the NTs were a fruitful recruiting ground. Building the ketch of his POW camp dreams would be done in his own time.

The Volta River, a sovereign river 1,000 miles long from its source in Upper Volta to Ada in the Gulf of Guinea, awaited them.

Chapter Thirteen

VOLTA RIVER

In summer 1956, John, aged fifteen, flew out to the Gold Coast. Almonds drove to meet him late at night in Accra. On the way back to Kumasi, they stopped several times on that lonely road through the jungle, alive with the sounds of Africa: vibrating insects, bush baby shrieks and honking fruit bats. The two travellers walked around the car several times to shake the tiredness from their eyes.

Once home, there was no time to catch up on sleep. They were going on the journey down the Volta River. No records of this ancient waterway existed. Sir Robert Jackson[1] asked Almonds to correct the scant aerial map, take soundings, keep a log and film the trip. Jackson wanted data input to the impending 'Volta River Project', to dam and flood the Volta River basin to provide hydroelectric power for industry. Jackson promised to provide the necessary equipment, but due to the shocking local communications systems, none of it ever arrived.

For good stability, Almonds made the canoe wide: 4 feet, 6 inches extreme beam with a 9-inch freeboard. She could carry four people sitting in pairs, one behind the other. A large open cockpit separated small decked areas. Under these decks went the passenger gear; with more behind the forward seat. Propulsion relied on four large, very heavy, mahogany paddles, each 5-feet tall, with a blade that was 2-feet long and 8-inches wide.

The other two crew members were the assistant adjutant, Gordon Robson, a young lieutenant from the King's Own Scottish Borderers and a

Ghanaian cook corporal, Danyata Gerunchi. They would cover 300 to 400 miles, from Yeji, 140 miles northeast of Kumasi, to Ada on the Volta Estuary in ten days. The summer holiday was a good time to do it. By November, the river would rise even higher with water from the rainy season, the current would be stronger and many rapids would no longer exist.

Almonds gave John the job of writing the log, as well as compiling lists of stores and kit.[2] They had no life jackets, no radio, no river map (other than a vague blue line on a Texaco Petrol road map), a minimal first aid kit and no means of contacting anyone in an emergency. When John asked Almonds how they would know when they had reached the sea, he replied, 'You'll know all right. The water will taste salty'.

On Monday 27 August 1956, skipper and crew left Kumasi for Yeji in a convoy of four 3-tonners laden with supplies for the army garrison at Tamale in the NTs. They tied *Discovery* upside down on top, with their own stores and equipment. One crew member sat beside the driver in each lorry with Almonds leading.

The journey was long and uncomfortable on the hard, unsparing seats. The heat of the engine, on which John was forced to place his feet, penetrated his canvas shoes. The warmth sent him off into long daydreams, from which he would wake when his feet got too hot. The trucks stopped many times for silly things, mostly minor mechanical problems, which should have been dealt with beforehand. John kept going over the list of stores and equipment, trying to make sure that he had not forgotten anything. He was responsible for clothing and personal items for himself and his father, as well as equipment common to the whole expedition such as the medical kit and fishing tackle.

Along the road to Yeji lay African villages of red laterite mud and wattle houses, some with corrugated roofs and some covered with *attap*. As the convoy passed, the inhabitants waved frantically and shouted greetings in their own African languages, which John returned. '*Broni!* Bye, bye, *Broni!*' they shouted (meaning white people).

At Yeji, the convoy halted near the ferry. Here, the Volta was about 150 to 200 yards wide, with steep ten-foot banks on either side, giving way to flat ground covered with small bushes and elephant grass. The water, the colour of dark tea, was hardly moving. While the drivers untied the ropes of the leading convoy truck, many curious Ghanaians watched. They lent a willing hand to ease the boat off the lorry, turn her the right way up and launch her onto the water. The unloaded kit was placed in a pile on the bank. One of the drivers guarded it, while Robson and Gerunchi went to find something to eat. Meanwhile, father and son stowed the gear into *Discovery*.

While waiting, John watched their four departing trucks take the ferry, one at a time. There were two ferries (or pontoons), one of which was not working. The latter was a large wooden-decked iron construction with a precarious rail, made from an assortment of materials. A small motor tugboat was lashed to its starboard side for propulsion. The ferry conveying the 3-tonners across the river was different. The basic pontoon and unsafe rail were the same, but its locomotion was provided by a diesel engine, housed in a small wooden construction on one side. It looked like a ramshackle aircraft carrier. The cube-like housing was strangely assembled: three of its walls had horizontal boarding, while the fourth was vertically planked. The craft was prevented from drifting downstream by a chain, which ran through a pulley on its upstream side. On its other side, another chain disappeared down into the water and across the riverbed. The engine passed the chain over a toothed wheel, gauged to fit, and so hauled the ferry across the river.

Robson returned and said that Gerunchi was coming. Almonds and John left him preparing his photographic equipment for action and went into the small town. They met Gerunchi coming down the sloping concrete ramp to the ferry landing point and asked him if he would buy them a saucepan (Gerunchi would be able to buy it for a lot less than a British Army officer). However, Gerunchi did not seem to understand so Almonds desisted and he and John went to buy it themselves.

Yeji had one main road with a few side alleys. On either side were familiar mud huts with corrugated iron roofs, some painted a dull khaki green. One or two had whitewashed or distempered walls. Small shops were everywhere, with their goods on display outside under awnings. A heavy stillness pervaded; it was now half past one and the sun beat down. As the two white visitors strolled down the street, the shop owners plied their wares. 'Good day, sir! I say, good day, sir. You like to buy this one, sir? Very cheap. I give you for 3/6d, sir. You no like? I give you for 3s. You don't want?' When the vendors were certain that they 'no want', the cries changed to either grins or curses. The man and the boy went into a small bar, no more than ten feet by four. They bought drinks. Almonds declared himself not hungry. John concurred so they did not bother with food, but drank half their beer and lemonade respectively, saving the rest for later. They went in search of a saucepan and enough bread to last them as long as it would keep.

Saucepans were not lacking in Yeji and they had plenty of choice. After selecting one on a stall run by a little old lady, they asked its price. The woman could not speak English, so she called to someone behind her. The piece of sacking over the entrance to the shop interior swung aside and a boy of about twelve appeared and said in fair English, 'Good afternoon. What is it you want?' They showed him the saucepan and asked its price. There ensued an exchange between the woman and the boy, which ended with him pronouncing that it was for sale for 12 shillings. Almonds immediately showed his displeasure. After another conversation between the two vendors, the boy said, 'She like your face so you can have it for ten shillings.' The bartering continued until they got the saucepan for 8 shillings.

Bread was not so easy. Large, beautiful, golden-brown round loaves, like fire hose coils, glinted in the sun. They bought one for a shilling. With a little squeezing and shoving, they just managed to get it into the saucepan, which amused several young girls looking after the store. Their shopping done, Almonds and John returned to their boat. Arriving at the *Discovery*, Robson announced that Gerunchi had gone to buy a saucepan. Almonds groaned and said they already had one. However, there was nothing they could do but wait for Gerunchi's return.

While waiting, the boy watched the local women doing their washing on the riverbank. He imagined what the English housewife would say about having to do the family wash in the brown soupy water of the Volta. Each had her own large, round stone jutting out of the water. On these stones, the women pounded and scrubbed the articles for wash, rinsed them in the river and spread them out on the grassy bank and bushes to dry in the hot sun. Before long, Gerunchi returned. All were relieved that he had not bought another saucepan (the saucepan they had was their only utensil and in it they fried, roasted, boiled and made tea).

They took up positions in the boat: Almonds paddling to starboard and John to port in the rear seat of the craft. Gerunchi sat forward to port, leaving the starboard side to Robson. About to cast off, Almonds discovered that he did not have his beer. He had left it in one of the shops. Robson casted off and, with a few strokes of the paddles, they had way on her and headed out into midstream, the CSMU firmly strapped to Almonds's right hip.

Paddling hard for ten minutes, they covered about a mile, towing a large spinning lure on 20lb nylon. But as the pace began to tell on them, they were forced to take it in to prevent it from sinking to the bottom. The boy thought it a shocking effort to be so tired after only ten minutes, but he reasoned that none of the party was particularly fit and the sun, from which they had no protection, was just past its zenith. Its powerful rays seemed doubled as they reflected off the water. Later on, they were forced to paddle under much worse conditions, hour after hour, with only occasional breaks as Almonds pushed the pace. When they looked back on that first afternoon, it had been a feeble effort.

They passed a long, narrow island. It was possibly not an island when the river was at its highest. At either end lay a small point of golden sand, while the rest was hidden by a mass of tall elephant grass, waving gently in the faint river breeze. These islands, formed easily by the November flood waters, gave rise to elongated sandbanks that remained long after the river had fallen again. Seeds of abundant elephant grass had germinated in huge numbers on the sandbank, covering it entirely, giving no other plant a chance.

After ten minutes, Robson suggested that the forward and aft pairs take turns to paddle. So each pair paddled five minutes on, five minutes off. This pattern took them along at a painfully slow but steady pace. To be rid of the guilt of their laziness, they told each other that it was not good to overdo things on the first day as they would be stiff the next day. During a rest period, Almonds loaded his .22 rifle with high velocity dum-dum bullets.

After half an hour, Gerunchi pointed downstream and said one word,

'Crocodile'. Immediately, all John's dreams of the past week leapt at him: reveries in which crocodiles had tried to overturn the boat and had been driven off by hefty clouts from the paddles, only to be caught later and their skins kept. He followed Gerunchi's pointing finger and saw a bump above the water: a snout, with two eyes sticking up behind it. The boat drifted while the croc swam upstream, leaving a broad V-shaped wake behind it. The respective courses of *Discovery* and the amphibian were such that they were going to pass each other at about three yards' distance.

Almonds told them all to be quiet, as he had done in occupied France when in a jeep with three other SAS men, surrounded by a passing German convoy. He had brought them safely out of danger. Now, he told his crew that crocodiles were timid unless hungry. They should wait to see what it would do. Gerunchi looked doubtful. John suggested, to no one in particular, that they ram it, which would certainly have done for the croc, as the boat, plus equipment and crew, weighed 60 stones. However, his suggestion was ignored. A good thing, too. As *Discovery* passed the croc, they saw that it was the top of a forked stick, poking up above the water, with weed draped around it and the current causing the supposed wake, making a very realistic croc.

John felt slightly annoyed; the wonderful castle he had been building in the air suddenly fell to pieces. He asked Gerunchi what on earth a forked stick was doing poking up in the riverbed. Apparently, it was the centre pole of a hut swept away by the rising river and possibly all that was left of a temporary village. This statement ignited a burst of paddling to move the boat into deeper water. There might be more centre poles left just a few inches below the surface, ready to make short work of the canvas of their canoe.

They passed to starboard a small village, no more than a collection of huts. The occupants, emerging to see the travellers, began to laugh and point at the boat. When asked the cause of the hilarity, Gerunchi said that they were laughing at white people in a boat, a sight never seen before on the Volta River. During the course of the afternoon, they passed islands, mostly covered with elephant grass, but now having competition from small trees and bushes. The riverbanks began to be covered with thick scrub.

Some of the larger islands still had temporary fishing villages, not yet threatened by the rising waters. Each was a cluster of a dozen or so wooden huts, thatched with elephant grass. Different villages had different types of houses, though most were either a round hut like an enlarged beehive or a ridge tent. Most villages had one larger oblong building, with a ridged, thatched roof supported by six poles. Inside the building ran long beams on which were skewered many fish, hanging tails down. Gerunchi confirmed that these were drying houses. Myriad boats lay moored at the water's edge, but could not be seen clearly as *Discovery* glided by. Above the boat moorings, white nets hung from high poles, drying in the sun.

They passed an island to port. A fishing village lay abandoned, the water already lapping a few feet from the nearest house. Robson called out, but the usual laughing crowd did not appear. There were no boats, nets or fish in the drying house. That afternoon, two birds appeared. The first was a white-headed fish eagle, sitting on the topmost branch of a dead tree, silhouetted against the sky. A bald-headed eagle, it had black plumage with white wing tips. The other bird was a wader, black-feathered with brilliant orange legs and a long, pointed bill.

At half past four, the explorers looked for a flat, clear camping ground with trees from which to hang their mosquito nets, at least five feet above the river in case of flash floods. The river divided into two channels around a large island. In the distance, they saw down one channel some small, steep-sided, sandy islands with grassy tops. *Discovery* paddled down the long stretch of water. Halfway there, they heard it: a dull roar in the distance. Quickening speed warned them of trouble ahead. Rapids! They took that in their stride, but the 'islands' were just large bunches of tall reeds that had turned brown at the bottom, giving the appearance of earth.

Suddenly, with rapids ahead and darkness falling, they were desperate to camp. It would be madness to start shooting rapids on the other side of which lay they knew not what. Rocks, a waterfall, a whirlpool? Rapids might be only a line of bubbling water or they could stretch for 20 miles, in which case they would end up shooting them in the dark.

At last, the river converged into one channel. They saw a game track leading down to the water's edge and made for it. After a hard pull across the river, against a current made faster by the nearby rapids, which they could hear but not see, they made it and tied up. As Almonds walked up the track, he startled a baboon that had come down to drink. It vanished into the bush.

After choosing a stretch of level ground about 25 yards away, Almonds returned to the boat where Gurunchi and John were unloading. Almonds asked Gerunchi to get busy with the saucepan and make tea. Father and son then went back to the camp with the equipment. Robson already had a fire going and was away searching for more wood. They laid out their bedrolls. John's was a groundsheet (the waterproof case in which it had been stowed), a blanket, a mosquito net and his night clothing: a pair of long denim trousers to protect him from mosquitos that got inside his mosquito net; a long-sleeved shirt; a pair of long socks; and a pullover, in case it was cold at night. It was the first of many nights in his life that John Almonds would spend in tropical jungles.

He laid out Gerunchi's bedroll while he made a cooking fire. He took a machete and hacked a slit trench in the ground about six inches wide and 1.5 feet long. He took some glowing brands of wood from the other fire, put them in the trench and placed the full saucepan of water over it. John changed into his night clothes and took the empty bottles they had acquired in Yeji to fill them with water. Night had fallen, so he was glad of his torch. It had a good beam, with which he swept the path ahead. At the bank, he climbed into the boat and held first one bottle, then the other under the water, watching all the time for the slightest swirl in the water that would betray anything below the surface. He had read of a man being taken by a crocodile while filling a water bottle. With two full bottles, he made his way back towards the fire he could see flickering through the trees.

Robson then showed the boy how to use the sterilising kit. He had to drop one white tablet into each bottle of water, leave it for thirty minutes and then put in a blue tablet. The voyagers were very thirsty and all had a good drink. The water was horrible, but it was wet and so tasted 'smashing'. The sudden drinking emptied both bottles, but the arrival of the tea saved the situation. John lay on his groundsheet and calculated where his hip would be when he lay down to sleep. Having found the spot, he punched a hollow in the earth to accommodate his body shape. He tried his bed for comfort. It still left much to be desired. Finishing his tea, which was, according to Robson, 'Without exception, the best I have ever tasted', the younger Almonds started off to refill the water bottles. He was told to be quick as 'grub up' wouldn't be long. He returned to the camp with full bottles, almost stepping in a plate of boiled rice, beans and curried corned beef left on his bed. The others were already eating. He set to with a will, determined to catch them up.

Gerunchi went down to the river to wash up, while John, after fixing up his mosquito net on a tree branch above his bed, tucked it in all round the bottom, got in and began to write the log by torchlight. As he did so, they heard movements in the undergrowth. He and Robson shone their torches around, while Almonds was too tired to be bothered and Gerunchi was already asleep. The beam of John's torch picked up a shining pair of eyes, which disappeared as the animal looked away. Almonds murmured that it was probably a baboon or hyena, neither of which would attack four of them, especially if there was an ember in the fire that would burn until morning. The boy finished writing the log and switched off his torch. The last thing he remembered was Robson leaving his bed to put some more wood on the fire.

Next morning, John awoke to the pleasant smell of wood smoke, wafting in his direction. He sat up. Pressing his face to the net, he saw Gerunchi had raked over the fire to get it burning again. Almonds was tying string around his bedroll. Robson was just surfacing. John was aware of a long, continuous noise, which was, at first, incomprehensible to him. Then, he remembered the rapids. Quickly, he took down his mosquito net and rolled it up. After putting on his shorts and leaving out the blanket, he rolled up his bedroll and tied it securely. Father and son would sit on the folded blanket during the day to save their posteriors from the hard wooden seat. He sterilised more water. While Almonds and Robson packed up the remaining gear and Gerunchi cooked, the boy went down to the boat and baled out water with a china mug. Surprisingly, there was not much. The day before had been *Discovery*'s first day afloat for any length of time (she had previously only been in the Kumasi swimming pool for about fifteen minutes). John returned to camp, where tea and a hunk of bread awaited him. He shared the tea from Robson's mess tin.

After breakfast, the boy took a pile of kit to the boat. He got in, took bundles from the others and stowed them in a semi-scientific way under the decks. He tied one bundle that wouldn't fit to the bilge boarding, along with the fishing rods and rifle, as a precaution against capsizing in rapids. Robson took a photograph of the campsite. He and John checked that they had left nothing behind, retrieving an oil rag that Almonds had used to clean his rifle. Back at the boat, John got in, leaving Robson to cast off the bow warp. *Discovery* slipped out of her moorings and headed off downstream, hugging the left bank until they were almost into the rapids.

The roar became ever louder. Some way off, columns of water were leaping up into the air. Dancing white foam betrayed the existence of rocks in the water. The rapids stretched for some 20 yards downstream where the river fell about two feet over an obvious ledge of rock. Getting closer, they saw two indistinct objects at the river's edge. Two fishermen were standing in the shallows where the rapids began. They waved that *Discovery* should get over to the other side of the river. The canoeists realised that they were being directed towards a good channel through the rapids. With a few hundred yards to spare, they did a quick dash across the river at 90 degrees to the current (a most dangerous procedure near cascades). Having turned side on, they slipped quickly towards the rapids. Half way across the river, they knew that they would not make it. They decided to shoot the rapids near the two fishermen.

Almost there, they had to straighten up their craft and point her bow downstream again. Not quite quick enough with this manoeuvre, they again slid sideways. This miscalculation carried them through a clump of reeds, which, due to the speed of the current and their own weight, they flattened. They shot through a few more swirls and into calm but fast-flowing water. Passing the fishermen, they bade them a polite 'Good morning', to which they received a grunt in reply. Almonds asked Gerunchi to ask them the name of their village, which they could now see over on the left bank. A long stream of discourse came from Gerunchi, but the fishermen just stared and soon the current had carried the boat on too far for any further conversation. 'Happy, sociable chaps,' said Almonds, as they resumed paddling.

They carried on, working in alternate, fifteen-minute shifts over swift-flowing waters where the river had flooded across former bends, straightening out its course while in temporary spate. At times, they chose to go with the flood water, between the tops of small trees and large bushes sticking up out of the water. Although this stratagem made their journey quicker, it was not without risk. Unseen obstructions were more numerous than if they had followed the midstream, but somehow the boat's canvas skin remained intact.

They met several fishermen in boats. Asking them the names of their villages to help with navigation was painfully slow. Some refused to cooperate and stared at the boat. Some gave false village names, the names of villages already passed or those that still lay ahead. And for every village mentioned on the map, about fifteen were unmentioned. Many supposedly mapped facts about the river's course were also incorrect, including the confluence of tributaries shown on the Texaco Petrol road map. In fact, the map proved useless. It had been created by aerial survey and simply joined up known points of the river by a straight blue line.

Throughout the morning, they paddled on, still taking alternate rests in pairs. During Robson's rest periods, he took photographs, while Almonds took a shot at some waterfowl. At about 12.30, they found a convenient, shady spot and pulled into the bank for a rest. Their mooring was a flat piece of land about a foot or so above the water level. The ground was covered with dead leaves and shaded by a mass of tangled creepers. Lianas twisted up through the tree branches. Almonds, Robson and Gerunchi got out while John found the tea, sugar and milk. He handed them across, along with the ubiquitous saucepan and a packet of hard biscuits. Gerunchi soon had a fire going, with the saucepan full of water over it. They shared out the biscuits and tea. They reloaded the boat, sat a little longer and then set off again downriver.

After leaving the bank, their paddling technique, by an unspoken order, changed: all four paddled together and continued like this for the rest of the journey. They stopped for a rest every half an hour for five minutes, drifting with the current. Alone in the middle of that wide river, all was peaceful. Only the sound of the water gurgling around their dragging paddles broke the silence. John, being a non-smoker, kept the boat on course while the others had a cigarette. Since the brand was called *Tuskers*, the rest periods became known as 'Tusker time'. They met two fishermen in a boat. The men were different from those they had seen before. Amiable and polite, they seemed glad to be of service to the unusual travellers. One of them spoke a little English, so they asked him how far it was to Kete-Krachi. 'Kete-Krachi, Yeji, Keti-Krachi she near,' he said. Gerunchi confirmed that this meant Kete-Krachi was nearer than Yeji.

The fishermen's boat was a long narrow canoe, made from five roughly-hewn boards. The flat bottom, made of one board, was cut to the required shape. The sides consisted of two boards, each joined together in the centre of the boat by an unusual joint, not seen in European carpentry. They were also joined at right-angles to the bottom. There were no nails, just wooden pegs, holding the craft together. At either end, where the sides just met and joined, they were fastened in some way without the aid of a stem or stern post: a small, triangular piece of wood held them together across the gunnels. At odd intervals down the length of the boat were thwarts, one of which had a hole in it, presumably for a mast. Nonetheless, the boat leaked like a sieve. John thought that it would have been a good 'contrast' advertisement for small boat stoppings: 'this boat uses so-and-so's waterproof stopping – but this one doesn't.' The water inside the boat did not seem to worry the fishermen in the least, but all the time one was talking, the other was baling, using half a coconut shell.

The men were fishing with a cast net and had a good catch in the bottom of their leaky boat. They gave *Discovery* two fish, then continued casting their net, a large white circle of fine mesh with a chain around the perimeter to sink it quickly, while from the centre came a drawstring rope. To throw it, one fisherman stood in the bows of the canoe and took the net by its centre, from which the rope emerged. He coiled it onto a thwart, keeping one foot firmly on the loose end. Taking the net in an elongated bundle around his arm, he put one link of the chain into his mouth. Then, with a twirl like someone doing a highland fling, he hurled the net into the air. It opened out and dropped in a perfect circle onto the water. Pulling up the net slowly by the rope gave the chain a chance to come together along the riverbed and so trap any fish. Gradually, the net appeared above the surface, but this time the fisherman had caught nothing. With a few waves to each other, the two boats glided away in opposite directions.

Discovery was soon out sight around the next bend in the river.

Chapter Fourteen

RAINFOREST, ROCKS AND RAPIDS

At about four o'clock came a loud roar of rapids. The adventurers shot over them, without any idea of what was on the other side. As they went down the left bank of the river, more rapids appeared, much bigger, with more and much larger rocks. The surrounding area was also very rocky; both banks were covered with huge black stones and boulders. The prospect of shooting these rapids was grim. A little further down, they saw a tributary flowing into the Volta. They came nearer and were almost sucked into it. The channel was a fork in the river itself. They saw, too, that it dropped very steeply, the water boiling like a cauldron over hidden, submerged rocks that could occasionally be seen through the foaming water. This was not the route for them.

Having narrowly escaped the channel, more fishermen appeared, shouting to them wildly in a local language. After listening for a few moments, Gerunchi said that the men were warning *Discovery* not to go straight on as the river 'did many bad things' and that frequent huge stones lay beneath the surface. 'Ask him what we do then', said Almonds.

Gerunchi ascertained that they should go down a smaller channel, around an island on the right riverbank, where the rapids were not too difficult. To avoid repeating that morning's performance at the rapids, they set off across the river immediately. However, they travelled even more quickly sideways and were not quite half way across when they saw an island – nothing more than a pile of boulders showing above the water. Making the other channel was a close-run thing. They turned *Discovery*'s bows downstream to avoid being swept sideways down the rapids into a large bluff, which stuck up out of the river.

Shooting through a small gap between the bluff and the island, risking any rocks just below the surface, the swift current dashed them against the rocks of the island. John and Gerunchi fended off on the port side. But there came a sudden jar. They had hit a rock. Feeling with his paddle, John felt a ledge of stones, over which they then slithered into deeper water. He looked for damage, but *Discovery* had not been holed. They dashed forward again into a fast-flowing smaller channel, tossed among great swirls and waves, taking in water over the bows, which soaked Robson. Avoiding plenty of rocks and the worst of the turbulence, the heap of boulders that separated them from the main channel became low, revealing glimpses of the main river about six feet below them. It flowed free of rapids, proving those on the main channel to have been short but very steep.

After half a mile, the two channels joined again. John was sorry to leave the rapids behind. *Discovery* shot into the main river, which flowed slowly, flecked with foam and froth from the rapids. At 4.30pm, they looked for a place to camp and fish. Just the spot appeared: flat ground immediately below the rapids at the confluence of a tributary.[1] They guided the canoe into its mouth, tied up and started to make camp.

John handed across the kit and Almonds and Robson took it to the campsite a few yards away. Gerunchi again set about the fire and cooking. They laid out their bedrolls and John tied a length of string about four feet between two trees, from which to hang their mosquito nets. Robson went in search of a main road, as they could hear vehicles not far away. Almonds sat down and began to clean his rifle, which had got wet while shooting the rapids. John went fishing, using as bait the head of one of the fish they had been given. He used a 20lb nylon hand line with a piece of fine 4lb nylon, a small hook and three lead shot weights on the end. After adding a float, he sat in *Discovery* and fished. Half an hour later, only a few tiny fish had played with the bait, making the float twitch slightly. Called for grub, he left the line over the side, fastened the other end and rejoined the others.

Supper was excellent chicken noodle and mulligatawny soup. Halfway through this repast, Robson reappeared. He had found not a road but a village 300–400 yards away. He was sure it appeared on the map, so they could fix their position. They drank tea and talked of reaching Kete-Karachi the next day and enjoying a good night in a rest house. John returned to his fishing. It was getting dark, so he put a matchbox-sized piece of fish and a large hook on 20lb nylon, removed the float and threw it in. He cut up the rest of the fish, threw it in as well, washed his knife and returned to the camp. Taking soap and a towel, he waded into the river and washed before smothering himself with insect repellent. He then got into his nightwear, hung up his mosquito net and turned in.

Just before they went to sleep, Almonds pointed out a thunderstorm in the distance where lightening played and danced over the darkening jungle. They put all the remaining kit in a pile and covered it with the spare groundsheet. If it rained, they would change back into their day clothes, take up the bedrolls to keep them dry and sit on them in the rain. A few minutes later, it was clear that the storm was not coming their way. They fell asleep to the roar of more rapids downstream.

He woke second on that Wednesday morning, 29 August 1956. He had something important to do. But what? Then, he remembered his fishing line. Fumbling his way from his mosquito net, he dashed off to see if he had caught anything, hardly bothering to return Gerunchi's greeting of good morning. He put his index finger under the line to feel for that welcome wriggle, but not the slightest movement betrayed the presence of any fish. He pulled up the line. The bait was untouched, so he threw the line back again.

Gerunchi packed and started the fire, Robson's head emerged from under his net and Almonds stirred. John assembled their equipment. Back at the boat, he started baling out water from the rapids, a tiny amount inevitable by this stage of the trip. Robson appeared and took over.

At the campsite, Almonds was finishing his breakfast. He invited John to help himself quickly to the saucepan's contents because Gerunchi wanted to brew tea in it. The boy quickly emptied tinned tomatoes and beans onto his plate. A fishing boat arrived. A man stepped ashore and went to a fishing trap nobody had noticed the night before. He took out a fish about eight inches long. The trap was a beehive-shaped basket of liana creeper with a funnel protruding into it from the wider end, rather like a lobster pot. The man wished them all a good morning, but that was the extent of his English. Gerunchi asked how far it was to Kete-Krachi. After discussion and violent gesticulation, Gerunchi said that they could get there that night if they travelled fast. The river was difficult further on with many big rocks. They should keep to the left and take the next channel. The fisherman smiled, climbed into his boat and paddled away, while the crew of *Discovery* sat down to drink their tea. John now sported a new drinking utensil: the tomato tin, saved for this purpose. Almonds had smoothed its cut edge.

After stowing the gear in the boat, they cast off and, keeping close to the left bank, paddled on downriver. At the side channel, they could still hear the rapids, hidden from view by a bend in the river. The fast current sucked them in. It would be a long hard paddle to get out again if they needed to retrace their steps. They sped along at great speed. The channel probably didn't exist when the river was not in spate. It was very shallow. Dodging in and out between the tops of bushes, they nearly hit a large waterlogged tree trunk, with only the tiniest bit of it poking up above the surface. A few hefty digs with the paddle on the starboard side and John using his paddle as a rudder brought them round quickly – too quickly – almost side-on to the current. The port-side paddles had to work overtime to bring them up straight.In the narrow channel, minor rocky rapids made the water gush very fast. Huge waves curled up and over the rocks, creating mesmerisingly impressive coils of water. While darting in and out among the tops of bushes, they once again misjudged the speed of the current. To avoid some minor rapids that stretched halfway across the river, they aimed for the clear side between a bush and a big clump of elephant grass. They could just glide over it by flattening it down. 'Go left!' shouted Almonds. As they brushed past the clump, John saw a large jagged rock inside it that they had just missed. For the only time in his life, the boy swore at his father: 'Bloody hell! Did you see that fucking great rock?!' But Almonds just shook his head gently, smiled and said, 'Didn't see a thing'. And all the time they were fighting to keep the canoe in one piece. After that near miss, they avoided even the most innocent-looking reeds and took to the rapids where they could see what they were doing.

On a long, open stretch of river, they paddled better as a team and with less effort than they had on their first afternoon. *Discovery* slid easily through the water. The port and starboard paddles worked better together so when the current brought the bow off the point they were making for, one side's paddlers slackened while those on the other side dug deeper. Then, when the bow came back on course, the side that had slackened met it with a deep dig to steady her. They settled down to a steady stroke.

During the morning, they shot several sets of rapids. Some were averagely difficult, while others could hardly be called rapids and were dubbed 'ripples' by Robson. Passing over some flooded land to shorten their journey and bypass more rapids, they saw a crocodile. Manoeuvring through bushes, there was a sudden splash. From a small island nearby, something shot into the water. It swam at right angles to the current with its snout above water, then submerged and they did not see it again.

A strong wind blew upriver. Its opposition to the current kicked up some choppy water, slowing them down considerably. Keeping close to the windward bank (the wind was a few points off from blowing straight upriver), they gained the shelter of trees but still had to contend with the waves. As they approached the sea, the wind menaced. The Sahara Desert, north of the Gold Coast, was drawing in air from elsewhere to compensate for its hot air rising upwards.

Robson, Almonds and John were all sunburnt. At 09.30am, strong sunshine forced them to put their shirts on. But even when cloud hid the sun, they still got sunburnt. Almonds's and Robson's shoulders and backs were badly burnt. John's skin, although not so bad as theirs, was tender. His worst sunburn was on his legs, which when stretched out while paddling caught the full force of the sun. His father's legs were badly burnt where they were usually covered by his uniform long socks. Almonds would dip his hand over the side, scoop up a handful of water and wet his burnt legs. John adopted the same tactic, but did not find it any protection. He learned to paddle with his knees under his chin and his legs under the shadow of his body. They joked about why Gerunchi didn't have a problem.

Travelling slowly down the right bank, they saw a baby monkey, caught by one foot in the top of a bush just above the water. Gerunchi wanted a monkey, so they turned and paddled back upstream. But the little monkey was dead; it had caught its foot in a forked branch and got trapped hanging upside down with its head in the water. It was light grey, with a long tail and a big ruff of fur behind its head. They left it where it was and continued on downstream. Floating among semi-submerged bushes, they heard crashing in the higher branches of a tree leaning over the river. A small monitor lizard about a foot long dropped onto a nearby log. For a few seconds, it lay motionless, looking for all the world like a piece of wood. Then, with a scurry, it leapt up and dropped with a splash into the water.

Almonds racing his home-converted US jeep, the 'Silver Bullet' with my brother John, aged seven, hidden beside him. Chester, 1948

A British major-general, wearing SAS wartime operational breast wings, bows before the Emperor Hailie Selassie as he presents gymkhana rosettes – handed to him by Major Dudley Apthorp, Addis Ababa, 1950

*Emperor Hailie Selassie watches British-trained troops on exercise, briefed by a
BMME officer. Seated, L is Crown Prince Asfa Wossen. Ethiopia, 1950.*

THE BRITISH MILITARY MISSION TO ETHIOPIA

*The Ethiopian emblem of the British Military Mission to Ethiopia. The words above
say 'Emperor Hailie Selassie' and those beneath 'The Military War Office.'*

A shooting expedition, Almonds at the wheel of his jeep. Ethiopia, 1950

*Batie market in Danakil country, with the gallows in
the background – used frequently! Ethiopia, 1950*

L to R, Crown Prince Asfa Wassen, Duke of Harar, and his brother. Almonds and Apthorp had tea with them in the ducal palace, Harar, Ethiopia, 1950.

The Eritrea Police Field Force

The insignia of the Eritrea Police Field Force.

Left: The British Administration Eritrea Stamp (dated 4 July 1951).
Right: Straight out of a spaghetti Western: One of Almonds's
Field Force patrols makes a river crossing, Eritrea, May 1951

POLICE NOTICE

The rewards mentioned below will be paid for information leading to the arrest of the following shifta or to the person producing their bodies, dead or alive.

NAME OF WANTED MAN	RESIDENCE OR TRIBE.	Amount of Reward.	Crime for which wanted.
Hamid Idris Awati	Antora Village	£ 300	Already notified
Uoldegabriel Mosasghi	Barachit Abbai	£ 200	Already noti..ed
Berhe Mosasghi	Barachit Abbai	£ 200	Already noti.ied
Hagos Temanu	Debre Adi Zadih	£ 150	Already notified
Asserassie Embae	Arresa	£ 100	Already notified
Ogbanse Igigu	Sciumanegus Tatai	£ 50	Already notified
Gnebre Tesfazien	Deda Village	£ 100	Murder
Debessai Abraha	Habella	£ 25	Murder
Sebhatu Damas	Habella	£ 20	Murder
Tecle Asfaha	Corranacudo	£ 20	Murder
Chidane Demsas	Habella	£ 20	Murder
Teclehaimanot Sereche	Corranacudo	£ 20	Murder
Berhè Haptezghi	Magurca (Anseba)	£ 30	Murder
Uoldessilassi Adal	Leban (Serae)	£ 30	Murder
Abraha Zamarian	Zighib	£ 25	Murder
Grazmac Ilfai Asfaha	Corranacudo	£ 35	Murder
Mengusteab Seum	Adi Conzi	£ 30	Murder
Berecheteab Andenchiel	Deda	£ 20	Murder
Tarahe Urrèda	Tigrai (Ethiopia)	£ 20	Murder
Andemariam Zere	Debri (Liban)	£ 20	Murder
Berhè Leggiam	Decchi Dascim	£ 20	Murder
Medhin Cassai	Irob (Ethiopia)	£ 20	Murder.
Abraha Suba	Tigrai (Ethiopia)	£ 20	Murder
Ghirmazien (Ex Haile Abbai gang)	Tigrai (Ethiopia)	£ 20	Murder
Mebratnu Techlenchiel	Habella	£ 20	Murder
Gheremedhin Cnefela	Adi Uur (Serae)	£ 20	Murder
Omar Aluru	Ass Alisen	£ 20	Murder
Khalifa Omer	Subaco Ore	£ 20	Murder
Zater Saleh	Tigrai (Ethiopia)	£ 20	Murder
Issak Aly	Tigrai (Et'iopia)	£ 20	Murder
Aly Ioris	Hanzer Tribe	£ 20	Murder
Aly Hudera	Dancalia Tribe	£ 20	Murder
Khalifa Aly	Hazu Tribe	£ 20	Murder
Aly Umer	Tigrai (Ethiopia)	£ 20	Murder
Ghirmai Hailu	Mogo	£ 20	Murder
Amare Embaie	Arresa	£ 20	Murder
Ioris Awati	Barla Tribe	£ 20	Murder
Gaile Anouri	Cunama Tribe	£ 20	Murder
Snababi Tana	Cunama Tribe	£ 20	Murder
Osman Longni	Cunama Tribe	£ 20	Murder
Abbakair Gaile	Cunama Tribe	£ 20	Murder
Agage Haitin	Cunama Tribe	£ 20	Murder
Gaile Ambi	Cunama Tribe	£ 20	Murder
Awati Busu	Cunama Tribe	£ 20	Murder
Tecle Ghilegaber	Decchi Scihai	£ 20	Murder
Hapte Ghilegaber	Decchi Scihai	£ 20	Murder
Chidan Hapte	Decchi Scihai	£ 20	Murder
Chessete Tesfalidet	Decchi Scihai	£ 20	Murder
Fesseha Fessazien	Decchi Dascim	£ 20	Murder
Melleke Bairan	Decchi Dascim	£ 20	Murder
Chelete Gheresghir	Decchi Dascim	£ 20	Murder

Asmara, 7th January, 1950.

(Sgd.) T.W. FITZPATRICK,
Commissioner of Police and Prisons,
Eritrea.

The 'Wild West Wanted' poster which encouraged bounty hunters to catch the shifta bandits. Instead, Almonds and the Eritrea Police Field Force hunted and caught them.

Almonds, second from left with a captured shifta spear. Discussion was about how the shifta never killed Englishmen unless they went off the beaten track – which Almonds did frequently! Western Province, Eritrea, April 1951

Digging shifta bandits out of hiding in the hills. Two British officers are directing the fire of two Field Force men lying on the ground. Ethiopian Eritrean border April, 1951.

Duncan Cumming, Britain's Chief Administrator, responsible for bringing shifta terrorism under control in time to implement the UN Resolution federating Ethiopia and Eritrea under the Ethiopian crown. Asmara, 1951.

Cumming centre and Almonds, second right of centre (standing below a bank at the back) at a meeting with local chief Abraha Tsemma about shifta banditry on the Ethiopia-Eritrea border

The Auster light aircraft Almonds used for chasing shifta bandits – and for joyrides!

Above: A typical Field Force patrol – not enough rifles to go around, Eritrea, 1951

Left: Tecle Asfaha, the young shifta bandit leader who declared war on the British. He eluded capture until he surrendered to Almonds, July 1951.

Duncan Cumming, top hat in hand, witnesses the end of
British Administration in Eritrea. The band of the South Wales
Borderers marches past. Asmara, 15 September, 1952.

The Malayan Emergency: Almonds as OC 'B' Squadron, 22 SAS, back row, fourth from
left just after a parachute jump. His 1938-pattern webbed belt is blackened with boot
polish. The RAF PJI is second from right, third row. RAF Changi, Singapore, 1953.

Alf Gould, the 'genial bruiser' with a reputation for total fearlessness and one of the toughest men Almonds ever knew. Gould followed Almonds to Malaya where he killed CTs. Malaya, 1953.

Major 'Gentleman Jim' Almonds, Royal West African Frontier Force, preparing to parade at the Kumasi Fort. Gold Coast (later Ghana) 1956.

Almonds designed and built (by hand) a four-person canoe, Discovery. *He shot the Volta River rapids from Yeji to the estuary with son John (R), the Assistant Adjutant, Gordon Robson and Corporal Danyatta Gerunchi of the Gold Coast Army, Gold Coast, 1956.*

Relaunching Discovery *at Keti-Krachi ferry, Gold Coast, (later Ghana) 1956.*

Not a single power tool. The ketch Almonds designed and memorized while in 'solitary' in an Italian PoW camp under construction in our garden. The second layer of planking is fastened to the frame, Kumasi, 1956.

Soldiers help to turn her over, Kumasi, 1957.

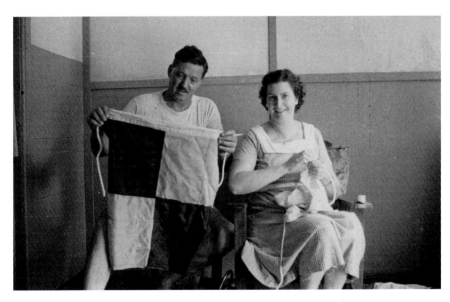

Almonds and Lockie making the SS Kumasi's ship signal flags, Kumasi, 1959.

Ghana Army carpenters Emmanuel Bruku and Samuel Kwame Deghun help speed up the end of the job Kumasi 1959.

Above: The long low lines of the ketch SS Kumasi. The start of the journey, Takoradi Harbour, Ghana, 15 May, 1960.

Left: At sea. Almonds at the helm with 'the Brute' in the background, mid-Atlantic Ocean, August, 1960.

The lagoon at Abidjan, Skipper Almonds at the helm,
Alan Cameron L, Ivory Coast, June, 1960.

Left: Almonds sorts out the rigging, Pico Island, Azores, August, 1960.
Right: Near catastrophe! Kumasi's mast almost caught the bow of the
Cestos of Monrovia, 364 miles from Land's End. September, 1960.

Journey's end: L to R, Alan Cameron, Almonds, Gordon Robson. After 5,000 miles at sea, all had lost weight, looked temporarily aged and could not walk properly. Weymouth.

Goodbye from the skipper. With Gordon Robson, late Kings Own Scottish Borderers, Weymouth Harbour, September 1960.

Major 'Gentleman Jim' Almonds, L Detachment, 1st SAS, aged 84,
visiting the New Zealand SAS, New Zealand, 1984.

Just before a tea break, they met a dugout canoe coming upstream. Via Gerunchi, they asked the inevitable question of how far it was to Kete-Krachi. The man had left it at 11am; as he was going against the current and it was still only 12.30pm, the distance was not great. Their hopes rose, but not too high, since they knew how unreliable local information was. They promised each other a proper night's sleep in a real bed in a rest house, while Almonds and Robson pledged one another a large bottle of cool, sparkling beer.

They pulled into the bank, tied up, got the kit out of the boat and put the saucepan on to boil. The tea was 'jolly good'. But the place was teeming with small black ants, so they could not sit and drink it in peace. Local canoes coming downriver saw their moored boat and came to investigate. First, one canoe nosed its way into the bank alongside theirs, then another and another until eight had moored up. After exchanging greetings, the newcomers wanted to know who the voyagers were, where they had come from and where they were going. Gerunchi satisfied their curiosity and they seemed thrilled but puzzled by the canvas boat. They touched and poked it, gradually more violently until Gerunchi warned them to be careful, at which they stopped immediately.

The reply to the eternal question of how far it was to Kete-Krachi made the *Discovery* crew think twice about whether they would sleep in a proper bed that night. Kete-Krachi would only be achieved by sunset if they travelled very fast. So the explorers set out with their new friends as a small fleet, giving rise to a bit of competition. *Discovery* made good progress. She took up position behind and to starboard of the lead canoe. The other boats followed in a bunch behind on either side of them. The leading canoe set a fast pace, obviously to see if they could outrun the army boat. *Discovery* went at slightly under her usual pace. From time to time, the lead boat suddenly put in a burst of speed and *Discovery* would increase her stroke to a little above the normal pace. The boats continued in this way with the pace gradually telling on the Ghanian paddlers, so that they slackened off. *Discovery* did the same. Eventually, the friendly fleet pulled into their villages and *Discovery* continued alone.

They saw the snout of a monitor lizard, but it turned out to be the head of a water snake. It came close enough to be touched with the paddle, then disappeared, only to reappear on the port side. Rounding a bend in the river, they saw a tin-roofed building and made for it. A roar announced more rapids, so they pulled in. Going up a track, they saw Kete-Krachi in the distance. Robson went into the town and returned with the District Commissioner of Police, a Mr Bather. He put their kit into his car and drove them (at last) to a Government rest house. He also offered a truck and portage for *Discovery* around the dangerous rapids.

In town, they replenished their stores before retiring to the rest house. That evening was spent with their policeman friend, having drinks at the house of the government agent before returning to the commissioner's house for supper. Then, back to the rest house to sleep in proper beds. They awoke refreshed. While packing up, a message arrived telling them to go to the commissioner's house for breakfast. They drove in a police car to the police station. A truck arrived with their upside-down boat. More willing hands lifted it into the back and soon they were off to the ferry. Robson took a photograph of *Discovery* being relaunched before they loaded up, said their 'thank yous' and 'goodbyes' and set off again.

After shooting four sets of rapids at half-hourly intervals, they arrived at a place where the river divided, divided again and sub-divided into a maze of channels and islands. Some channels were almost continuous rapids. This time, they chose the right way through, where no rapids barred their progress. The river flowed for long stretches with a following wind. They experimented with a groundsheet 'sail', but it did not work. During the morning, it rained on and off.

At 12.30pm, it stopped, so they landed on a very steep bank to brew up and eat Ryvita and tinned cheese. It then rained again, heavily. They sought shelter under small bushes or trees. John had grabbed the groundsheet, so managed to stay dry. It was no joke, although John and Gerunchi were killing themselves laughing. Slapstick came when they decided to move on, picked up the kit and started down the now very slippery steep bank. Suddenly, Almonds, who was carrying the remains of the tea in the saucepan, slipped and fell on his back, the tea dregs going all over him. John also skidded, spilling items from Gerunchi's kitbag, which he was carrying. By the time they were underway again, it was still raining, but due to their paroxysms of laughter, morale was high.

That afternoon, a duck idled by. They opened up at it, but the duck just glided on into the reeds. Staying the night at a local village, where they were given a hut with no walls, they set up their beds, had a good stew, a good brew and went to bed. Next morning, they awoke to the sound of villagers sweeping the compound. After packing, eating breakfast and taking a photograph of the village chief and villagers, they set off at speed for an uneventful two miles. More rapids shot, they found themselves in a fast current. Resting on their paddles, they came to a fork in the river and more rapids. Some nearby fishermen told them that a port-side channel was the safest as there were waterfalls down the other. The *Discovery* crew groaned as they had to paddle upstream against the current in order to go down the better channel. This done, they rejoined the main river and were furious as they saw that the rapids down the other channel could have been traversed easily.

They aimed to land at Akroso for supplies. On passing a large village and asking fishermen if it was Akroso, they were told that it wasn't. So they carried on, only to find out later that it *was* Akroso.[2] After a midday stop and brew up, the sun began to let them have it, blazing down. Paddling became exhausting. They passed to port a range of small hills. The current was swift, so they rested, drifting slowly downstream. Almonds and Robson fished with spinners, without success. Towards 5pm, a storm approached. They pulled in near a village and made camp in another wall-less hut. With a little tinned grub, they enjoyed an excellent stew, followed by a chicken they had bought. In this village, the girls wore almost nothing. The younger Almonds had never seen bare breasts. From the repressions of an English public school, this was really something for a boy of fifteen. After the standard tea, they retired for the night.

On Saturday 1 September, they awoke to the bleating of goats. After some porridge, the four packed up and set off again downriver. The sun was hot, the current fairly slow and another stiff headwind kicked up little waves, hampering their progress. Tempers frayed. Gradually, the wind dropped and they passed between some high hills. In the hot sun, they relished their midday break. Gerunchi made some tea and a sudden shout from Robson alerted them to the fact that he had found some sort of fruit. It tasted 'smashing', but none of them knew its name or even recognised it. It was about the size of a plum, with both yellow and green fruits growing on the tree. The flesh was very soft, but there was not much of it due to the large size of the stone. It was marula fruit, much beloved by elephant. When they gorge on it, they become drunk and potentially dangerous. However, it did not have this effect on the four men. John wandered a little way from camp and found a still for making alcoholic drink. It was a 44-gallon drum over a fire. From it, a pipe passed through a hollowed-out tree trunk full of water, which acted as a coolant. The other side of the tree trunk had an outlet pipe for collecting the drink. He thought the apparatus was probably distilling the marula fruit, which almost distils itself.

After lunch, they paddled on slowly until about 4pm. A large outcrop of rock appeared, sticking out over the water, leaving a very small channel between the rocks and the bank. Rather than lengthen their distance, they went into the channel. About halfway through, they hit a submerged rock. It holed *Discovery* twice. Drifting free of the rocks into the main channel, they began to fill rapidly and lose speed. They beached and ran aground at an unsuitable spot, but there was nothing else for it.

On touching the bank, Gerunchi and Robson leapt out, followed by Almonds. They caught the kit that John was already slinging ashore. When they and all kit were ashore, they dragged the canoe out of the water and turned her over to drain out the brown water. Almonds and Robson opened up the repair kit and John began to mend the holes with Bostik sealant, which he had used to repair *Wug* in Singapore. Almonds and Gerunchi looked for a place to sleep, but there was no good spot nearby. They considered relaunching the boat and trying to move on to the next village in the last half hour of daylight. This option would ruin the sealant on the patches, which were not yet dry, though they would be able to repair them and leave them to dry again overnight at the village. They decided to risk it and found a village only a few yards away along the bank.

Putting in for the night, they repaired the boat again. After 'chop', they brewed some tea. The villagers helped to carry the boat from the water and turn it upside down. Later, they brought an oil lantern and John continued to write up the log. To his right, the menfolk of the village sat in a circle making a fishing net from ordinary string. Gerunchi had gone to bed and John soon followed.

On Sunday 2 September, they awoke early. The paint on the patches was still tacky. After a breakfast of 'bully' beef and beans, they put the boat into the river and began to reload her with the help of villagers. Setting out again about half an hour after their usual departure time of 7.30am, they paddled on, stopping for five minutes every half an hour to rest. John kept the boat on course as they drifted downstream.

They passed more hills, some of which featured rocky outcrops. One formation looked just like a monkey's head, so the expedition named it

'Monkey Head Rock'. The light breeze that had been against them since they started began to strengthen, hindering their progress even more. They sought shelter from the bank, where Almonds shot a black and white monkey. Gerunchi cleaned and skinned it and asked permission to keep its long white tail, which Almonds granted. They spread the monkey carcass on the deck to dry in the sun; they would eat monkey steaks that evening.

Pulling in for chop, Gerunchi made tea while John found some plantains and bananas. As he ran back to camp over some burnt-off ground to get a machete, the boy failed to see a large black snake against the charred background. At the last minute, he jumped right over it. About four feet long, it vanished at terrific speed. Shocked at such a narrow escape, John hardly dared let his feet touch the ground as he danced around in a daze. It was a black mamba. Unlike its arboreal relations, the black mamba hunts by day and sleeps at night. Its deadly bite can kill in twenty minutes if no anti-venom is available. It usually avoids humans, but will attack if disturbed.

The encounter having shaken him, John picked up a stick in lieu of a weapon and proceeded with caution. He returned with Gerunchi to the spot, both of them with *parangs*, and cut some plantains – the bananas being too unripe to eat. They resumed paddling and came to a large village, where John remained in the boat while the others went shopping. While he waited, two African boys came down to the water's edge to see him. In pidgin English, they discussed general things, mainly the shooting of the monkey by so small a weapon. John explained the principle of the dum-dum bullet.

After leaving the village, *Discovery* ran into a really strong wind, which again threw up a steep sea against the current with waves reaching about three feet in height. Some swept the monkey off the foredeck into the cockpit. They ran for shelter at the bank. That evening, they camped at a village of snail eaters. The chief had blood poisoning in his foot, as well as a guinea worm. Keen to help, and conscious of the need to win hearts and minds, Almonds administered a penicillin injection. He was no medic; John winced as his father used the syringe like a harpoon! That evening, Gerunchi cooked the monkey, steaks and liver. They all ate some, except for Almonds. It was interesting meat, rather like tough pork. That night, John went to bed early. The meal of monkey had probably been a bit too close to cannibalism.

On Monday 3 September, a week since the day they had set off, they breakfasted on bread, fish and butter before resuming their journey.

All went well for an hour, but then the wind began to increase and the going became heavier. After the midday brew and continuing through the afternoon, they asked an African boy fishing by the riverbank the location of the camp for the Volta River Project. The boy persuaded them to pay a short visit to his village, Ajena[3], then got into their boat and showed them the way.

The camp turned out to be the Volta Dam construction site. Here, early survey work was underway in preparation for building the dam. Almonds and Robson went to negotiate beds for the night, in return for information about the Volta River, with the project and site boss – a relatively young, European engineer. John remembered having met his wife on his flight from the UK. They loaded their kit into a Land Rover and jumped in. After a late night, they slept in proper beds in a mosquito-proof house and went to another nearby house to eat.

On Tuesday 4 September, they woke later than usual and wandered around the site offices looking at plans for the Volta River Dam. These included some interesting cross-sections. While looking at one drawing, John realised that the dam would be made of just loose rocks and clay. He got talking to one of the engineers about the dam, who explained the principles of 'rock fill' dam construction and under what circumstances it is used. This remained forever in the boy's mind.[4] Suddenly, a wave sadness swept over him: the fishing villages, the rapids, the people they had met and the whole way of life they had seen would be swept away forever in the name of progress. The Volta River Project would flood them all.

That morning, Almonds, Robson and John discussed whether or not to finish the journey at Senchi. Robson favoured ending the trip there, while Almonds was undecided. John wanted to continue to Ada. The others pointed out that it would take another four days to reach Ada, two days to drive back to Kumasi and that he would be flying back to England on the thirteenth. In addition, the army leave that Almonds and Robson had taken was due to expire on the ninth. The expedition objective was from Yeji to the sea and Senchi was on the estuary where the water was brackish. Faced with these facts, reluctantly, the boy concurred.

After breakfasting with their hosts, Almonds telephoned 89 Coy RASC in Accra, asking them to send a three-tonner lorry to Senchi ferry at 3pm. The four said their goodbyes, loaded the boat and got underway again. There was no hurry that morning; it was only seven miles to Senchi, while their usual morning distance was ten miles. As usual, the strong headwind made for a choppy surface as they passed slowly downriver.

The people at the dam project had told them that a new bridge, similar in design to Sydney Harbour Bridge, was under construction a little way downriver. They began to hear the sound of cranes, derricks and hydraulic machinery. Just before rounding a bend in the river, they saw the top of a crane through a gap in the trees. Later, they saw that it was perched on the highest point of the bridge arch. Suddenly, they came in full sight of the bridge. Its arch was completed, except for being painted; workmen were starting to hang its roadway. It was the Adomi Bridge, which would enable traffic to cross the Volta instead of having to take the pontoon at Senchi. In 1956, the only places where the Volta River met the road and ferries crossed were Yeji, Keta-Krachi and Senchi. Robson took photographs and when *Discovery* stopped right underneath the bridge, he got out and went seeking more photographic vantage points.

He approached a European and asked him when the bridge would be finished. The man replied in broad Scots, 'I dinna know and I care less', so Robson withdrew to the boat. They pushed off but after a few yards realised that Robson had left his paddle on the bank. Returning under three paddle power, they grabbed it and set off again.

Once more, the river divided into many channels, each with its set of rapids. Those in the channel they chose were absolutely ferocious. Large jagged rocks and semi-submerged boulders threw up huge waves as the water leapt and bounced over them. John thought them the most exciting they had encountered throughout the whole trip. Kumasi's altitude is higher than that of Accra and they had reached the dramatic escarpment usually seen from the road. The Volta River also went down over this rocky edge. Bounded by unyielding rock, the river speeded up and gushed down a long, steep gorge. *Discovery* gathered velocity, too, and flew down the narrow channel between the rocks. At its end, the river hit a high wall of rock. All the water turned in a sharp, thirty-degree turn (which felt like more) building itself up into a huge, black curling wave, awesome and terrifying to see. Tons of smooth, fast-flowing river water suddenly changed direction. The canvas boat barrelled round this curve like a rider on a motorbike wall of death. The occupants mentioned certain members of the holy Trinity as they shot round it at high speed.[5]

Amazingly, boat and crew stayed upright. They sped on down the river. To the young Almonds, they had just shot more rapids, since he had never experienced any others. He met no similar challenge again until he canoed the 'Devil's Cauldron' Rapids on the Salmon River, Idaho in the early 1990s. Further downriver, they came to their last set of cascades: the Kpong Rapids. They constituted the last slide of the Volta River into the tidal estuary. Also fierce, they were nothing like as hair-raising as those in the gorge. At the end of the rapids lay Senchi ferry.

Since they still had plenty of time before 3pm, Almonds, Robson and Gerunchi went to the police station, leaving John on guard at the boat. They sent a signal to Mr Bather at Kete-Krachi, reporting on their exploits since they had left him. They sent another one to the OC in Kumasi and to Lockie, telling her when they would be arriving (neither of these two signals ever reached their destinations).

Left on guard, John opened another tin of bully beef and ate the lot himself, finishing it off with some sweet 'mammy bread', on which he plastered high concentrate butter. After nine days of hard, physical work and meagre rations, he needed to build himself up. This was his first experience of the 'post operations' phenomenon, which he would know again, many times.

By 3pm, there was still no truck. At 7.30pm, the three-tonner finally arrived. John was just relieving Gerunchi, who had been watching the boat while others dined in the rest house, when the truck pulled up. A lance corporal driver got out and saluted John. He returned the salute and called Almonds and Robson. Together, they loaded the boat and equipment and followed them onto the lorry. Almonds had not allowed any rest days, so they were all exhausted. They had been on the water six hours each day, covering on average 25 to 30 miles a day. So, in nine days, they had covered between 225 and 360 miles. Apart from Gerunchi, they were blistered and sunburnt. However, all four were satisfied with their assault on the Volta River.

Chapter Fifteen

TREKS, TRACKS
AND ELEPHANTS

Kumasi has a picturesque fort, built during the Ashanti Wars, with red walls and a thatched roof. It formed the backdrop to ceremonial parades of the British and Ghana Armies. When my father was practising his sword drill, in advance of acting as parade commander, Gloria would pass the cheese to him at dinner, speared on her knife, by carrying out the sword drill salute. He would solemnly respond with his knife. On the day of the parade, the Ghana soldiers marched past in their khaki uniforms and bright red waistcoats. Almonds wore his red tunic and sword.

As usual, the British Army in Kumasi socialised; everybody entertained everybody to dinner. House boys did their best to provide a high standard of service. They knew that hot plates were essential. Our houseboy even used them to serve ice-cream. He did the same with jelly. At one of Lockie's supper parties, much to her embarrassment, instead of using her elegant gravy boat for the sauce, he served it in an old cracked mug. Whenever this kind of thing happened, everybody played the game and said nothing while the boy was present. It was very important not to damage his sense of dignity when he had tried so hard. Houseboys from different households worked together in ingenious ways. Out for dinner one evening, my mother commented on the beautiful china dinner service, saying that she had one the same – only to discover that it was indeed her own.

We mingled, too, with the Boys Company. The imam held regular Koran recitals in the evenings. Gloria and I went as part of the audience. It was a big event for the boys. Each one had memorised a Koran passage and took his turn sitting cross-legged, not in uniform but in white, on a red carpet. Each recital lasted a long time; we marvelled at how the boys could remember such huge chunks of text. We also attended boxing matches between the different Boys Company platoons. These were smart occasions; my father wore his mess kit with white jacket and miniature medals, while Gloria and I wore dresses. British and Ghanaian PTIs working together organised everything. When the boys took a swing at each other and their boxing gloves flew off, it was difficult not to laugh. At the end, my father presented the cups.

My parents were members of Kumasi's European Club (tactfully renamed the Kumasi Club after Independence). Here, Almonds met Swiss, Armenian, Greek and British businessmen, some of whom ran timber companies. At the dinners and dances, local bands played Ghanaian 'highlife' music, featuring jazzy horns and guitars. The dancing that accompanied it consisted of small, almost shuffling steps, partners opposite each other, with arms akimbo. Highlife was Ghana's own original music, which incorporated modern instruments and gradually spread to other countries, so Ghanaians were rightly proud of it.[1] In the club one evening, the dancing stopped and we all stood still, listening to a radio broadcast about the Suez crisis.

In our house was a bar where my father kept whisky, rum, gin and bottles of the different cup numbers of Pimms. Two houseboys looked after us. One was a soldier batman, who looked after my father's uniforms and kit. It soon became clear that my father was not the only person consuming the alcohol. Since my mother and the rest of us did not drink, the house boys came under suspicion. My father made pencil marks on the bottles, level with the waterline, and the bottles were left alone. He turned them upside down and marked them: the level of the contents appeared above the mark and the stealing resumed. On one occasion, the thief added water to replace the missing alcohol. To his despair, the contents of the bottle turned cloudy.

While the army boy was away for a few days, my father was able to confront the other boy, who admitted to being the culprit. He was sure he was going to be sacked, but my father, in a gentlemanly way, pointed out to him why his stealing was wrong and how it damaged the trust he had enjoyed in being allowed to be in our house. There followed a scene of great contrition, with the boy quite upset and my father very stern. We were unsure how genuine the repentance was, but there was no resumption of the stealing.

One hazard, for every household, was the risk of being burgled by thieves known as the 'teef men'. These seasoned robbers wore nothing but oil, so that if anybody grabbed them, they could slip free. One NCO and his wife woke one morning to find that absolutely everything in the house had vanished, except the bed in which they were sleeping. When the teef men came to Royal Palm Avenue, we escaped their attentions, either because we had two house boys or we had nothing worth stealing. That night, the teef men robbed all the Royal Palm Avenue houses, only missing out ours and that of the Chief of Police.

Another danger was the fauna and flora. On entering the dining room one morning, Gloria and I saw a large spider high up at the top of the wall (the ceilings were very high). About the size of a saucer, the spider was wide, dark grey and had a thick furry body and legs. The house boy brought a long pole. As he lifted it up to dislodge the spider, it sprang onto the end of the pole and was smashed against the wall. It was a tarantula. One day, our gardener came to my mother on the veranda, the back of his hand swollen and transparent into a huge blister. He had been bitten by a spider on one of the flowers. My mother went over to the Mess and rang the MRS, insisting that a Land Rover come to get the gardener, before the poison had time to circulate. One morning, I found what I thought was a boil on my leg. Having put a plaster on it, the next day when I took it off, a big fat maggot emerged. I had been bitten by a *tumbu* fly.

My mother had been right to say in the Red Sea that we children would see many unusual things. One day, Abinama, the wife of John Daghati, the soldier batman, had a baby in their little *giddah* (house) in our compound. After quite a time of bellowing, Abinama delivered her baby with the aid of two women, one of whom had gone in carrying a big stick. A pool of blood spread out from under the door, dripping down the step onto the earth. My mother arranged for an ambulance to come and take mother and newborn baby boy (who looked surprisingly pink) to the hospital. John Daghati gave my father the honour of naming his son, whom he called Leo, after Leo Africanus, the 16th-century Moorish Andalusian diplomat. Later, Gloria watched Abinama put a big dead spider into a ball of clay, bake it, peel off the hairy outside, then mix the flesh with fou-fou.[2] When cooked and cooled, she fed a little of it to the baby. My father suggested that Dhaghati should not follow the local custom and scar the baby's face, but before long there were the cuts with ash rubbed into them.

My sister and I attended a service children's school a short walk away from our house. We had a cat and even a tame toad called Horace, who lived under an ornate plant pot on the veranda steps. He would wait for us all if we had been out in the evening and would accept a few lightly stunned flies. Gordon Robson brought me a young duiker, a tiny deer of the rainforest not much bigger than a small dog. At first, it thrived on bottled powdered milk, but then it became sick. I held it all through the night, breathing on it so that it would know it was not alone, until it died.

We acquired as many pets as possible. Help with this aim came from an unlikely source. A 'Hausa-man', a Muslim northern chieftain of the Hausa people, came to pay his respects to my father. The tall, stately man, in a flowing *babban riga* gown and *jalabia* robe, wore a white turban with long ends wrapped across his throat. Accompanied by four men, he came to the steps that led up to our house and began to call down blessings.

When my father appeared, the Hausa chief bowed low. On being invited onto the veranda, he took out a small bottle and, with more benedictions, poured a libation, probably of *akpeteshi* wine, onto the red cardinal floor. His bearers then laid gifts before my father: a large, wide basket of some three dozen or so eggs; a huge platter of different kinds of fruits (oranges, pineapples, tangerines, bananas and guavas); and two struggling chickens, a cockerel and a hen, their feet firmly bound. The Hausa men wanted advance agreement that their boys could join the Boys Company. Almonds was courteous, but explained why he could not accept the gifts. He spent a long time talking to the Hausa man and offered him and his men soft drinks. He made clear that every potential recruit could only be accepted if he passed certain educational tests and satisfied specified medical conditions. But he did agree to recruit in the areas where the Hausa were to be found and to look out for the boys in question. At this point, Gloria and I asked if we could rescue the chickens. The Hausa man said,

'Very good chop', to which we replied, 'No go chop-um'. My father thanked the Hausa man and said that as the chickens were not going to be eaten and were being given to his daughters, he would accept them. The rest of the gifts were politely declined.

Lockie was not bound by the rules in quite the same way. When John went back to England to school, she missed him terribly. One day, a young

Ghanaian boy with one leg bent sideways at the knee came to our veranda. The house boy brought him inside to where my mother was sitting in an easy chair. The boy, whose name was Appiah, had been rejected by the Boys Company because of his twisted leg. He could not face going back to his village in disgrace and pleaded with her to give him a job. Appiah was the same age as my brother. My mother sat with an unusually stony face, knotting and twisting a white handkerchief in her lap. She was trying to hide her feelings from the boy, while at the same time thinking how on earth she could help him. We already had two house boys. She asked him to come back again that evening. By the time he did, my father had come home and, between them, they had found a way to take him on.

The cockerel and the hen, Simon and Martha, became our special pets. They lived in a small brick room adjoining the house, meant for garden tools. Almonds quickly installed some broom handles from wall to wall, on which they could perch at night. Each evening, towards dusk, we would leave the door open and the two fowls would appear, cautiously making their way to bed. They scratched for food, but we also gave them fresh corn from the cob, rice, oats and the occasional bacon rind. As they grew tamer, we were able to pick them up easily, tuck them under an arm and walk around the compound feeding them titbits.

Simon and Martha began to meet us at lunchtime when we came home from school. At the edge of the compound, they would lead us to the biggest logs under which quantities of termites (large white ants) could be found and make a particular 'feed me' me sound. As we turned over each log, the chickens moved at top speed, gobbling up the delights. Each day, they met us earlier and earlier as we were coming along the road from school. Eventually, the day came when Gloria and I were still sitting in class, which had open shuttered windows, when from outside came the unmistakeable 'feed me' sound. I caught Gloria's eye; outside, two chickens, heads cocked enquiringly on one side, were waiting to walk us home.[3]

In summer 1957, Gloria and I went on trek with the Boys Company to the NTs. We wore shorts every day and travelled in the back of an open three-tonner truck. As we drove northwards, the jungle began to peter out. The land became dry, with sparse scrub, huge stones and tall elephant grass. Hardy, strangely beautiful baobab trees, with bulbous trunks, seemed to squat on the ground, their branches twisted up against the bare skyline. The Harmattan covered us, the trucks and everything with thick red dust. Each vehicle threw up a cloud of laterite. Guinea fowl became plentiful; *akpeteshi* was made and sold locally. We lived on a combination of army 'compo' rations and market-fresh fruit and vegetables.

When we arrived at Tamale, a smartly dressed young subaltern met us, saluted my father and offered to guide us to the Government rest house, where we stayed. What a euphemism. We shared the accommodation with bats and rats, who inhabited the roof space. Each night, as we put up our camp beds, bending the metal struts that had to be inserted to keep the beds taut, we listened to the pattering of the rats' feet above, hooting fruit bats and yowling bush babies. Power cuts were frequent, so we were ready with oil lamps and candles.

That evening, we saw two Boys Company boys, who were travelling with us, trying to open two curled-up hedgehogs with lighted cigarettes. Gloria wasn't having that and took the hedgehogs away. During the day, we fed them from the tops of evaporated milk tins. They travelled inside our shirts in the back of the three-tonner. At night, they needed to be put somewhere safe from predators, including the boys. On the third night, and several hundred miles north of where they had joined our trek, they escaped.

The next morning, scores of hopeful young men appeared, wanting to join the Boys Company. First, they had to pass a medical test: there was no point in assessing them for anything else if they were not fit and healthy. Some failed immediately for obvious defects, such as legs crippled by Guinea worm or partial paralysis. The rest had to produce urine samples to test them for diseases that it was not possible or economic to cure. These included river blindness[4] and bilharzia[5], both endemic in Ghana at the time.

The boys quickly realised the importance of the urine test and some tried to obtain what they thought was 'fine, fine past Takoradi corned beef" urine. This inevitably involved some dash. But they had no way of telling whether the bought urine was any better than their own. Even the Boys Company boys travelling with us could have become reinfected with bilharzia. The boys who passed the urine test then had to pass aptitude tests. Gloria and I (now twelve) helped to administer the puzzles and questionnaires, inwardly willing the boys to pass. Some who did went on to successful careers in the Ghana Army and probably a better life than they would have had in the NTs.

On later recruiting trips, Almonds refined the approach. Some villages had 'press-ganged' their sons into applying to join the army. The recalcitrant boys 'climbed a tree to hide. 'Right', said my father, packing some grit and gun cotton into a small container. 'There will be no more stupid puzzle tests. When this gravel goes up the tree, those who stay up can obviously take the flak, so they are going into the Air Force. Those who go to ground like sensible soldiers are going into the Army!'[6]

While at Bolgatanga, we visited a lake. Here, local boys tied live toads to lengths of elephant grass and attached the other end of the grass to stout sticks. With these, they enticed the crocodiles out of the lake. When the crocodiles finally ate the poor toads, it was a ghastly sight. We thought it an early attempt at earning money from tourists, but we were not holidaymakers and did our best to discourage this awful practice.

My father and Gloria met a crocodile of their own, as well as some wild elephants. Between the crocodile lake and our rest house ran a nearly dried-up creek, crossed by a small, flat road bridge. After testing the boys one afternoon, my father dismissed them and his driver. He wanted to go back to the bridge because he had noticed some movement in the trees. Gloria went with him. He carried his 0.22 rifle. They left the jeep and set off downstream on the left bank. Suddenly, he stopped.

'Up ahead. Crocodile', he said. 'A big one'. Gloria looked. The huge creature lay almost parallel to the rivulet in the centre of the creek with its snout near the water. It was waiting for them.

'It's watching our every movement', said Almonds. Then, he added, 'Don't worry about the front end; watch the back end. If it gets you with its tail, then worry about the front end.'

They made such a wide detour of the crocodile that they were almost at the top of the bank. Something had crossed the creek diagonally in front of them. Huge, dinner plate-sized holes pockmarked the mud: elephant tracks. The closer to the water they went, the deeper the footprints. Gloria took size six shoes and she could put both feet into one hole. 'Snap, snap', came from beyond the top of the riverbank. 'Elephants', said my father. 'They're feeding.' At the top of the bank, they saw broken bushes and smelled the most awful stench. 'We're downwind of them.' Gloria heaved a sigh of relief. They retraced their steps and, back at the bridge, set off again downstream, but this time on the right bank. As they got near the elephants, they saw a long avenue in which all the trees had been knocked over. The low rumble of the elephants and the snapping of branches grew louder. The stink became overwhelming. Each snap sent up a large cloud of buzzing black flies.

The cleared path stopped a little way ahead, so they turned left towards the river. Carefully, they parted the lush bushes growing on the bank and peeped through. About 20 yards away, five elephants, with a baby, were yanking the treetops into their mouths. They were down in a dip towards the river, so their trunks were on a level with the eyes of their human observers.

'You know this 0.22 won't stop them,' said my father. 'Be prepared to climb a tree.' Gloria was terrified. The only trees around were branchless saplings, thin and spindly as they competed for the light. Slowly, father and daughter withdrew to the bridge and the waiting jeep.

Also at Bolgatanga, we found the Lobi tribe. Wearing only small bunches of leaves, their lips had been stretched by inserting increasingly larger, flat wooden discs until they reached the size of saucers. We were told that the practice had begun during the slave-trading days as a means of ensuring that they would not be taken. These ladies were shy at first, but when they got used to Gloria and me would allow us to approach. It was difficult to communicate with them as when they spoke, the discs made a clattering sound, but they smiled with their eyes.

At Kintampo, the local chief made quite a fuss of my father with his staff car and convoy of army trucks. That evening, the chief invited my parents to a special party. Since it was not to be a late evening, Gloria and I went, too. Almonds and Lockie, wanting to be good guests, joined in the dancing. Later, they discovered they had taken part in a fertility rite. It must have given the chief ideas because he offered my father a flock of goats for me and promised to make me 'Number one wife'. My father kept threatening to take up the offer if I didn't behave.

Something mysterious happened at Navrongo. A local chief had died and that night a huge fire burned in the distance. His funeral was taking place. The army boys kept telling us that evil spirits would be roaming around during the night. Despite the appalling heat, they all locked themselves into one small brick outhouse of the Government rest house after dark. We had about seven jerrycans full of petrol (we had to carry fuel with us). To prevent them from being stolen, my father lined them up on the veranda, slipped a length of chain through all the jerrycan handles and padlocked them to a metal post at the corner of the veranda wall.

That night, there was a full moon. Gloria awoke to the sound of the chain rattling. Curious, she went out onto the veranda. Each one of the jerrycans, in turn, was lifting itself a few inches off the ground and then going back down again. As it did so, the chain was pulled through the handles of the other jerrycans, causing the rattling sound. She watched as the chain tightened and then slackened each time. Gloria was not afraid, only keen to understand what was happening. She bent down and looked underneath the cans. Moonlight was falling on the wall when each jerrycan was lifted up. Nothing could be seen and there was no explanation, so she went back to bed.[7]

Before we left Ghana, there was a happy ending to the story of Appiah. After a while with us, he left to 'go back to his people'. About a year later, when my father was on parade and we were sitting watching, one of the soldiers in the rear rank of a man-service company called to us. It was Appiah, now eighteen, his twisted leg perfectly straight. A *juju* man had healed it. He came once again to the veranda and asked to see my mother. She was amazed by the remarkable healing. Appiah said he had given dash and gifts to his village *juju* man. He had wrapped Appiah's knee in boiled leaves and herbs and put it in a splint. At the same time, he broke the leg of a healthy chicken (we did not like that bit). Appiah was not allowed to put any weight on the leg for weeks. Every few days, the treatment was repeated and the leg rebound. The bird received the same treatment. When the chicken was healed, Appiah got up with a straight leg and went off to join the Ghana Army.

During my brother's last summer holiday with us, he and my father trekked to and climbed Mount Afadja, the highest mountain in Ghana at an elevation of 885 metres (2,904 ft). Known to us as 'Afadjato', the mountain was in the Agumatsa Range in the Volta Region, near the border with Togoland.[8] The trek was another recce for a later Boys Company Exercise. Almonds, John, now seventeen, a brand-new, out-of-Sandhurst Ghanaian Lieutenant called Alf Ketah and another Ghanaian soldier set out towards Togoland. They were all in uniform (John quite illegally). While climbing Afadjato, they surprised a band of smugglers trading across the border. The traffickers outnumbered the Boys Company patrol by several to one. However, on seeing the army uniforms, the smugglers broke and ran, probably thinking that they had run into the lead scouts of a larger military force sent to deal with them. John thought it a lucky escape. Almonds did take the boy soldiers there later and got into trouble because they crossed the border at some point. Diplomatic notes started flying back and forth about border incursions and invasions.

The hoo-ha did not bother my father. He had much bigger adventures to come.

Chapter Sixteen

THOSE WHO GO DOWN
TO THE SEA IN SHIPS

s Almonds said, 'Whether they bring it to the fore or not, every human being has the survival instinct and the desire to create. Building a boat and sailing it home to England is about having your dream and satisfying it.'[1] It was also about seizing opportunities. He had promised himself in the Italian prison cell that he would one day build the boat of his dreams. The plan was still in his head. In Ghana, he had the chance to do it. Timber such as teak, mahogany and oroko was ideal for the task and plentiful. He was on a four-year posting and so he had the time, although being so close to the equator meant that there were no light evenings.

As in the desert days when he had built 'L' Detachment's parachute training rigs, Almonds's effort was met with incredulity, not encouragement. His brother officers simply couldn't believe that he could build a viable, ocean-going ketch and make it back to England. The work was hard, especially in the afternoon heat. But when Almonds bought the wonderful West African wood, he knew it was going to work. He made the frame from the best mahogany. Elsewhere, he used oroko and teak. In summer 1957, just before we left for three months' leave in England, he laid the keel, weighting it down in strategic places, in the garage beside our house. The keel was so long that it stuck out through the garage doors. He covered it with tarpaulin against the tropical rain.

From ex-service sources, Almonds bought a bubble sextant and took sightings of the ceiling electric light bulb. John, who was by then at Welbeck College (and studying maths as one of his A level GCEs), wondered what his father would do with the angles he recorded. Almonds had learned no trigonometry at Stixwould School.

In Boston, Almonds bumped into his brother-in-law, Ricky Kopyt, in the chandler's shop. Almonds was buying a Johnson's Seahorse Outboard motor, new but US Army surplus. Still in its crate, he arranged its shipping to Ghana.

'What's your plan?' asked Kopyt.

'No plan. It's all in my head', said Almonds.[2]

He made the smaller items of ship's chandlery, which were unobtainable in Ghana, using old brass shell cases for the blocks and the gimbal compass housings. He plaited parachute cord to make the rigging lines and fashioned harpoons with which to spear fish on the voyage. On the return journey to Ghana, Lockie had pulley blocks and cleats packed among her underwear.

After the age of twelve, there was no suitable school in Kumasi. So, in September 1957, it was the turn of Gloria and me to be separated from our parents. Thereafter, we saw them only once a year in Ghana for the August holidays. At the end of each summer term, we joined crowds of children gathering at the BOAC Victoria Airways Terminal in London to catch flights to parents abroad. The separation was sad, but there were benefits. We knew it was for our good and communications were more meaningful. We probably said things to each other in letters that we would not have said while living in the same house. In summer 1958, John joined us in Ghana for the last time. He went off to the Royal Military Academy, Sandhurst the following year.

The SS *Kumasi* – there was never any doubt that this would be the boat's name – was named by Mrs Ellen Staffierne, wife of the Kumasi District Manager of the United Africa Timber Company. Almonds spent every spare moment designing and building. He turned the pressed keel upside down onto several trestles and began the frame and hull. In Ghana, the British Army working day started at 7am, with a return to the house for a half-an-hour breakfast at half past eight – known as the 'Ghurkha breakfast' – before finishing at 2pm. Almonds, therefore, had about four hours of daylight for boat building.

While brother officers slept in the afternoon or went to the races, Almonds worked on his boat. After the early tropical twilight, he carried on with preparations for the next and subsequent stages: planning the next day's work, the tools and materials needed, and shopping lists for more timber to make parts. I can see him now, leaning on the end veranda wall in the gathering gloom, looking at the boat, a tankard of Heineken beer on the wall and the occasional glow of his cigarette as he thought and planned. When he worked in the afternoons, I sometimes hung around, watching and smelling the aroma of newly sawn wood as piles of sawdust fell onto the earth. He had no electric power tools. The timber arrived as huge planks and he sawed them by hand. The CO's wife thought that the piles of wood in the compound were cooking stove fuel. Whenever I asked him what he was doing, he explained it to me. But when I asked what he was going to do next, he always said that it depended on how the current stage went. There was no written plan and he had no paperwork with him as he worked.

Colleagues sometimes resented Almonds's focus. The British Army organised horse racing in Kumasi and officers were paid to be officials. But my father would not accept any invitations to do it. Eventually, he responded that the Queen paid him and he needed nothing more. This annoyed one or two who almost made the duties a full-time job during the racing season. Many came to see the mad major building a boat in his compound 200 miles from the sea. Even a noble lord involved in a timber company came to look. On his knees beneath the upturned keel, he looked up inside and marvelled at the construction. Almonds never doubted that he would finish the boat and sail her home to England.

There were many difficulties, some almost insurmountable. They related not to building, but to acquiring certain marine engineering parts or international navigational clearances, or persuading the army to grant unpaid leave in order to make the voyage. Almonds enjoyed making the rigging, thinking of the rope-making he had done in the past: a new set of bell-pulls in the church at Stixwould and the sennit lug-line he had made in the Forest of Orleans. [3] It was now used, fitted with a finned device, to log the mileage as *Kumasi* sailed to England. He even made the sails, with Lockie's help, from surplus light khaki material used for making Ghana Army uniforms. The SS *Kumasi* also needed a full set of International Maritime Code signalling flags and pennants. So, Lockie made twenty-six flags for the letters of the alphabet on her sewing machine, ten numeral pennants and three 'substitutes', using strong linen in the colours needed in the flags: red, yellow, white and black.[4] Almonds stowed them on board in a specially built flags locker.

We were still there in September to see the upside-down boat, now with planked hull, turned upright. A large company of soldiers came to help, but even with many pairs of hands and Almonds guiding the operation, damage occurred. At one moment, two of the spars extending a foot from the hull touched the ground. With the whole weight of the boat resting on them, they snapped off like matchsticks. My father just repaired them. Building the decks, the cabin with two bunks and the cockpit could now begin. The work proceeded without any problems.

In summer 1959, Gloria and I went to Ghana for the last time. My father did not come to Accra to meet us. Instead, we flew in a little aeroplane up to Kumasi. The aircraft had only six seats and we were the only two passengers; apart from a truly massive hornet. We discovered it about ten minutes after take-off. By then, we were airborne over the dark green jungle canopy. The insect's long dangling appendages included its stinging equipment. Our dilemma was whether or not to tell the pilot and risk distracting him, so causing an accident. But if we didn't, he might suddenly be stung and crash the plane. For forty-five terrible minutes, we kept avoiding the hornet in that tiny enclosed space. We also flew through a tropical storm, buffeted and tossed about as rain hammered on the windows.

Although Almonds detested admin, seagoing paperwork was different. He prepared an itinerary of fourteen possible countries relevant to the trip. For each country, he listed its ports, whether these had a consul, railway, telegraph system or a radio station (many did not), whether refuelling and repairs were possible, whether pilotage was compulsory and what form it took. Immigration was a potential problem. So he wrote to all the British consuls or vice consuls in each possible port of call, who in turn wrote to their respective chief immigration officers asking that the skipper and crew of the SS *Kumasi* be offered every assistance.

Collecting this information took months. He sent his itinerary to the Royal Naval officer in Takoradi responsible for Ghana harbours. He replied asking for full particulars of 'the yacht' and offering to send the information to all shipping agents, all harbour authorities and to the Admiralty in a 'Ghana Notice to Mariners'. If *Kumasi* came across a British ship, she should signal asking for her position to be passed on during its next radio transmission. By this means, *Kumasi* should be 'passed' all the way from

Takoradi to Boston, Lincolnshire, not only by harbours at which she called, but also by passing ships.

Gradually, the Job's comforters became fewer. By the end of 1959, the SS *Kumasi* looked like a respectable, oceangoing vessel. People became actively interested and by early 1960, ready takers wanted to sign on as crew. Dan Calvert wrote from Newton Abbot in Devon saying he wanted to come. Peter de la Billière's brother replied to a letter from Almonds asking about his experience of a similarly adventurous trip.

'You need a bloody big bottle and a damn good life insurance policy' was his only advice. Gordon Robson, by then out of the army and tea planting in India, wanted to build on his Volta River experience. And at the last minute, Alan Cameron from Dundee, the Government chief regional officer, who was leaving Ghana, asked to join as well. Neither had ever sailed. Robson was from Edinburgh, so Almonds had an all-Scots crew.

Even the War Office caught the spirit. After finally granting the unpaid leave, they wrote again saying that 'PR3' had displayed 'a lively interest'. They went on, 'Almonds, of course, cannot be compelled to become a vehicle for Army publicity, but we would be grateful if you could persuade him… providing, of course, that he is successful!'[5]

The timetable pressed. Almonds needed paid help to finish the work. It came in the shape of two Ghana Army carpenters: Sergeant Emmanuel Bruku and Corporal Samuel Kwame Degun, assisted by Kwesi Sam of the Garrison Engineer's Department. Each afternoon, Almonds set them to work while he finished the masts, centreboard and cabin. He still used his USMC knife when the job called for it. The Ghanaian carpenters speeded up the job and seemed to enjoy it. Almonds, too, found it a pleasure. As when he had used two Italian POWs to help him build the towers for Stirling's wartime parachute training rig in the Western Desert, he had someone to chat to. In due course, the carpenters accompanied SS *Kumasi* to Takoradi for her sea launch and their role was acknowledged in the Ship's Log: *The Maiden Voyage of the Ketch Kumasi.*

Kumasi had an overall length of 32 feet (28 feet at the waterline) and maximum beam of 9 feet, 6 inches. An iron plate ran along her keel, encasing the centreboard so that as it went up and down, it did not damage the wood. Her draught with the centreboard up was three feet and seven feet with it down. The timber company obligingly sawed up old metal railway tracks for her ballast. She had triple diagonal planking and a deadweight of 8.5

tons. Her sail plan was a gaff ketch rig consisting of a jib, staysail, main and mizzen.

Almonds designed and built an ingenious and novel system for raising and lowering Kumasi's two masts without the need to un-ship them every time. She would need to passage in and out of the River Witham, under its bridges on the way to her ultimate anchorage, Stixwould. The method was rather like that used to achieve a masted ship in a bottle. Both masts were hinged in tabernacles and a pulley system from the forward end of the bowsprit raised the forward mast first. Then, a second pulley from the top of the now erect forward mast to the top of the mizzen mast pulled the latter also into vertical. To lower the masts, the process was reversed. Almonds registered his boat at the port of Takoradi, Ghana – her club being the Takoradi Sailing Club.

Launch day came. More soldiers loaded SS *Kumasi* onto a massive boatyard container, used to import cars at Accra, and pushed her across to the Officers' Mess for her dry land launch. My parents issued a formal invitation for Tuesday February 25th, 6pm to 8pm. At her naming, Mrs Ellen Staffiere, wife of the United Africa Company District Manager, smashed a bottle of champagne against her side. Frank Duffy of 'HBWR & Co' presented Almonds with a handsome brass ship's bell engraved with 'Kumasi' and his firm's letters. Then, she set off for Takoradi on a timber lorry, followed by people from the launch party. The local press carried a feature entitled, 'The boat that was built with Ghana wood'.[6] Not long afterwards, a Ghanaian man, Kwadjo Amure Dankyi, wrote on 8 April 1960 from Takoradi, saying that he had been to see the boat and was keen to join the expedition.[7]

Riding at anchor in Takoradi harbour, the SS *Kumasi* was a pleasing sight: a gaff-rigged ketch of hard chine construction. She had a clipper bow with bowsprit and a transom stern with tiller steering. Her fore hatch was separated from her self-draining cockpit by the cabin, with five windows on the port side, four windows on the starboard side and two skylights. Her gleaming upperworks were varnished and her bulwarks painted black, while her topsides were white with red boot topping. All this set off her buff-coloured sails. Almonds had also made a 14-feet dinghy to help with getting ashore.

My father was leaving Ghana for good, so had to fit in the usual farewells and arrange his next posting. In Accra, he met a visiting War Office officer dealing with secondment policy. Would Almonds consider a post commanding the Training Company of the Royal Sierra Leone Military Forces in Freetown? He should go and see the brigadier as he sailed through. He was given an application form to send off from Freetown – '… if you like them and they like you!'[8] He had planned to sail solo, but eventually decided on two crew: Gordon Robson and Alan Cameron. In them, Almonds had found, as he put it, 'Two equally inexperienced crew members, brave or perhaps foolish enough, to come with me'.

Almonds himself had no recent sailing or navigational experience as the three men set sail for the UK. They had no lifejackets or clip-on safety tethers.

Chapter Seventeen

MAIDEN VOYAGE OF THE KETCH KUMASI

On the beach at night stands a child with her father,
Watching the east… ships sailing the seas, each with its special flag or ship-
signal… a chant for the sailors of all nations,
Fitful, like a surge… the white-grey sails, taut to their spars and ropes.[1]

Almonds was an unorthodox soldier – and an unorthodox sailor. Like his boat-building, his sailing was self-taught. At the time, none of us in the family gave it any thought. He had immense self-confidence and drive, which communicated itself to us. The first craft he built as a boy, made from a bacon box with two toffee tins as outriggers, he launched on Stixwould village pond. At fourteen, he made a large model sailing boat, but it wouldn't float without listing slightly. He gave it to his schoolteacher, who was delighted and had no intention of sailing it. But Almonds had learned from his mistake. So he did not consider that boat a failure.

It was a significant year to make the trip: during 1960, seventeen African countries would become independent. During the war, while in the Middle East, Almonds had built boats, even making one on request for David Stirling. But most of his boatbuilding skill came from making his canoe in Eritrea and *Wug* in Singapore. His only maritime sailing experience had been in the Jahore Straits. But Almonds's lack of education in naval architecture, navigation and sailing did not deflect him from his purpose. There were probably not many men in 1960 who had sailed 5,000 miles in a boat they had designed themselves and built by hand in their back garden.

It was too late to abandon the idea. As he said,

'The great day came. We took it down to the sea, lifted it off with a crane into the water and it floated. There was no time to try it out because my posting was up and I had already broadcast what I was going to do. A notice on the board in the Accra Airport departure lounge said that Major Almonds was going home in his own boat.'[2]

Alan Cameron had spent ten years in the Colonial Service after reading modern languages at the University of St Andrews. He offered to keep and write the log of the maiden voyage, while Robson was keen to be navigator. So Almonds delegated these tasks. He took not much interest in the log, though he did keep a brief record of his own. However, he also continued to navigate himself. As John had discovered on previous sailing and canoeing expeditions, his father appeared to delegate navigation but was always one step ahead, navigating by the sun and the stars.

'You're in charge of this', he would say and the boy would busy about trying to do his best, only to find that behind the scenes his father had everything already sewn up.

The last-minute crew had to learn on the job. The Takoradi Sailing Club had invited *Kumasi* to a send-off. On 15 May 1960, they cast off at noon and motored out of Takoradi Harbour to the nearby club[3]. The members were waiting on the jetty. *Kumasi* gave them an example of seamanship by crashing into the jetty, breaking the bobstay and almost wrenching the bowsprit from its housing. The tow rope of the dinghy they wrapped around the outboard motor. They stepped ashore to raised eyebrows.

After cold beer and pleasantries, with the bobstay repaired and the last provisions and petrol stowed, they cast off again at 2pm. They motored out to sea, accompanied for about a mile by some of the club's sailing dinghies. The brand-new crew stopped the motor and put up sail. The jib and stay went up smartly. The copper rings of the main and mizzen stuck fast. It was five minutes before they were under full sail. A small tear in the mainsail served as a memento. Cameron had handled a halyard for the first time in his life.

They began from the centre of the world. Ghana is also unique for its position on most global maps. It is the country closest to 0 degrees Latitude (the Equator) and 0 degrees Longitude (the Greenwich Meridian). From 4.9167° North and 1.7667° West, they set a course north-westward, out of the Bight of Benin and up the western seaboard of Africa. The dinghy they towed contained a special firkin of concentrated Rose's lime juice from Cameron's friend, Bill Cummings, in Cape Coast and a colossal inflated aeroplane tyre inner tube, as an emergency buoyancy bag. In the choppy sea, the painter snapped. Back they went for the dinghy. Having secured it, a mile later, the painter snapped again. They looked at each other. The dinghy was but a handicap impeding what little progress they were making in the heavily laden *Kumasi*. So within the first hour, they abandoned their dinghy and lime juice. Too bad if they all got scurvy.

Robson and Cameron began to be sick. They felt all right in the open air, but wretched when they went below. Almonds remained on watch. The wind took them slowly southwest. By 1900 hours, the lights of Takoradi twinkled in the distance. The wind fell and they drifted. Cameron wondered if the Takoradi Sailing Club was going to see them again. He took over a tiller for the first time in his life. Almonds explained what he had to do and left him to it. A mug of tea wasted in the sea and Cameron began to feel better. Robson had it rough below. Almonds's head appeared out of the hatch every half an hour to check that all was under control. Cameron was tensed up with the novelty and responsibility; the slightest heel of the boat seemed alarming. But all went well and the feel of the wooden tiller was reassuring. Just after midnight, Robson took over the helm. Cameron went below and lay on the bunk, pondering the deck (sic) 6 inches above his nose.

During the night, the wind died. Next morning, Almonds started the motor. While lying at anchor in Takoradi, the petrol tanks had rusted up. Originally, refuelling was to be a simple operation: a pump would deliver the petrol right to the motor. Instead, they would have to pump the tea-coloured petrol into a two-gallon can, while filtering it through a cloth and funnel before adding oil to the petrol and mixing well. Since the engine was mounted on the port quarter, one of the crew had to sit on the deck beside the motor while a second stood or knelt between his legs. The first then grabbed the legs or thighs of the pourer with one hand and with his other hand held the funnel. They swayed back and forth with the seas while petrol splashed on the deck and in their eyes. At night, it was worse. Someone had to hold a torch to see where the petrol was going. In heavier seas, the operation was highly acrobatic and positively dangerous. The deck and rear hatch became slippery with petrol and oil.

Despite no wind, they made for Cape Three Points. After drifting into a little bay, they anchored to spend the night. A canoe with husky-looking paddlers came out to greet the *Kumasi*. Their anchorage was safe and out of the surf. They ate their only meal of the day, a stew of potatoes, onions, 'bully' beef and peas, and relaxed on deck. The night was calm, but someone remained on watch in case of a sudden squall or a dragging anchor. On 17 May, they had a mug of tea for breakfast and then motored out to sea for about 10 miles. They got a fair wind, but still no sign of Cape Three Points. In the evening, they could still see Takoradi. They were making very little progress.

On 18 May, rain squalls arrived in the night. The boat heeled over. Cameron's heart was in his mouth as water rushed in through the scuppers. 'Quite an alarming experience at night for a complete novice,' he noted in the log. But they made Cape Three Points and progressed westwards. Next morning, a line squall with rain arrived under grey, sultry skies. Calm again, they drifted slowly northeast towards land. Almonds decided to anchor again until the wind was more favourable. At dusk, they approached the shore near Appolonia and what they thought was the village of Atuabo. In calm, oily water and hearing breakers ahead, they caught the lights of the village. They dropped anchor outside the surf.

Bad decision. In ten minutes, the surf suddenly rose 50 yards out to sea. There was no wind to take them out again and the motor was *kaput*. Quicker and heavier came the boiling surf; huge combers crashed down upon the *Kumasi*. She shuddered while everything moveable was swept from the deck. About every seventh breaker was bigger than the others. Almonds dropped a second anchor to avoid being swept ashore on the rocks and reefs that lined the beach. The villagers could probably see *Kumasi*'s lights, but would have been unable to come out by canoe through the seething surf. 'Is this the end of our hopes and our ocean voyage?' Cameron noted. 'Jim has spent four years building his boat and dreaming of this voyage!'

It seemed impossible to survive the night in such surf. They donned life jackets. Two remained below while a third took turns to stand on the cabin steps and call out when a particularly big breaker was bearing down on the boat. They braced themselves. A sudden huge thud and water poured over the boat into the cockpit, down into the cabin and through cracks in the cabin windows and skylights. Everything was soaked. By midnight, the shout of 'A big one!' came more and more often. At times, they felt the hull thumping on the seabed. No damage yet; the bottom was probably sand and shell – but that gave even less grip to their anchors. They could do nothing except lie or sit in the cabin, half dozing all night, knowing that any breaker could be the final death blow to the *Kumasi* – or, for that matter, to themselves. Just inside the cabin door, Almonds had installed a large felling axe in a quick release bracket. Typical Almonds. It was there in case all else failed – to cut rigging free or even a mast. He was almost moved to use it in the surf that night.

Dawn on 19 May. The boat was still in one piece. 'Thank God', Cameron noted, 'that Jim has built a boat so solid and secure.' The surf abated slightly. Almonds tried the motor, a perilous manoeuvre. As he pulled the starter, a huge wave sent him flying into the cockpit, breaking two ribs and a forearm. 'His bones might be broken or cracked', recorded Cameron, 'but he shrugs it off'. In the cool fresh morning air, the surf moderated a little more but was still dangerous. They waved to the villagers crowding the shore. Half an hour later, a long surfboat with eight paddlers poled and paddled its way towards them through the reefs. At first, the canoeists were reluctant to come near, calling out that it was too dangerous. *Kumasi* threw them a line and the new arrivals tried to tow the ketch out beyond the surf. They used the harpoon line, but the canoe tilted too awkwardly in the swell for the heavy ketch to be towed. The surf continued to reduce; seven canoeists were persuaded to clamber aboard with their paddles. They soon dug in, singing a paddling song that sounded like 'heavo-ho'. Slowly, *Kumasi* moved out about 60 yards into safety beyond the surf.

For half an hour, the white men and the villagers sat in the sunshine, resting and chatting. A noggin of whisky for the crew, and for the worthy village helpers, their favourite, some gin. After a palaver, Cameron went ashore in the canoe for petrol, bread and fruit. He got soaked again in the surf as the canoe performed crazy acrobatics in the foaming breakers. He stepped ashore onto the sand and then flopped down as he discovered he had lost his sense of balance. After five minutes, he lurched wildly up to the mud village, followed by scores of children and villagers. He imagined they must have thought he was from the moon. None could ever have seen a bearded, scruffy white man staggering in from a sailing yacht. [4]

At the United Africa Company village store, Cameron had a cup of tea, made a phone call to Takoradi, paid the canoeists £5, got the stores and took off again back through the surf to the *Kumasi*. Almonds and Robson had dried out the ship and all the bedding. Almonds put new spark plugs into the motor and checked it over. They set off again and made 31 miles south west on the motor to give themselves plenty of sea room.

That evening came sudden line squalls with rain. They had only one pair of oilskins, so somebody always got wet when changing watch. The rainy nights were quite cold. When scudding along, Robson and Cameron used Cameron's white topee to keep the rain off their faces. Almonds showed them how to hold the sheets (there are no 'ropes' when sailing) in their hands during a blow and when to let air out of the sails in a hurry. The winds were fickle; on 20 May, they were becalmed nearly all day. Then came a light breeze for an hour. Cameron took precautions against sunburn and wore a shirt most of the time. Nevertheless, he got burned about the thighs and on his back. He wore his topee or straw hat when at the tiller.

The lack of wind surprised them. They expected southerlies to be blowing fairly steadily. 'At this rate, we will never make the UK in time', noted Cameron. He and Robson bathed in the sea, while Almonds kept a keen lookout for sharks. They sighted Alban Hills, the log reading 22.5 miles. Still drifting in calm, oily seas, they tried to keep the boat heading northwest or southwest. The rainy season was due and Almonds wanted to keep in front of it. Away to the east, thunder and lightning flashed; the squalls were probably forerunners of worse weather to come. However, their main problem was lack of wind.

They started the motor and went west, but then came engine palaver. After refuelling, the motor refused to start. They tried using less oil in the mixture, but the engine continued to splutter and cough. They took turns at pulling the starter. Occasionally, the motor would start, go for half an hour and then die out. 'Jim', recorded Cameron, 'who knows the motor inside out, keeps replacing plugs and doing other mysterious things with no great success'. They still hoped to make Abidjan, in the Ivory Coast, the next day – if the motor worked or the wind blew. They ate only one meal a day in the evening, with a mug of tea or coffee for breakfast. They had already lost weight. Cameron thought he had lost a stone.

In the afternoon, they played about with Almonds's .22 rifle, firing at tin cans. The cabin was shipshape, but they were all a mass of bruises from falling against sharp edges. Almonds's chest and arm were very painful, and their bottoms were raw and pimply from sitting on the wet oily deck. They found the cockpit seat too low and so sat half perched on the rear hatch and deck. But they were beginning to get their sea legs. Robson suggested that *Woman's Own* magazine could advertise their type of sailing as an infallible means of slimming. Before midnight, they enjoyed two hours' light wind. A school of porpoises kept them company – excellent for the lonely helmsman.

On 22 May, they discovered that the compass was affected by the metal jerrycan at the side of the cockpit. They steered west northwest and ran the motor, which performed intermittently. A hot sunny day enabled all sails to be run up and a light breeze became a fairish south southwest wind. On the northern horizon, town light reflections appeared. Grand Bassam or Abidjan? They couldn't see a lighthouse or any red or green lights. In a dark but starry night, they must be at the mouth of the Abidjan Canal. With the motor misbehaving, they tacked back and forth in front of the entrance, about which they had very little information. An emerging pilot boat ignored them completely. They were alarmed as the wind began to blow them on shore. They tacked to the east of the canal, just managing to keep away from the roaring surf.

Next morning, they got further out to sea. Daybreak and rain arrived. They put out their pilot flag, but the pilot boat took no notice. The chart told them that they were over the Bottomless Pit, so great was the depth beneath them. A terrific swell at the mouth of the canal meant that sailing through it was totally out of the question. The seas were stained by the yellow waters of hundreds of lagoons pouring out from the canal mouth. They had to try the motor. Almonds, still in pain from his broken ribs and arm, worked on it for over two hours before it started. Then, just as they entered the swell, the motor conked out. Cameron and Robson were ready with the anchors to prevent the boat from being swept onto ugly-looking rocks. No wind for sailing.

Finally, Almonds, by then pouring with sweat, got one cylinder of the engine working. They chugged slowly past the huge breakwater into the safety of the canal. A hundred yards in, they moored by the bank to get directions from some locals about the different channels to use to get to Abidjan. A large British cargo boat slipped slowly by. With one cylinder working again, *Kumasi* moved upstream. The air was overpoweringly hot and sticky.

At the Abidjan Port entrance, a motor boat guided them to a jetty next to an old Liberty ship. They tied up. The mate of a nearby French ship, M.

Arosdidier, offered them beautiful cold beer and, best of all, a hot bath. There was no fuss about immigration, police or health. The harbour master came to welcome them and was kind and helpful. He had received advance notice of their arrival from Captain Everard of Takoradi and had sent out the motorboat to meet them. They all found *terra firma* not very firm. On board *Kumasi*, it was impossible to walk normally. The longer they were at sea, the more they lost the ability to walk properly on land. They went ashore in the evening and sat on the veranda of the Hotel de Parc with glasses of cold beer and sausage and ham sandwiches.

The centre of Abidjan was very French and very beautiful with some wonderful roads and flyovers. It put Accra to shame. Gendarmes, white and black, strolled around in kepis. Cafés lined the sidewalks, while teenaged white girls flirted around in Parisian summer dresses. Motor scooters whizzed around furiously. White and black women bustled about with long French loaves under their arms. Many of the shops had European assistants. Almonds was exhausted after his efforts that morning, as well as his injured chest and arm. Cameron found himself a room in the Hotel International, while Almonds and Robson had an early night on board the *Kumasi*.

On 24 May, Cameron enjoyed a ham and egg breakfast with fresh milk and fruit. He got to the boat at 9am to find M. Arosdidier advising Almonds to see a specialist. At the hospital, an X-ray confirmed two broken ribs (and a broken right radius bone). A doctor injected cortisone and novocaine. He strapped Almonds's chest with bandages, redolent of the wrappings of an Egyptian mummy. He refused treatment for the arm; it was impossible to sail a boat with an arm in plaster. The next day, he wrote to Lockie without mentioning any injuries: 'the trip has not been too bad so far… as a crew we are settling down quite nicely.'[5]

Back at *Kumasi*, Robson had restocked the provisions. Almonds began to overhaul the engine, but couldn't get it to go. He was eventually persuaded to spend the night at the hotel before all going off to the La Pergola restaurant for a good dinner with French wine. After Robson had returned to the *Kumasi*, Almonds and Cameron had a few drinks in the hotel bar. The proprietor's wife was English. Initially very reticent, she arranged to buy all their fresh provisions for them, while the proprietor, M. Fioux, said he would find a young French engineer who specialised in outboard motors.

Next morning, they took the hotel proprietor to the boat. Cameron changed a cheque into dollars and sent off cables to the UK. The motor started beautifully, but then flopped and had to be taken to the garage. The young French engineers were very talkative and slow. Consequently, *Kumasi* was unable to set sail that day. The motor arrived back at the boat, but again refused to work. That evening, they had dinner as guests of the proprietor and his wife – octopus and red wine – before getting to bed at midnight.

On 26 May, they went down to the boat in the morning. The engineers played around with the carburettor, condenser, plugs, points, timing, fuel feed and just about all of the engine's innards. Almonds was totally exasperated. After lunch, everyone went back to the boat. The motor ran, but without acceleration. Again, the engineer dismantled everything. Robson now christened the engine the 'Brute'. Finally, the exhaust outlet was found to be completely choked with carbon and soot. This cleared, the Brute worked beautifully. The manufacturers' instructions were clearly wrong about the mixture of petrol and oil. The Brute's cantankerous nature was a mystery, especially since it was about the only bit of kit that Almonds had bought new in Boston.

They motored to the fishing quay for petrol, but nobody was there. Robson went off water-skiing with the young Frenchman. Later, the engineer, M. Garrard, invited the three men to supper with his family. After a pleasant evening and a beer in town, they finished letters home and went to bed – Robson sleeping inside a lorry on the quayside, while Almonds and Cameron returned to the *Kumasi*. Next morning, they were up early, brewed tea and moved to another berth, followed by two French minesweepers. The sailors fired their rifles as they hoisted the French and Ivory Coast flags.

The fresh water taken on the day before was now rusty. Cameron fetched kerosene, filters, fruit, meat and other provisions. They said farewell to the port captain and his assistant, then motored to the Shell Quay for petrol. There, they were delayed for two hours over customs – according to Cameron: 'typical West African nonsense'. The West African clerk couldn't do anything without his superior, but the superior wasn't available. They took on another 260 litres of petrol and 24 litres of oil. Everyone was exasperated at the delay.

At noon, they were off down the lagoon into the canal. At the canal exit, *Kumasi* bounced up and down furiously in very heavy swell. The pilot boat stood by, but with the Brute going full throttle, they made it out to sea. Some days behind schedule, they motored steadily southwest for 25 miles. Then, the engine stopped: the propeller pin had broken.

Cameron cursed like mad. The Brute was living up to its name. While straddling the shaft over the water, Almonds cut a new propeller pin from the end of the soldering iron and replaced the broken one. They restarted the motor and motored southwest. And every two hours, they carried out the very trick and dangerous refuelling operation. The Brute also made a 'hell of a noise'.

On 28 May, Abidjan lay 60 miles behind. But *Kumasi* was becalmed. With a backing squall, they sailed well until midnight. On a northwest course, they made 35 miles. The next day without wind, they lowered the sail to get rid of the constant rattling. More rain squalls; course west northwest. Robson was busy plotting their course on the charts. After half an hour's pulling, the Brute deigned to start. The propeller pin broke again. Almonds made another new pin from a quarter inch bolt and Robson went overboard to replace it. Four hours' repeated pulling failed to get the Brute to start. In the evening, they raised sail in a light breeze.

30 May saw them on course two points north of west. The wind freshened again 'small, small' (they were still using Ghanaian Pidgin), but they made little progress. Becalmed again, Robson and Cameron went for a swim. The motor failed to start, but *Kumasi* appeared to be out of the shipping lane. Cameron managed to make a decent cup of coffee from water left to settle overnight in the pressure cooker. Robson didn't care for tea, but Almonds preferred it so Cameron shuttled between the two. Every evening, they had their *Ein Topf* – an 'all-in' stew of everything that needed to be used up. Almonds dismantled the engine again and examined the plugs, carburettor and condenser, but without success.

A large shark with two sucker fish on its side appeared. Robson tried to harpoon it, but it stayed just out of reach. They put out a line with a hook and salami sausage – both were bitten off. They tried a stronger hook, but the shark was now wary of a hook diet. Still becalmed, Cameron sunbathed while Robson repaired the clew of the jib. It was getting rubbed on the pulpit rail. Almonds greased the blocks and puttied the port cabin window. They replaced the mainsail, which was torn in three places. The new main went up, but the eyelet in the luff was also torn. Despite the mast having been slightly greased, the rings still stuck as they hauled the sail aloft. Sometimes it took two of them, even three, to do the job.[6] The throat of the boom was also wearing the mast slightly. For supper, they had their first steak and kidney pudding with potato and onion.

On 31 May, the wind freshened from the southeast, then veered to the west. Waves were running in from the south. *Kumasi* had made 42 miles since the day before. The fresh fruit was ripening too quickly, except for the oranges. They found their last bottle of gin in the forward hatch and squeezed the remaining limes for a gin and lime. At noon, they reckoned their position to be approximately 30 miles south of Scranton Corner. The current in the area was allegedly very strong, but it was difficult to assess its effect on the boat. Everyone was in a better humour due to the good breeze. The sores on their bottoms had healed, their beards were looking more respectable and Cameron could take the sun without burning.

At noon, a fickle wind from the southeast meant little progress. They sat becalmed with the rigging 'in pain'. The noise was amazingly trying on the nerves. Then came a southwest breeze and they began to make about two knots on course two points north of west. Six large shoals of mackerel boiled up near the surface. Robson rushed for the rods. The fish waited just until he was ready, then disappeared. A few swallow-like birds darted and swooped just above the surface. The log read 447 miles. Gusts of stronger wind arrived. Clouds raced across the sky. A ship to starboard was travelling west southwest. *Kumasi* was probably just inside the Cape Palmas shipping lane, but heavy mist or cloud obscured the horizon, while thunder and sheet lightening flickered in the southwest.

On 1 June, they were suddenly becalmed. The rigging rattled and the boat creaked – horrid music in their ears. A breeze sprang up from the southwest. Their course was barely west northwest, with a heavy swell from the south. Two ships to port were spotted travelling west northwest. Rain arrived. The log read 480. Becalmed again with the rigging racked with pain, they had a light snack of beans and a gin. Almonds started fiddling with the Brute and – *mirable dictum* – after only half an hour, he kicked into life! Course west northwest and in fifteen minutes, land-ho! However, they could not recognise it from the pilot. A dark storm cloud with a broad front loomed. They hauled in the Brute and lashed everything down. Only the staysail remained up. False alarm. There was rain, but only light gusts of wind. And once again, they were becalmed.

On 2 June, after a cloudy, misty night, they drifted. Having started the motor again on a course west, they again sighted land. Were they west southwest of Cape Palmas? Was that the outline of the Cape and six little hills to the northwest? Almonds reckoned they were about 30 miles east of Palmas. Rain squalls continued all the time and it was a bugger pouring liquid food into the Brute every hour. The cabin was filthy and wet. Breakfast was chewing gum and a mouthful of Henco brandy. Everyone was cheesed off. The cockpit was an ice rink of oil and petrol. They badly needed another set of oilskins.

At 9am, the log read 518 miles and at 1pm, 540. They were making little headway against the current and the choppy seas. Still uncertain of their position, they peered through grey skies and intermittent light rain. A school of porpoises paid the *Kumasi* a visit. Refuelling was a strain on the back and leg muscles, but at least the Brute was working. Cameron recorded that the lack of wind might mean their voyage would end at Freetown since Almonds had to report to his regimental depot by the end of September. Moreover, braving gales in the Atlantic or the Bay of Biscay in the autumn would be risky. The trouble was that none of them had any experience of Atlantic weather. Almonds shared none of these doubts.

They recognised Kablake Lighthouse. So that morning they had been off Grand-Bérébi, not Cape Palmas. The current had taken them northwards and delayed them by at least 30 miles. In the evening, the SS *Aureol* passed close by. She did not alter course, though Cameron guessed that there must have been at least sixty friends and acquaintances on board. They were too far off to identify anyone. On a course west southwest, they were reckless and burned fuel until they saw the reflection of Cape Palmas in the sky. At 10pm, they saw the lights. All sails were up, but they barely kept on course west northwest.

Almonds wrote Lockie a blue, folded airmail letter:

'From: Major JE Almonds, SS *Kumasi*, At Sea'.

Dear Lockie,

100 miles southeast of Monrovia, 7 June, 1960. We now have a favourable wind and a good chance of making Monrovia tomorrow. We have been delayed at sea for a number of days due to calms, a late start from Takoradi and an extra-long stay at Abidjan and are now nine days behind our programme. I did not mention it in my last letter but the long stay at Abidjan was due to the fact that I broke two ribs and the radius in my right arm as I was thrown about during the run from Takoradi. I got the ribs fixed at the hospital in Abidjan but did not mend [sic] the arm for fear of

being delayed even longer. Things are now alright, with no more trouble from my injuries.

In the last week, it has rained day and night and has been rather miserable so we are all looking forward to a chance to dry out and get clean clothes in Monrovia. I did not think much of Abidjan, although the people were quite helpful and kind. But we were all too tired to enjoy the stay. I now feel much stronger and have lost my 'paunch'! *I really enjoy fighting with the elements.* [My italics.] We have now according to the ship's log covered 745 miles. Gordon and Alan are doing alright.'

In cold rain and mist, Robson tacked west northwest for an hour, then south for an hour, then back on west northwest. At 7am, they saw Cape Palmas town. 'About time too', noted Cameron. The swell was irregular and the wind began to drop. Once past Rockton Point, they hoped to alter course a few compass points to the north. Everything on board was wet and clammy. With no real sun for three days, their clothes reeked. The cockpit cushion made of kapok stank to high heaven. Without ceremony, they consigned it to the deeps. Visibility dropped to half a mile. The coast looked dangerous, with outlying reefs and rocks only 2 feet below the surface. The log at the Cape read 594 miles. Squatting aft on the toilet bucket, plunging up and down in the rain and swell, was anything but comfortable.

The wind died completely and they drifted south. Heavy rain squalls hit them with rough seas, but they made little mileage due to the strong current driving them back to the Cape. Two ships passed going west. All *Kumasi's* torches except one were *kaput*, due to salt water damage. They had to be careful at night in the busy shipping lane in rain and poor visibility. Various little leaks in the cabin skylights and windows annoyed all three men and wearing wet pants gave them pimples on their bottoms again. Liberia's weather was as bad as its politics! Cameron dropped a brandy bottle with a note inside into the sea. It promised a pound to the finder. Rain and feeble wind kept up until midnight. The current had driven them back to a position southeast of Cape Palmas. Quite exasperating!

On 4 June, in a night dark with heavy rainfalls, they seemed near the Cape, so Cameron tacked south southwest. The rain fell away with the wind. He kept flashing his torch when any steamer came near. At dawn, the sun came out fitfully for a few hours and was followed by more light rain. At noon, they were again just past the Cape. Three cargo ships passed by.

Cameron had an infected right knee and it was slightly swollen. Almonds suffered from a barnacle on his bottom. His ribs were slightly better, but his arm was still not back to normal. According to their schedule, they should have been in Freetown. At noon, the log read 618 miles. They shared a tin of jellied veal for lunch, which Cameron had bought in Kumasi over a year before. They continued to drift, the current pulling them back southeast on a thick, oily-looking swell, without a single ripple on the surface. Sunset was grey and blue with streaks of pale gold. Almonds changed the centreboard sheet. Dark night; no wind; no light; no ships. They must have drifted well to the south of the shipping lane. A large, unidentifiable object surfaced 200 yards to starboard. Whale? Submarine? Or the Loch Ness Monster?

On 5 June: No wind until dawn, when light gusts filled the sails, but were not strong enough to turn the mileage log. Tea for breakfast. The sun came out and the log turned occasionally. They dried out the bedding on top of the cabin and discussed sextants – the thingamajigs they saw Royal Naval captains posing with on the bridges of their ships. *Kumasi* had two sextants. The log read 622. They must be in an area that had not seen ships since the days of sail. Modern ships usually kept to the shipping lanes. Almonds thought a lump in his right forearm meant that it was still cracked. To curb the rattling rigging, they used lazy guys on the main and mizzen. The sunny Sunday weather was such a welcome change that they felt in a happy Sunday mood. Hot sun all day. A tin of peaches for lunch. It was difficult to tell if they were still drifting to southeast. Almonds thought they were some 15–20 miles south southwest of Cape Palmas.

They forgot the danger in the deeps beneath them.

Chapter Eighteen

LONELY SEA AND THE SKY

I must go down to the sea again, to the lonely sea and the sky,
And all I ask is a tall ship and a star to steer her by;
And the wheel's kick and the wind's song and the white sail's shaking,
And a grey mist on the sea's face and a grey dawn breaking.[1]

Cameron nearly met his end. He was below, snoozing, while Almonds and Robson remained on deck. He awoke to hear Robson shouting, 'Alan! On deck – quick! Shark!' Cameron staggered, half asleep, on deck. Robson was casting a line towards a silver monster a few yards away. It darted towards the boat. Cameron craned forward to get a better look, put his hand on the mizzen boom, stumbled and fell overboard, smack on top of the shark's tail! Within ten seconds, he grew wings, grasped a stanchion and hauled himself back on board. Robson leant out immediately to help. But the man overboard, desperate as he was, avoided the outstretched hand for fear of pulling Robson in. The shark disappeared in a flash, probably more frightened than the humans. Cameron observed with *sang froid* that according to Jacques Cousteau and Hans Hass, sharks were merely curious. Almonds looked at Cameron as if he were nuts. They were lucky that the boat was becalmed; otherwise, the creature might have ended up with indigestion from a surfeit of lean meat.

The shark returned. While Almonds played around with a hooked line, Robson pranced from side to side with a raised harpoon like an ancient gladiator ready to deliver the *coup de grâce* to his adversary. But the shark kept its distance. It probably disagreed with the song they had sung: 'A Gordon for me'. The wind freshened from the south and the mileage log began to turn. In honour of the occasion, they polished off a bottle of red wine. The log read 628. The wind was fair until midnight.

On 6 June, both wind and sea strengthened. With a good south wind, they altered course to west northwest. The skies were grey, but without rain. Heavier seas sent the scuppers under water most of the time while waves broke over the bows. That night, in a strong wind, they reduced sail to the stay and the main. Heavy, choppy seas kept breaking on the port quarter.

From midnight, they held the same course with heavy seas. Steering was a continual struggle with the tiller, which meant putting up the helm to allow the seas to sweep under the stern. The helmsman needed his head continually cocked over his shoulder. Fortunately, the moon gave some illumination through the clouds. Two heavy seas swept over the deck, coming unexpectedly at a steep angle. They swamped the binnacle light, making it difficult to see the luminous points on the compass. With the boat heeled over, even sleeping was difficult. The port bunk was the worst. The occupant would brace himself in, with his left leg against the centreboard table. New leaks developed over the port bunk, delivering drips down the neck or on the stomach. In this clime, they used no blankets or sleeping bags. The log read 745.

The morning dawned wet and grey. Becalmed for so long off Cape Palmas in strong currents, their position was uncertain, but was possibly 15 miles off land. Cameron's topee proved an excellent wind gauge as it howled under the sweat band. It was also a useful baler and windbreak when lighting a cigarette. They all smoked sixty cigarettes a day. The cabin and deck were littered with wet matches and boxes, disintegrated by salt water. Cameron's right knee continued to swell; undiluted Dettol and neobacrin kept the infection under control. Suntan and dirt were indistinguishable on their bodies. The wind began to fail and the boat wallowed in heavy swells. There came a fairish breeze with rain for the rest of the day.

On 8 June, fair wind and rain continued and they sighted land. In heavy drizzle, the wind fell and they made little progress north northwest. The land was unidentifiable from the pilot. It was a very disappointing day. Then came a proper downpour; the sun peered out of a watery sky. For three hours, they attempted to start the Brute without success. Almonds greased and tightened the stays. On course northwest, at noon, the wind was moderate.

Robson repaired the clew of the jib where it had been wearing against the stanchion. Raising the main and mizzen was still difficult. They hoped to see Monrovia that night. According to their timetable, they should already have been in Conakry. Near the headland, they tacked south southwest. At midnight, the log read 850; they were back on course north northwest. The wind fell away again as a full moon skidded between scattered clouds. They felt a land breeze, but land was barely visible and they could not fix their position. In the distance were more mountains than were described intelligently in the pilot. In 1850, Captain Vidal had seen the mountains from the west round to the northwest, rather than from the south and east. After a verbal storm in a teacup that morning, the future outlook was serene. The log read 853. The day was sunny and hot.

Great excitement just after noon! Almonds caught a sailfish over two feet long. It changed colour when caught from green to electric blue, then olive green to green and black, then back to its original colour. Robson photographed it, then made a fine meal of sailfish steaks and onions. A southerly breeze sprang up; so, after experimenting with the whisker pole, they sailed goose-winged. A large oblong building appeared on the skyline, towering above everything. The pilot gave no trace. The American mission on Cape Mount? Or a water tank? Or a new mansion for President Tubman? They steered straight for it.

After supper at 6pm, a lighthouse started flashing two seconds every ten near the object on the skyline. This confirmed the land as Monrovia. For some time, Almonds had been wondering if they had overshot Monrovia and instead should make straight for Freetown, Sierra Leone. By late evening, the *Kumasi* was off Monrovia, but they could not find the entrance to the harbour. Being virtually an ironbound coast, there was only one possible place to anchor: Monrovia's artificial harbour. Where the River Saint Paul reached the sea was a nasty bar, with a wild breaking sea as the outflow ran fast and high. Heavy surf pounded on the rocky coast the other side of the port.[2]

The leading lights did not match the description in the pilot. At the helm, Almonds tacked again, wove his way between five ships and anchored off the harbour. They glided landwards, found the breakwaters and sailed silently between them into a large, bare harbour. Avoiding some fishing nets and canoes, they took the western channel, then anchored just outside the main canal. The log read 870. After hot Ovaltine, Almonds and Cameron turned in while Robson remained on watch. The night was calm and moist, with fine rain. 'Great', Cameron noted, 'to be able to relax, knowing you are safe in harbour.'

'On deck this morning, found a stranger', Cameron confided to the log on 11 June. It was Robson with the dirt washed off. He had busied himself tidying up the boat, sheets, halyards and other items that needed to be re-stowed. He had also climbed the main mast to sort out the tangled jib and stay sheets. Twice, he had climbed it – never a pleasant experience at sea. 'Almost circumcised doing so', noted Cameron. By 9am, Almonds had cleaned up the Brute's plug points. Cameron and Almonds had a quick wash, before starting the Brute and motoring past President Tubman's State yacht towards the quay.

After an hour, they were allowed to tie up near a smelly fishing boat. A Liberian doctor and immigration and customs officials came on board. Four forms, all in quadruplicate, were duly filled out and fees of fifteen dollars paid to the doctor and ten dollars to the officials. No official receipts were provided, just scraps of paper torn out of a notebook. 'The doctor and officials must be rich men!' noted Cameron. *Kumasi* anchored 50 yards off the quay. Her crew visited the harbour master, a 'dried-up Yankee', but no letters awaited them.

They set out by taxi to the Ducal Palace Hotel, the large building that had puzzled them from the sea. Opened only ten days before, it was an ostentatious affair of 106 rooms. They enjoyed a beer in the roof bar and discovered a cockney working as a steward, who gave them an illuminating description of his ten days' experience in Liberia. The hotel towered over the sea and town. It quite outshone the Ambassador Hotel in Accra. After an excellent lunch in the Heinz Maria Restaurant, they found two air-conditioned rooms in the Hotel Ambassadeur and slept from 3pm to 3am. They got up only for hot showers and went back to bed. 'We literally slept like logs', Cameron recorded.

Sunday 12 June: awake at 7am, Cameron went to church while Almonds and Gordon had breakfast and returned to the boat. After removing the sails for sewing, they tidied the cabin and cleaned the tools. Anchored off, but without their dinghy, they had to depend on the charity of an Italian fisherman to take them to and from the quay. A little motor vessel was moored nearby, owned by an elderly Spaniard. In broken English, he told the *Kumasi* crew that he was from Las Palmas. 'I am crazy,' he said. 'I go anywhere; I no like work; maybe Kenya, maybe South Africa.' His boat had no sails and was a blunt, sturdy fisherman-type about 30 feet long with a steering cabin amidships. A real beachcomber.

By midday, *Kumasi* was clean and the sails were with a tailor for mending. Cold beer at the Hotel Ambassadeur, where they had decided to stay, was followed by a superb lunch and afternoon siesta. In the evening, they met a young French girl, Nadia, who was serving behind the bar. After a visit to the country club, they went to the Heinz Maria for drinks and a sandwich. The white people there were continental: Germans, Italians, Belgians and 'of course, there were Yanks'. Unattached European women acted as hostesses and barkeepers. The proprietor and staff were helpful and friendly. Cameron tried to phone the Ghanaian Ambassador, but the line was out of order. The proprietor told them Tubman had ordered no bills to be paid until the British company had installed 'efficient systems'.

Monrovia was odd. The shanty town area was not as bad as the worst in Accra, but there were fewer fine buildings or shops. Pitted roads had American-style traffic lights at each junction. Some houses were built in the old southern States style. Local people said that Monrovia was basically rich and boom time was not far off. Certainly, there were great undeveloped forest reserves and ore deposits. The *Kumasi* crew found the Liberians pleasant and not openly hostile to white people. Cameron wished he had the opportunity to see the Firestone plantations and the real bush, as there were apparently some good roads into the interior.

On 13 June, they were up early, with Almonds talking of leaving at 6am the following day. The wind was fresh and strong. 'He has the fever in his blood', noted Cameron, 'and wants to be up and at it. He always likes to be doing something.' If it kept up, they could reach Freetown in two days. Quite a thought! And a pleasant change from lying becalmed in the rain at sea. Robson and Cameron posted cards and letters, the former's consisting of busty nudes. It would be interesting to see if they were confiscated in Ghana.

At 11am, they received a hospitable reception at the Embassy of Ghana. They met Ooto – the First Secretary, Kobina Kessie, was absent. Cameron waited for a doctor to look at his knee. The infection was spreading. At noon, Almonds appeared in the hotel bar, his face like a thundercloud. He was short of £70 in Travellers' cheques while in taxis in town – all his money!

His passport was also missing. Having reported his loss to the central police, a detective accompanied him. They searched his room. Almonds provided details of the cheques, passport and taxis. He dashed a police constable £4 to make enquiries. There was little hope of finding the money and they risked being delayed by several days.

They went down to the boat to pick up Robson – same palaver with the dinghy. After returning to the hotel for consoling drinks, Robson suggested that they looked in their rooms and hey presto! Passport, cheques and wallet were all found.[3] Almonds was very relieved and sheepish. The Belgian hotel proprietor advised against informing the police, as they might accuse Almonds of blaming Liberians maliciously. That evening, they met a cockney Jewish diamond merchant. He talked like a machine gun, knew everybody and everything – money and contracts. He also talked of a number of Nazis 'living it out' in Monrovia. During dinner, heavy storms caused a power cut. Three young Arabs boasted in the bar of killing Americans and Jews. A Dutchman prepared to squash them. A German doctor prescribed antibiotics for Cameron – suppositories for Robson!

On 14 June, Almonds wrote to Lockie:

'As you can see, we're rather late on our trip. The weather has been so bad… and is unlikely to improve before we reach Dakar when we should speed up considerably. Leaving today for Freetown, where I hope for definite news of our future.[4] I fixed an appointment with the Brigadier, HQ Sierra Leone. I am alright Lockie and grateful to you for allowing me to do this trip, which *is the last time I shall do such a thing. The thirst for adventure is wearing out.* [My italics.]

After an egg and bacon breakfast, Cameron paid the bill of $90 for three nights for two of them. Down to the boat for the dinghy, oil and water palaver. However, *Kumasi* had dragged her anchor during the storm the night before. They had lost the horse scissors and a raincoat and a stanchion was bent. Most boats had drifted. They tied up at a floating dry dock. An elderly Danish captain, broke and out of a job, wanted to come with them. He was over sixty, but knew the coast inside out. Robson favoured taking him. The others hesitated. He might be a liability if they had to end the voyage before reaching the UK. His seamanship and navigation skills would have been useful but…

Having collected their laundry, they weighed anchor and motored five miles out to sea. The log read 870. They set the main, stay and jib in a slight breeze; course west northwest. By midnight, they were becalmed in showers of rain. They downed sail and started the Brute, who actually cooperated; perhaps he appreciated the canvas cover they had started to use when he was at rest. They motored on and found themselves off Cape Mount. A strong wind sprang up, accompanied by squalls, thunder and lightning, then dropped. After a night of no progress, the rain stopped. They changed the engine gear oil. The Brute worked until 5pm when they got a good breeze, course north northwest. At 6pm, the log showed 967. They should be off Sierra Leone and hoped that the breeze and weather would remain fair. On 17 June, a storm hit them. At 5am, Almonds routed out Cameron. Land was in sight and surf roaring. Could they get on course away from the land? Eventually, they gybed around, but were barely moving west southwest. To their relief, the noise of the surf slowly died away. It had been confined to one spot and this indicated the Sherbro River Entrance.

No one wanted another night in the surf like Apollonia's. Just before 6am, Robson and Cameron turned in. The next thing they knew, they were rudely thrown out of their bunks to the sound of pans, books and the chart drawer being flung about. The wind howled, the rain poured in and, according to the clinometer, the boat listed 50 degrees to port. The port window was under water. The barometer showed 30.3 millibars – the highest they had seen to date. At 7.15am, Almonds had been making tea with the boat almost becalmed and the sky clouded, but by no means ominous or threatening. Immediately, he let go the main and mizzen sheets. The boat still heeled over alarmingly while the mainsail boomed and cracked.

In a flash, Robson was on deck, downed the jib, hampered by the length of coil round the cleat (*Kumasi* had no self-jamming cleats). Meanwhile, Almonds got down the mizzen, but the loose main was still heeling the boat over. As Robson struggled with the main halyards, the gaff bolt snapped and the main came down with a loud crack. *Kumasi* righted herself and within five minutes, the worst was over. They wallowed in the seas and rain. The list had been over 50 degrees and Almonds had seen the boom dipping in the sea.

Surprisingly little damage had been done. The cabin was a mess of books and charts, but nothing was broken and the skylights had stayed above water. After fifteen minutes, they set the stay and sailed west to southwest with barely any wind. The gale had apparently come out of an unusually U-shaped cloud they had noticed to the west at 5am. It had moved landwards, then suddenly swung out to sea again. Thank God they had not anchored near the surf earlier. The log read 999 – perhaps Father Neptune resented them nearly achieving the first 1,000 miles of their journey. The skipper reckoned that the little boat had been in a Force 8 or 9 gale. They lay, thankful for once to be becalmed, until 11am.

But the day's events were not over. They motored northwest. At 9.30pm, while Almonds and Robson were refuelling by the light of the masthead lamp, the lamp ignited the petrol fumes with a great flash. The rear deck and engine were suddenly both on fire. Quick work with the cockpit fire extinguisher put out the blaze with no damage and no burns. So ended three serious episodes, which was more than enough for one day. They passed a bell light, the log at midnight showing 1,050 miles. At dawn, they sighted the Banana Islands and Shilling Cape. A light breeze sprang up, accompanied by intermittent rain. Then, out of the blue, another gale hit them, estimated at Force 7. They downed sails, except for the stay, closed the hatches and endured lashing rain for fifteen minutes. Afterwards, again becalmed, they sighted Cape Sierra Leone about 15 miles away.

It was another ten long miles of sailing before, with the help of the motor, they entered a broad estuary and Freetown Bay. Almonds had last been there in 1941, on board HMS *Glenroy* with 8 Guards Commando and 'Layforce' on his way to an unknown destination. It had turned out to be the Middle East, where the Siege of Tobruk and the founding of the SAS awaited him. Last time, crowds of natives in canoes and little white-painted boats had come out to sell fruit and dive for pennies thrown from the ship.[5]

Dusk. After a vain search for a berth, during which they hit mud and rocks near the jetty, they anchored in Man O'War Bay. Without a dinghy, instead of a hot bath and bed, they had to remain on board. After breakfast, they motored round to a bay, which, they were informed by the harbour pilot (whose boat they rammed), would afford them protection from tornadoes, which were frequent at that time of year. The inlet was shallow and, as luck would have it, they went aground. A group of nearby naval workers waded out to their assistance.

Sierra Leone was a British colony. Military aid appeared, in the form of a corporal and five men, kindly lent by the commanding officer of the

1st Battalion, The Royal Sierra Leone Regiment. *Kumasi* was hauled up a slipway and given a thorough overhaul. Thereafter, the detachment of soldiers reportedly daily to offer assistance. The boat's masts were unstopped and patches of hide nailed over the sail parts chewed by the gaffs. Numerous little jobs, which ought to have been done in Takoradi before departure, were also completed. All ship's stores were re-stowed, and worn sheets and halyards replaced. After repainting, varnishing and putting a new coat of anti-foul on her bottom, the ketch *Kumasi*, still on her maiden voyage, looked as trim as any little vessel Cameron had seen.

On Saturday morning, the crew were guests of the Governor of Sierra Leone and his wife, Sir Maurice and Lady Dorman, at the residency. Cameron could only imagine what passed through the minds of the other guests as the *Aide-de-camp* announced three bearded mariners in scruffy attire, quite unbefitting to the occasion. During their stay in Freetown, the three men lived in the Officers' Mess, hospitably entertained by the mess members, including the CO, Colonel Keymer, and the Royal Naval Port Officer, Commander Davies.

Almonds was supposed to go and see the brigadier commanding the Royal Sierra Leone Military Forces about the potential post as OC of the Training Company, as set up the previous February, but he did not bother. What better way to end his army days than sailing home from Africa? On 28 June, they breakfasted early, collected their mattresses and were down to King Tom at 9am.[6] One of their hawsers had broken during the night; unfortunately, this had been spotted by the watchman. The white paintwork was already marred by harbour oil. They paid £18 for another slipway. Robson and Cameron organised customs, Elder Dempster and 'Winneba' for one case of whisky and 4,000 cigarettes.[7] 'British Colonies do run on red tape', noted Cameron. They bought extra onions, potatoes, oranges, bread and sausages and a 46-gallon drum of aviation fuel to be delivered to the jetty. 'Will we fly with it!?' mused Cameron. At last, they cast off at 1pm with Colonel Keymer there to wish them *bon voyage*.

The Brute misbehaved, but finally they were off in dull grey weather – the log reading 1,086. Setting course northwest, they motored for two hours before sailing on in a light breeze. At midnight, Robson was feeling off colour. The next day, the sky darkened – another storm was on the horizon. They reduced sail to the stay and mizzen. A line squall hit them. This time, they were well prepared with all sails already down except the stay. 'A pity we have to take storm precautions and then the storm doesn't break', noted Cameron. 'We missed a good wind this afternoon and evening'.

Next day, they sailed under jib and mizzen, then took them down again for another squall. A dark and ominous sky covered the moon. They identified a light flashing every five seconds northeast as the *Isles de Los* lighthouse. They motored west northwest for two hours before picking up a good wind. Almonds puttied and varnished the cabin windows, managing to cure all the leaks except two. Their clasps had broken loose due to the pressure of the seas, wave on deck action and rusted up iron washers. A bolt on the motor mounting was working loose and the tiller had developed a rather rough, grinding movement. The Brute worked, if unwillingly, with coughs and backfiring.

Threatening little line squalls appeared all around, with low temperatures. But they kept all sails up on their course northwest. The sky cleared – somewhat. The seas became heavier, with spray flying over the boat. The log at 4pm read 1,166 miles and kept going strong. At 8pm, it was 1,179. Clouds darkened around them and they lowered the main. On 1 July, the wind slackened further. Down sails, out Brute and they motored west northwest for 25 miles. At 1pm, they raised sail and made steadily northwest in bright sunlight with hazy light cloud. They were all eating more fruit. 'It won't last until Bathurst!' noted Cameron.

Their main difficulty was making enough westing to clear dangerous shoals around the Bijagos Islands. Strong winds forced them too far towards the north and east. They all felt uncomfortable at night close to unknown land. Health-wise, nobody had any new sores. Next day dawned dark and damp, with a faint wind veering further south. Only the jib and main were up due to an overcast sky and lightning. Their north northwest course was only held with difficulty. Almonds chose this moment to deliver a soliloquy on the hardships they could expect after Dakar! Small, swallow-like birds and boobies followed *Kumasi*. Two ships passed close by; their own estimated position at 7.30pm was Latitude 10 degrees, 13", Longitude 15 degrees, 39". The seas were heavier and choppier.

Porpoises entertained them for an hour. Then, the three men discussed the possibility of reaching Ryde by 2 October and their various alternatives. If a month late, they could face autumn gales. They tacked vainly about in heavy seas, followed by dark, ominous clouds. Seven ships passed them between 5am and 10am. All except one seemed to be going north or northwest.

They were uncertain of *Kumasi*'s position. The shipping lane suggested they were further out to sea than they had thought. Then, while Robson was examining the sextant, the paper calibration table blew away! Little progress was made until 5pm, when the log read 1,320, the course having changed frequently with backing and veering. The wind, in fact, freshened so much that they were making two knots to northwest. During their few leisure moments, they tried to catch up on their sleep. They had done no reading since they had left Takoradi, apart from looking at the pilot and reading a *Daily Express* bought in Freetown from cover to cover. The wind freshened again, so they held a course two points west of north. At times, *Kumasi* was doing five knots.

On 4 July, the wind dropped to a faint breeze. It was a good, sunny day. Eight ships passed to port or starboard, all sailing northeast. They filmed 'chop' being prepared. At midnight, the log read 1,401, course north northeast. However, at 10.30pm, while Robson and Cameron were below, there was a loud crack and down came the main. All hands went on deck to find that the bolt holding the main halyard to the gaff had snapped. Almonds quickly fixed a spare bolt and hoisted the sail again, but Robson had to scramble up the mast to the crosspiece to retrieve the halyard. He was much more agile than on the occasion of his first attempt off Abidjan.

During the night, the wind continued Force 3-4 from the west. At 8am, the log showed 1,430. Quite a good performance. Cameron started another course of antibiotics to deal with sores reappearing on his right leg. Robson's were healing. They estimated their position to be 100 miles from Bathhurst. They sighted land and a large, white, fort-looking building and water tower near a large-ish village. It was possibly the Cape Roxo lighthouse, but they could not identify the village and headland to the north.

The landfall puzzled them. The water in the bay was evidently shallow. Robson thought the headland was Bald Cape, off Bathhurst. Then Almonds, rather jokingly, suggested that Dakar lay ahead. Finally, they decided on Cape Roxo. The wind prevented them from rounding the headland. Everyone reread the pilot and re-studied the chart. They tacked backward and forward in the damp, misty night, trying to round the headland. While on the southwest tack, they found four ships at anchor to the southwest while a red flashing light was seen to the northeast. They made no progress and were still unsure of their position at dawn. A south-westerly blew up and they made way north, passing three more steamers.

The sun rose bright and clear. At 8am, a large, white building appeared on the horizon to the north northwest. Then came other buildings glinting in the sun. Finally, an island could be seen ahead. All of this mystified *Kumasi*'s crew. A mirage of Dakar was suggested! Then, they heard aircraft and realised, to their great astonishment, that they *were* at Dakar with the log showing 1,497 miles. Their navigation had been 150 miles out. Over the previous four days, the counter-equatorial current had been extremely strong and 30 to 50 miles in their favour. While in Dakar, they decided to keep quiet about their navigation!

They motored round the *Isle de Gorée* into the fine Dakar harbour and tied up at the pilot berth. A doctor came aboard, but no immigration or customs officials. Beside them in the filthy, oily water were two barques from Monrovia, both on their way to the UK. One of them belonged to an old man called Olaf Mueller. The other boat was skippered by a youngish Swiss, Fred Borling. He had bought the boat in the Baltic and sailed it out, singlehandedly, to Liberia to make his fortune, but had had difficulty in finding a cargo. It was a fine old wooden sailing boat, but had only two sails left. He was prepared to sell it for £1,000. Nearby was a beautiful, 60-foot yacht, the *Goches*, which was owned by a Portuguese and carrying passengers between Dakar and the Cape Verde Islands. The rigging and exterior were in rather tatty condition, but the hull and woodwork were still sound. Two Japanese 'tunny' vessels lay in the next dock – very modern with all the latest fishing and sounding gear. Robson went aboard one, made himself friendly and managed to buy a set of oilskins. Unluckily, they were rather small.

Almonds and Cameron went ashore. The harbour master had no letters for *Kumasi*. They had lunch with cold beer and returned to find *Kumasi* surrounded by young Senegalese. In the evening, leaving one of the Senegalese as watchman, they went into town. Cameron found a room in the Atlantic Hotel. They had a poor but expensive supper there. Almonds and Robson returned to sleep on the boat while the Portuguese yacht enjoyed a rum party.

On Sunday 10 July, after a week in Dakar, Cameron was up early 'and to kirk'. Afterwards, all three spent two hours searching for Brierley of the US Embassy, who had their jerrycan of kerosene. Finally, they caught him at the embassy. They bought 5,000 French cigarettes, 23 kilos of oranges and the kerosene, and got back to the boat at 10.30am. After stowing everything, they put to sea. With the jib up, they sailed in the lightest of airs, followed by the *Goches*. As they cleared the harbour and breakwater, the wind fell completely. They resorted to the Brute, sailing south southwest while the *Goches* took their photographs. A final salute as *Goches* dipped her red ensign and *Kumasi* was off with a stout-ish breeze and slightly choppy seas under brightly coloured skies. At 4pm, they rounded Cape Vert and the Almadies. To their delight, a good sou'wester blew up. Eventually, it proved too strong, so down came the main in the dark. At midnight, the log read 1,520 miles.

The challenge of the sea was terrifying, yet irresistible (to Almonds, at least). Totally exhilarating, it went on and on, like a never-ending rollercoaster ride. During the night, the seas became even choppier – and larger. Next morning, a Force 5 wind was blowing from the west. The waves were mountainous, their crests breaking. In wild waters, they tossed about in 40-foot billows. The gale sent the boat rolling while seawater drenched her, wave after wave. It was not for the faint-hearted. By noon, in a Force 9 storm, all sails were down. They attempted to lie to, with the stay and mizzen reefed and lashed to horse, using a bucket from the bow as a sea anchor. Eventually, they gave up and lay a-hull under bare rigging. *Kumasi* was quiet and rode the rough seas well. Cameron wondered if this was the typical Atlantic weather Almonds had promised, but they had not even reached the Atlantic.

The wind moderated but the seas were still heavy, with ugly crisscross swells. They ate a cold bread and cheese supper. The cabin was so full of petrol fumes from overflowing tanks that they dared not light the primus stove or light a cigarette below. Robson was slightly uncomfortable. After midnight, they sailed on with the main and mizzen reefed. At 5.30am, the bolt on the main gaff snapped again. The sail crashed down for the third time. When the seas calmed, Robson climbed the mast again and retrieved the sheet. The jib sail showed signs of wear. Robson, their needle expert, repaired some tears made by the anchor fluke and pulpit stanchion. They exchanged the mainsail for the spare. Despite roughish seas, they made progress north northeast.

Next day, they tried to sail westwards from Dakar, well out into the Atlantic for about 1,000 miles, but a storm blew them north. So they made for Port Etienne in Mauritania. A good south-westerly helped, with *Kumasi* doing 6 knots. On 14 July, they tried to estimate their drift in the gale and current of the previous few days. It was difficult to calculate, especially since the pilot was vague. After a spell of good behaviour, the Brute had a tantrum. At 5pm, with a west south-westerly wind, they made fair progress. The sky was a wonderful red. 'Red sky at night, sailor's delight', said Cameron. Then, at 9pm, came storm clouds and shortly afterwards a sudden line tempest with ferocious wind and rain. Almonds and Cameron just got the sails down in time.

They rode under the staysail all night. The air coming off the Sahara was very cold and they used jerseys for the first time. On 15 July, they sighted land again. Terns, seagulls and jellyfish appeared. Where was *Kumasi*? 'Lord knows', noted Cameron. They thought they were off El Mahaijrât or Mottes d'Angels. It was difficult to say as none of them could use the sextant. Shades of Christopher Columbus! If they were at El Mahaijrât, Cameron figured, then they had gained by being nearly 120 miles north of their estimated position. Could there be an error in it? The water was very shallow and the coastline yellow, bleak and forbidding with a dreadful lee shore. There was no sign of villages or huts. The pilot said, in an old-fashioned manner 'the natives are hostile'.

As Almonds tinkered with the innards of the Brute, he remarked,

'You know, many books have been written about people going to sea with little knowledge of navigation, but probably none about three men who went to sea with absolutely no knowledge of the subject.'

'No matter', said Cameron. 'When we reach the UK, we can tell the yachtsmen of fashionable clubs that the only time we took the sextant from its case was to clean it.'

At 9am, they started the motor and sailed along the coast. Robson repaired Almonds's trousers, while the latter screwed cabin windows down and puttied and varnished them. They had been leaking again during the storms. Otherwise, the boat was dry. Soon, they recognised the Piton de Chedallah and El Mahaijrât, though the pilot only mentioned two summits and they could see four. They noted that sea hogs (porpoises) had disappeared, but terns, seagulls and jellyfish abounded. At noon, they stopped the motor and set all sails on a reach, course north northwest. At 6pm, they sighted El Manghar and Cape Timirist. Ninety miles to Port Etienne! They were elated with their progress. The water became green and thick with floating rushes and reeds. Shoals of sardines surrounded the boat. Before midnight, the wind petered out as ships' navigation lights appeared to the west. At night, sardines illuminated the sea. The deck was heavy with dew.

On 16 July, with the sea like a millpond, they motored northwards across uncharted waters north of Cape Timirist. Racing through shoals of sardines, the water seemed to boil with tiny fish. The air was dry. In the morning, the boat was covered with fine, reddish Sahara sand, so out came buckets to wash down the decks and cabin roof. Without wind, they motored on. Robson tried fishing, but broke his hook on submerged rocks. Recklessly, they had extra cups of tea: a brand called 'Kettle', which Robson called muck, all stalks and dust, sent out by Liptons for the poor of Africa at a vast profit. As a tea planter, Robson should know.

During a perfect day, they sighted Cap Blanc at 1pm. Shortly afterwards, about twenty trawlers and drifters appeared. They were all Spanish or French boats, working in one of the richest fishing areas of the world. *Kumasi* passed the lighthouse on the bare promontory and sailed up the sea d'Arguin, past cruel-looking headlands and a few sturdy Moorish ketches. The bay of Port Etienne came into sight, its sandy shores littered with fishing boats of every description and giving off a strong, fishy smell. *Kumasi* hoisted her pilot and quarantine flags, but no boats came out to greet her. So, she motored in and tied up at a wooden quay. Her crew were told rather bluntly to move to another berth. There, they discovered old Olaf Mueller with his Baltic boat. He had arrived two days earlier. He helped them to moor next to him.

While they waited for immigration officials, swarthy moors crowded around, wearing blue robes and slung rifles. Finally, a French officer arrived to look at their papers and passports. The three men then washed and put on their best clothes – dirty shorts and grey-white shirts – and went ashore to find the town and a meal. There were no taxis, public transport or streets, just sand warehouses and mad French soldiers and airmen careering about in jeeps. After walking a mile, they found a French rest centre, where an airman took them under his wing. He got them a meal in the mess and, better still, a hot shower. After plenty of *vin rouge*, they took two French airmen back to the boat and plied them and Olaf with whisky. The captain of the *Frihed* and his other crew member, Leonard, joined them. He had lost a hand while playing with fireworks and looked after the diesel engine; in his spare time, he painted.

At midnight, they crowded into the jeep and drove madly to a wooden shack, draped with a tent inside. A Moorish girl welcomed them with ceremonial hot sweet tea. The girl, Rashitu, was pretty and eventually one of the French officers made a date. She was in the oldest profession, but evidently respected by the French. She was supporting three children and an old blind father. They left late and were driven wildly back to the boat, getting stuck in the sand once on the way. And so to bed, with Robson sleeping on the *Frihed*.

Next morning, Cameron went to mass, said by a white father with a tremendous beard. The congregation was just a few Europeans and blacks. He returned to the boat for a mug of tea, then 'stooged around' on the *Frihed* and wrote letters. The three-man crew of the *Frihed* threw a twenty-sixth birthday lunch for Robson of beans, sausages and tea. *Kumasi*'s crew provided whisky for the party from their small stock. After lunch, Robson and Cameron strolled through the sandy town, ending up in the rest centre where they drank beer with a French officer, followed by an excellent supper. Almonds was not fond of continental food and pined for Lincolnshire beef and green peas. He promised Cameron and Robson a herculean feast at Stixwould. Then to bed early, as they hoped to leave on the nineteenth, despite Olaf promising a change in the good weather.

During the night, Robson was sick with stomach cramps. In the morning, Almonds overhauled the motor and Robson did odd jobs, while Cameron had a frustrating time visiting customs, the post office, *Société Industrielle de Pêche* and the bank. The bank manager had the shakes. It took Cameron an hour to persuade him to change sterling traveller's cheques. He mistrusted anything coming from Ghana. Finally, Cameron returned to the boat with his purchases. Almonds was keen to stow everything away smartly. In his haste to comply, Cameron poured four gallons of kerosene into the petrol tank. 'No swear words from Jim!' Cameron noted in the log. 'Gentleman Jim' still lived up to his name.

By evening, they were all shipshape and had an early meal on board. Olaf made them a fine sea anchor, which they badly needed. He also offered *Kumasi* a tow to the Canary Islands, but Almonds knew that it would put too much strain on the little boat. The *Frihed* hoped to steal away in the early morning without paying 7,000 francs wharfage – encouraged by the white father and the port engineer. *Kumasi* was all set to leave at 4am. On 19 July, the alarm went off, but nobody stirred until 5.30am. It was a cold morning with a north wind. At 6am, they cast off from the *Frihed* and motored to Cap Blanc. The *Frihed* came out stealthily behind them, overtaking near the lighthouse with her diesel thumping away and mainsail up. The two crews waved goodbye to each other. Olaf was aiming for Rio de Orio and then on to the Canaries.

The SS *Kumasi* sailed on, out into the Atlantic – the wildest ocean in the world.

Chapter Nineteen

WILD ATLANTIC

Cap Blanc: *Kumasi*'s log read 1,816 miles. They sailed west northwest for nine miles, then north northeast. The seas and winds became heavier. Downing sail, they motored on, painfully slowly, through stormy seas. The bows thumped wildly into the waves. Refuelling became a dangerous operation. All three were wet and Almonds had the stomach bug from which Robson had suffered. At 6pm, they stopped the motor for a whisky and 'chop'. They lay, hull on, stay up and tiller lashed. The Brute refused to cooperate, so they lay a-hull all night in turbulent seas.

On 20 July, they tried for three hours to start the motor. Almonds and Robson favoured continuing westwards to pick up the Westerlies. Cameron was doubtful: their navigation was punk (sic); there would be an increase in the mileage; and the success of the Great Circle they were following would depend on favourable winds. The weather might get even worse. They would have to ration food and water.

Almonds listened to all this. Robson was the designated navigator, but Almonds was navigating, too. He knew that where they were, the Atlantic current ran in a clockwise direction, fast southwards, down the West Atlantic coast of Africa. Together with the north east trade winds, *Kumasi* was unlikely to make sufficient headway. So they should turn and make towards Bermuda, out across the Atlantic, until they could pick up westerly winds to bring them up to the Azores.

The bold decision was made. At 10am, they pulled in the Brute and hoisted the main, stay and jib. The log read 1,842, the wind was northerly and their course barely west northwest, so it was, 'Go west, young man, go west!' 'At least', noted Cameron, 'we know that the world is round, whereas Columbus had to discover it'. Cameron took over from Robson at the tiller. The winds were favourable, but the seas still heavy. A tanker loomed up close, going south. None of the passing ships took any notice of them. They might not even have seen tiny *Kumasi*, appearing only now and then from the troughs of huge waves. Their navigators were scanning the horizon, not looking down expecting to see a boat under their noses.

Almonds completed a bridle for the sea anchor. They tried it out in various places with the mizzen lashed, but the boat simply would not lie quarter on to the sea. She preferred to lie broadside on, with perhaps the stern angled a little to the seas. The crew consulted all seagoing books on board, but could find no solution to the problem. 'Anyway', noted Cameron, 'the good ketch *Kumasi* rides very well.' They started rationing. No tinned vegetables for supper. Gordon put in proper reefs on the main and mizzen, while Cameron re-stowed the cabin. It was cluttered with cases and jerrycans, but that was the way they wanted it for now. Almonds insisted on everything being below the waterline. He mentioned dismantling the motor and stowing it on the cabin floor. After supper, they raised the mizzen, stay and jib. Their course was averaging west northwest.

The night became calm and heavy with dew, no doubt from the Sahara. It was chilly and the sky misted over. A faint breeze from east southeast was not enough. They started the motor at 10am. A mug of tea for breakfast. The tanker *Marfik* passed close by. Almonds estimated that if the seas remained calm, they might make Rio de Oro. Cameron doubted it, as they were outside the northerly coastal current. However, the more northing they could make the better. There was still a chance of making the Canaries. They motored until midnight, when the log read 1,940. At 1am, they took in the motor and raised the sails in a faint breeze. After tea, they chugged northeast in the hope of reaching Rio de Oro or, further on, Tenerife or La Palma. Robson replaced the main stay and jib sheets, doing some real Gordonstoun splicing. At 4pm, they shipped the Brute and upped sails in a fair wind, course northwest.

On 23 July, after a night of fair sea and wind with light clouds scudding across the sky, the log read 2,012, course northwest. The heavens became bright blue with strong sunshine. By 3pm, the seas were rough, with a strong nor'easter. They lowered the jib and main and reefed the mizzen, but the sea kept rising. At 4pm, they took down the mizzen, main and stay sails. Trying desperately to ride bow to weather, they sailed with a reefed mizzen sail at the stern, as well as a sea anchor over the bow, to give them the best chance. But no matter what they did (they even buoyed the anchor), she would not lie to. Eventually, they lay a-hull with the stay up and the tiller lashed. Until midnight, the seas remained heavy, but the boat behaved well. It was Cameron's turn to have a dose of the 'skitters' – sitting on the bucket on the plunging deck in a Force 7 wind was terrifying.

All night, they lay a-hull. The gale lashed them, but one person always remained above on watch since there were only two bunks. A miserable night passed. At 10.30am, they put up a reefed main and mizzen, then eventually the jib, and braved the waves. The helmsman wrestled with a heavy pull on the tiller and looked out for steep, ugly waves. At noon, the log was 2,030. During the day, they lost Olaf's fine sea anchor. The lashings to the bridle broke away in the heavy seas. They had no heavy canvas left to make another one. Almonds proposed using an empty jerrycan instead. At 9pm, they took down the jib.

They had to deal with the Brute. That afternoon, Almonds did a herculean job, dismantling the cantankerous beast. They put his dismembered body to sleep on the port side of the cabin floor after struggling to get him inside the store cupboard. Even then he was a nuisance, getting in the way. There was no comfort in the cabin, what with the engine, jerrycans, boxes and other equipment. The boat, however, was more stable and secure, with less danger of capsizing.

Being on watch became an exacting business. A hard pull on the tiller could ensure that steep breakers passed under the stern, so every wave had to be observed to make sure that it did not break over the boat. Nevertheless, they got the occasional soaking. The cabin windows having been sealed, only a little water was coming through the skylights. But their clothing and the bunks were damp. All night, they sailed on under clouded skies. It felt quite eerie not being able to see until the last moment exactly when the next steep wave would break. The binnacle lamp was not working properly due to condensation on the inside of the glass, so the helmsman had to lean forward to peer hard at the compass. They all appreciated the beauty of the stars when one could steer by them. And the moon was a wonderful companion when alone on deck, surrounded by deep, rolling waters.

The log at 10am on 25 July read 2,080 miles, course northwest, wind east northeast. The seas were still heavy; Force 4 to 5 winds. At 4pm, they let out the reef in the main. It was difficult to get potatoes from the forward hatch. Robson crept inside. The Dakar onions were beginning to stink. Those from Sierra Leone were still fresh, being inside a small polythene bag. 'How we love 'em', noted Cameron. He and Robson suffered from wind, but like the Emperor Octavius, they did not believe in wiping noses or suppressing farts. 'Lord knows how Jim keeps quiet about his innards', noted Cameron. At midnight, the log read 2,127, course north northwest, wind east northeast.

On 26 July, they began less exhausting three-hour watches. At 8am each morning, Robson estimated their position on the chart. They were not too badly out, given the immense size of the ocean. Moreover, miscalculations cancelled each other out. On this, the seventy-second day of their voyage, their charted position was Latitude, 23 degrees, 40", Longitude, 19 degrees, 15" – they hoped! The seas and wind began to drop. Robson repaired a small tear in the mainsail. It was still difficult to raise the main and mizzen without the rings sticking.

At 6am, Almonds was up making tea. Robson and Cameron preferred theirs later. They tuned in their little receiver radio and listened to music from all over the world, but they couldn't get the BBC. They hoped to make the Azores, but Cameron was not optimistic about that unless they could get an accurate fix from a passing boat. The skipper was not in favour of that idea. 'I can see us asking eventually where Britain is!' noted Cameron. The day was cloudy but dry. They needed to refill their water tanks in case they missed the Azores. Cameron got out some old sheets to collect rain from the sails. 'We are all filthy', recorded Cameron. 'Gordon looks funny. His face is a greenish-brown – the green from the damp sleeping bag (he sleeps on his face) or from the Japanese oilskin parka. The brown is a mixture of tan and dirt. Our beards are quite luxuriant, if somewhat itchy.'

That afternoon, Almonds repaired the mainsail. At midnight, the log read 2,185, course west northwest. A wonderful dawn appeared of red, purple and gold-tinted skies. At 8am, they let out the reef in the mizzen. Gentle waves caressed a royal blue sea. They sunbathed. They tried a spinner, but without success. Having found that the rice had weevils, Cameron and Robson had a long discussion on fish and chip suppers and the possibility of frying in the pressure cooker. The wind fell again at night.

On 28 July, the skies were sunny and clear, with a light wind. Almonds changed the primus stove burner, which had been giving them a lot of trouble. They caught no fish during a rather pleasant day, but made little progress. The binnacle needed cleaning again. They were still unable to pick up the Azores wireless station on their little radio set. The sky darkened occasionally with clouds from the northeast, similar to the line squalls on the coast of Gambia, but containing only moisture and little wind. Three times they spread out their ground sheet and linen sheets, but there was still no proper rain.

29 July dawned bright and clear, with calm seas. Robson oiled the stays and shackles. A wooden box and some cardboard drifted by. The boat was so well trimmed that the tiller needed very little guidance, so they sunbathed and read. Cameron finished *The Long Ships* and began *Island in the Sun*. Their health was good, with bottoms clear of barnacles and pimples. Almonds took yeast tablets, while Cameron and Robson 'chopped' multivitamins. At 6pm each evening, they drank whisky – perhaps two or three tots each. Afterwards, they felt relaxed and cracked jokes. Almonds recited Kipling while Robson had a fine selection of salacious bothy or army mess ballads. There was little progress that day. At 7pm, the log read 2,334.

The wind freshened during the night. On 30 July, the Government's Cabinet was reshuffled. Almonds marked up the chart. At 10am, the log read 2,380 miles, position: Latitude 27 degrees; Longitude 21 degrees. They could not estimate the drift and current. The skies were overcast with a red sunrise. It was a calm day with sloppier seas. In a faint wind, they tried trailing red and yellow rags with a spoon, but had no luck with the fish.

On 31 July came a stiff breeze. One flying fish landed on deck. They had read about sailors finding shoals of flying fish on deck. *Kumasi*'s crew didn't! In the bright, sunny morning, two birds visited from north northwest. The men sunbathed for most of the day and had a two-hour discussion about the delicious meals they would have in the UK. Almonds repaired a tear in the oilskins, while Robson repaired his red swimming trunks with a red patch from the ship's Moroccan flag. It was doubtful they would see Morocco anyway.

They took some took risks in the culinary department. The first was to experiment with alum to clear away the red muck in their drinking water. Not too bad. They had to be careful how they made tea and coffee, otherwise their condensed milk curdled. One can was rusted up. The next risk was using the primus stove. Its jet was still tricky. It was probably too large and, when lighting it, the whole primus went on fire, filling the cabin with fumes. The problem was lessened by keeping the hatch and skylight closed, but that made the cabin very warm. Being alone on the ocean for days, they felt divorced from life. Cameron thought they should worry about their position and their route to the Azores.

On 1 August, the wind slackened. By 10am, they had completed only 65 miles on course one point east of northeast, the log reading 2,525 miles. A cloudy morning sky delivered a little rain, but not enough to collect. Just before noon, the wind died. It was very hot all day. They had a staggered lunch and in the evening, polished off the last bottle of Grant's Standfast and did some filming. Robson amused the others by writing a long note to the directors of the whisky firm, making mention of how their whisky had kept the three mariners alive after their water had run out. They put the note in the empty bottle and threw it into the sea, this being the sixth they had consigned in this way since leaving Dakar. They wondered where the bottles would end up and resolved to start on their Martell brandy the following day. The onions were all finished. Their one meal a day tasted 'lousy' without them. 'A calm, starry night when on watch is delightful', Cameron recorded.

At 10am on 2 August, the log read 2,560. *Kumasi* had only made 35 miles in twenty-four hours on a course magnetic north. They were probably out of the Northeast Trades and about 420 miles from the Azores. Cameron wrote in the log: 'Coffee for breakfast and a very learned lecture from Almonds on the beauties of Lincolnshire and the nature of bog oak. He has an amazing store of knowledge garnered over the years by attentive reading and interest in the natural sciences and geography.' The dorsal fin of a shark slipped through the sea not far away. They still had trouble with the primus. Robson talked longingly of haggis. Days passed peacefully. 'The calm before the storm perhaps!' noted Cameron.

One evening, they picked up the BBC – they always recognised it by its type of music. According to Cameron, some programmes were 'punk' and 'the female announcers had hot potatoes in their mouths'. Their estimated position was Latitude 30 degrees; Longitude 23 degrees. Cameron spotted two striped pilot fish, then a baby one. Robson caught one and they ate it for lunch. Almonds pleaded for the life of a second caught pilot fish. It was to be their mascot as they had no other. The others agreed. It was pleasant to sit up in the pulpit and watch it darting below in and out of the bow wave of

Kumasi. They named their little fish 'Pontius', a brainwave of Robson's. They
hoped he would not wash his hands of them! The sea became flecked with
small transparent blobs and brown specks. They searched the pilot to see if
this phenomenon was significant, in particular whether it meant proximity
to the Azores. The wind was soft during a hot day.

After a calm night with a three-quarter moon, on 3 August at 10am,
the log read 2,580. They could only manage a course west northwest. They
picked up Radio Montreal – talking about automatic flagpoles! They also
had a stowaway: a chirping cricket! On that hot, still day, the log did not
even turn. Almonds thought they were drifting southwest at least ten miles
each day. They became bored with inactivity.

Food and water were going down with no mileage to show for it. At this
rate, they would miss the Azores – a serious matter. The sea was like a mirror
– a banal expression but true. Almonds talked of reassembling the motor
and burning up the remaining fuel for another sixty miles. Cameron thought
they were in the area between the Northeast Trades and the beginning of
the Southwest winds. There came a faint breath of a wind! They staggered
northwest. On 4 August, the breeze was stronger and they held a course
northeast. A small rain squall arrived in the afternoon, followed by stronger
ones for two hours. They took down sail four times. A tanker passed by,
heading southwest. Suddenly, Pontius disappeared! They suspected that the
log might be under-recording when the wind was light. Seaweed and cork
floated on the water. There had to be land around.

Squalls hit them during the night. The helmsman had a busy time taking
down the jib. After reefing the main and mizzen, they continued on under
high clouds with narrow fronts, buffeted by five-minute gusts of strong
wind. They heard an aeroplane on course from northwest to southwest.
Could it be from the Madeiras or the Azores? It was dangerous to plot their
position by it. At 10am, the log read 2,675, estimated position Latitude 31
degrees; Longitude 22 degrees.

Concerned about their position, their rations and their lack of progress,
they remained close-hauled most of the time. They did not want to go
too far west and miss the Azores. So they tacked between northwest and
northeast. If they did not sight land in three days, they would have to make
an important decision and turn east for Portugal, the Madeiras, the Canaries
or the coast of North Africa. Their Atlantic wind charts and the Pilot had not
been much help. Their position based on the log and the compass could be

300 to 400 miles out, owing to the current and unregistered miles. Robson kept himself busy all day designing a luxury yacht, assuming he had won the Treble Chance. Cameron finished *Island in the Sun* for the second time: a sad, miserable book. 'Jim is devouring *The Long Ships*', noted Cameron. 'He would have made a fine Viking himself. He tells me his ancestors have been sailing men'.

The waves became rough. They took down the jib and ran before a Force 8 gale. Steep seas were breaking under the stern. A steamer passed by, but took no notice of *Kumasi*. By 11pm, they were lying a-hull with the stay up and tiller lashed. The next day, 6 August, was Almonds's 46th birthday and was celebrated by mountainous waves all night. *Kumasi* reached 32 degrees west. They had lengthy discussions that morning on their course, position, rations and water, but postponed any decision until the storm died down. Robson read out part of a letter from his aunt, 'You won't make it.' Not very encouraging. They tried a reefed main. It was heavy work with seas 30 to 40 feet high and pretty wet at the tiller, with secondary seas slapping and slopping over the side. They changed course to north northwest, but made little progress in the heavy seas. Eventually, the waves were too rough and they hove to.

Almonds made a new sea anchor out of two empty jerrycans, tightly fastened on a long cable and weighted with heavy chain. It didn't bring the bow right into the waves, but stopped *Kumasi*'s drift and made her ride more easily. They went mad and had a birthday lunch – a small piece of cheese and a basinful of Christmas pudding, bought in Accra for the occasion. The pud was very rich. Some of their other tins were a bit rusty. Almonds mentioned sailing through the Mediterranean and the French canals or making for Portugal. They all favoured Portugal, as there was no certainty of hitting the Azores. The North Atlantic in September and October might be too strong for them and they would not be able to use the winds effectively. 'There is no doubt we have been unlucky on this voyage', Cameron opined in the log. 'Jim has a difficult decision to make as skipper. Turning to the Med or Portugal would mean more expenditure; but more importantly, the end of his hopes for four years of sailing home up the Atlantic in his own homemade boat. We now know it is quite feasible; we could have managed it more easily if we had left Ghana on 1 April instead of 15 May. Moreover, leaving the boat in Portugal or France would mean heavy maintenance costs. He might not be able to collect it for months.'

Robson suggested remaining on the starboard tack until they hit the Westerlies; otherwise, they could only go back into the teeth of the Northeast Trades. By 8pm, the gale had moderated, so they raised sail, course north northwest. The wind fell during the night. Eventually, it disappeared and the sea was without a ripple under a hot sun and deep blue sky. They took the opportunity to clear out the forward hatch and do some stocktaking. They had enough food for thirty boat lunches and fifty-three boat suppers, but no onions and only twenty days' potatoes. This would hardly be comfortable if they missed the Azores.

Strict water rationing began. Almonds had faced the terrors of death by thirst in the Western Desert during the SAS raid on Sidi Barrani. The mental anguish of knowing they would almost certainly not find water was as bad as their raging thirst. When the rationed teaspoon of water per man per day ran out, the raiders had gone three days without anything to drink. Each man had kept his cool; then, they had stumbled across a cache.[1] Cameron and Robson had never known what it was to be really thirsty. Would the water last out until they made it to land or were they able to get some from a passing ship?

They suspected a leak or that both water tanks had not been filled completely at Port Etienne. Henceforth, they could only have one mug of water or tea in the morning and a drop for their whisky in the evening until they collected some rainwater. They had plenty of powdered soup, oatmeal, cocoa, Bournvita, coffee, tea and powdered egg, but these were no good without water. In addition, the solid fuel for the primus was running out. They resolved to use only the smallest amount when lighting up. Cameron had bought an American balloon distillation plant in Accra. They blew it up and floated it on the sea. Looking like a silvery beach ball, it was supposed to produce about two pints of drinking water a day. They managed to get only half a bottle of sour liquid. It was better than nothing and they used it for cooking.

Robson and Cameron had a wonderful swim. At 2pm, Cameron sighted five small whales, wallowing and blowing about 300 yards away. Luckily, they did not come over and bump the boat. They took some film of the bathing beauties and their 'cocktail party'. While swimming again in the evening, keeping a sharp lookout for sharks, they found some barnacles on the hull. Almonds tried out a distress flare and a parachute rocket. The former was damp, but the second very successful. It went up with a great whoosh, 'better than those launched at Cape Canaveral' according to Robson. He and Cameron waited to see Almonds's face turn brick red when a rescue ship appeared on the scene, but no such luck! The day remained hot and still.

That evening, Cameron took cine shots of their pre-prandial Martell brandy drinking. Almonds, while fixing a halyard, had the misfortune to see their Takoradi Sailing Club burgee drop into the ocean's depths. They raised the Freetown Sailing Club burgee instead. Still no luck with fishing, as the fish seemed to be at much greater depths. For supper, they had a tin of Wall's sausages, peas and potatoes. Egg powder, added to their stew, turned it into a weird mixture in the pressure cooker. After supper, Robson and Cameron bathed again in the still water. No sharks appeared.

Radio Australia and Switzerland came across very clearly, but the three adventurers had grown tired of hearing about the trouble in the Belgian Congo. They were glad not to be in the typhoon off Okinawa. Cameron began writing letters in the hope of posting them in the Azores. 'What a hope!' said Robson. He wrote a long letter to the weather clerk at Greenwich and sent it off to the UK in an empty whisky bottle. They both kidded Almonds that the finder of every bottle would obtain on demand a pound sterling from Almonds at his Lincolnshire address.

Next morning found them in a faint breeze and on course two points east of north. At 10am, the log read 2,750, which meant 15 miles covered in twenty-four hours. The barometer showed 1,030 millibars. The clouds looked flattened. Cameron tried the still from the moving boat. It continued to work. He tried it on top of the cabin. It was alright, but he doubted if they would get even a third of a bottle of water from it. He then cleared out the starboard bunk and dried out the bedding. Robson removed the ballast and got about two buckets of water from the bilges – very little, considering the length of time the boat had been on the seas. Some of the little drain holes were choked, but he managed to clear them with wire. They all hoped the bunk mattresses would remain dryer. By 12 noon on 8 August, the log read 2,772, course one point east of north. Five whales surfaced and spouted – 'just as one reads in books', noted Robson. Their little cricket stowaway was still on board.

On a port tack, Robson thought they had picked up the Westerlies. They had only 1,000 cigarettes left. If they missed the Azores, they would be celibate, teetotal, non-smokers by the time they reached the UK. In the evening, the sky clouded over. At 6pm, two squalls hit them. They got out the bed sheets and spread them on the cabin, but there was no rain. A ship appeared, going east. This might indicate that they were on the same latitude as the Azores or just north on the Gibraltar shipping lane. The wind improved at 7pm, but fell away at midnight.

Next morning, 9 August, a bird visited them, followed by three squalls. A little school of porpoises kept them company. They seemed to like the bit of speed they got around the bows of the boat. After the tempest, the log barely turned. A mug of tea for breakfast and the wind began to pick up from the west. The sky was overcast with light cloud, so their still did not work very well. In the afternoon, another whale appeared about 300 yards away. Robson was convinced that if they could manage progress west of north in the following three days, they were bound to hit the Azores, where they would be able to restock with everything they needed. Almonds proposed to turn east if they did not hit the Azores by 12 August. All were cheesed off by the uncertainty of their position and the lack of favourable winds.

At 7pm, a long tanker crossed their bow, going west northwest half a mile away. They could not recognise her nationality. Shortly afterwards, some porpoises appeared – the first they had seen for a long time. What with the odd flotsam and jetsam, seaweed, birds, porpoises and a fisherman's float, there was every hope that land was in the vicinity. Robson made omelette for everyone. Unfortunately, he put in too much seawater, so they were all thirsty for hours afterwards. He had fried it in olive oil – but for the excess salt, it would have been very good.

Before midnight, the wind veered north northwest and they were on a port tack heading northeast. They opened a tin of French corned beef Cameron had bought in Dakar. It was very inferior stuff. The skipper gave them a lurid description of the continental muck offered as food. This account involved his days with the *Maquis* behind enemy lines in France. Cameron was amused by Almonds's story of the German sentry who used to open the gates of the level crossing for their SAS jeep. They would honk their horn and he would come out, head averted (though he knew very well who they were). Later, they would return the same way and out he would come again to let them through. [2]

On 10 August, the wind petered away. They hardly moved. At 10am, the log read 2,835 miles. Almonds suspected that the log line was faulty, so he replaced the nylon line with a plaited line from the harpoon. After trimming the sails as finely as possible, they began to make three knots, on course northeast. The seas were small with rippling little wavelets. At noon, a passenger cargo ship crossed their bows, going west southwest, destination unknown. South America? In view of the recent wind directions and the ships they had seen, Almonds thought *Kumasi* might be passing east of the Azores. Cameron didn't know what to think. If Almonds was correct, they should just press on and not turn east as they had thought the day before.

Three kinds of birds visited the boat and a turtle ambled by. A few yards closer and it would have had a harpoon in its back! The day developed into blue sky and light, feathery clouds. The deck was hot. Their hooks were bitten off the spinner. Cameron thought their reel was tightening up by itself and the ratchet was too stiff when the fish bit. They scanned the horizon. At 6pm, Cameron started to cook supper. He poured out three brandies for their evening drink and went on deck. There, dead in in front of them, loomed a huge, conical peak above the clouds. It had no base below the cloud. Almonds saw a pimple on top of the peak: a mountain or cloud? Cameron suggested to Almonds, half humorously, that it was land. They had been deceived before by the shape and formation of dark clouds on the horizon. Then, to their delight, the clouds on the horizon changed formation but the cone remained! It looked like a volcano. Robson was roused and there began a feverish search of the pilot.

Azores? Canaries? The Madeiras?

Chapter Twenty

A TRUE VIKING

They hit the Azores spot on. *Kumasi* had reached the Mid Atlantic Ridge, running north to south in the Atlantic. Pico Island in the Azores, Portugal's highest mountain, almost 1,000 miles west of Lisbon, is part of that ridge, where it breaks the ocean surface as a seabed volcano. Almonds realised that the pimple of cloud was, in fact, the summit. Had they missed it, they would have turned east the next day. Like his Viking forebears, he had navigated by the sun. His method was not precise and they did not call at some of the ports on their itinerary, but it was good enough. It did not even matter where in the UK they made their eventual landfall (when the Vikings sailed for the Shetlands, it had not mattered to them that they ended up in the Orkneys).

As they drew nearer to land, the sloping shoulders of the mountain became more visible. However, the land mass below the cloud remained obscure. To celebrate, they had another brandy. From the distance, the peak seemed about 20,000 feet high, but as *Kumasi* sailed nearer, it became more like its true 7,700 feet.

Night fell, but they continued under full sail towards Pico Island. They repaired their rusty torch batteries and lit the navigation lamps for the first time in five days. Robson wrote furiously in his own log and made abstruse calculations on their course over the previous fortnight. He took three bearings on Horta, Lages and the east point of San Jorge, which were 315 degrees, 346 degrees and 51 degrees respectively, and transferred them to the Consul Chart of Portsmouth to the Canary Islands and Azores. This gave him a tricorn of about 2 square miles. Their new position he recorded as Latitude 38 degrees, 15" north; Longitude 28 degrees, 10" west. After twenty-three days without seeing land, they had sailed so far west that they almost reached 30 degrees Longitude. At 3am on 11 August, they handed the main. They did not want to approach the land too quickly and give a repeat performance of their arrival at the Takoradi Yacht Club. At 10am, the log read 2,890. *Kumasi's* official mileage by the log from Port Etienne was 1,035, but Robson reckoned that they had really done 1,350, so the log was under-registering by about 21 per cent.[1]

The morning mist was heavy with dew. They had plenty of coffee for breakfast and a huge lunch of ham, peas, baked beans and biscuits. Their shrunken stomachs could hardly take it all. At 1pm, they lay becalmed off Pico, which looked lovely with dark green fields, white houses and red roofs. Scores of silvery dolphins gambolled around them. In front lay the small town of Lages, but they could see no people. Was it siesta time? They didn't know if there was a sheltered harbour. Reefs appeared near a jetty and some breakers. There should have been some sort of a lagoon to enter, but they could not see an entrance. Then, Cameron saw masts behind the jetty. They ran up their pilot and quarantine flags. The bays looked open to the southeast and south. Since *Kumasi* was in southwest winds, they did not wish to drop anchor where they were.

At 5pm, becalmed, they drifted in rain and mist slowly towards the harbour. 'My God, the rocks around the entrance', noted Robson, 'and only a slim passage through them.' A cutter came out from the jetty, crammed with people: men, women and children. It circled *Kumasi*. Questions flew across the water until an old lady became their interpreter. The new arrivals took a tow rope aboard and they were off, in between vicious-looking reefs. To their relief, they anchored in a small, sheltered harbour. Thankfully, they had not needed to sail in by themselves.

Their charming interpreter advised the three arrivals to wait for the port captain and doctor. So they relaxed on top of the cabin, three bearded, filthy-looking ruffians. From the jetty and windows of the houses overlooking the harbour, many pairs of eyes and heads turned their way, accompanied by waves of welcome. The port captain, doctor and customs officer came aboard. There was no formality, only concern for their welfare. *Kumasi*, her three crew learned, was the first yacht to come to Lages. They asked about a hotel and bank and were told that all was 'taken care of'.

Artur, the manager of the island's canning factory, took the three visitors under his wing. In clean jerseys, they went ashore. In the village square, they had a brandy and then went to a pension for supper. After a stroll in the square, they met a schoolmaster and friendly children. They visited a factory where they discovered that the lady interpreter was its director. The superintendent and his wife had a large family. Strangely, no one would talk about money or banks. They finally went to bed in the spotless ward of a little hospital in the square and sank into a deep sleep.

On 12 August – the day they would have turned east had they not found the Azores – they woke refreshed at 8am. After coffee and biscuits, laid on for them by the ladies who worked in the hospital, they collected their dirty clothes from the boat. The garments were so filthy that it was doubtful they would ever be clean again. *Kumasi*'s arrival had been reported on the radio news at Ponta Delgardo and in the Horta newspapers.

Mount Pico looked wonderful in the morning sunlight, its peak still showing above white clouds. Senhor Bettancourt, the teacher and whaling master, said that if a whale was sighted, the *Kumasi* crew could go with the whaling boats. These were fragile-looking rowing boats with crews of eight. Cameron tried to change dollars, but nobody would accept them. Robson climbed *Kumasi*'s mast and changed the runner back stays, while Cameron made things shipshape below. Little boys swimming in the water surrounded the boat. Almonds and Cameron visited the port captain, while Robson 'got pally' with old José, a stone mason building the church. Cameron concluded that José did not want to finish the church as he would do himself out of a job. The three men visited the hospital superintendent's home. Senhora Olga Avila, with her nine children, received the visitors in a small, Victorian-like parlour. Her daughter, Helen Marie, gave a piano recital. When the senhora discovered that Cameron was a Roman Catholic, her face lit up and she fell on his neck.

After lunch at the pension, Arturo Brun and Bettancourt took the three visitors on a round trip of the island. It was very beautiful, with 148 volcanic craters, both high and low. Flowering shrubs lined all the roads. The seaside villages were clean and white. They went searching for locally produced angelica and spent three hours drinking in farm wine cellars with old farmers who reminded Cameron strongly of the crofters in Glenlivet. These men were not fat, sleek Portuguese, but big-boned, big-nosed and brawny with an uncouth sense of humour. One old boy, MTP, would have kept the three foreigners drinking for a fortnight if he could. The farms were built on lava; black rock walls surrounded all the vines and figs. The villages looked Mexican. It had been deserted when the visitors arrived, but after five minutes hordes of men, women and children arrived, wondering who the three bearded strangers were. Bettancourt knew everyone and was highly respected – a real *Scots Dominie!*

At 6pm, the party arrived at Maddelena, where they met Manuel Augusta da Costa and his wife. Da Costa seemed to be the big boy there, with a busy, energetic finger in everything. He was agent for many things and also ran a small handicraft factory in which whalebone was made into ornaments. A delightful couple offered the three guests whisky, brandy, vodka, *eau-de-vie*, anchovies and olives. Arturo looked a bit white and shaky from all the drink, but the three from the *Kumasi* were going strong and felt they could have drunk all night. Late in the evening, they got back to the pension for a fine meal, Robson having made a hit with a plump, mature daughter of the Senhora. After a chat and stroll in the village square to complete a marvellous day, they retired to bed.

Cameron awoke next morning to find his leg swelling with water on the knee. However, he did not want to see the doctor in case it meant a huge bandage for all the population to see. After breakfast, the three went down to the boat. Almonds talked of leaving the next day, 14 August, but Robson was against the idea. He did not see why they should not have at least one day of complete rest; besides, there was a local dance, a 'filharmonica', on Sunday evening, which it would be a pity to miss. So they arranged not to receive any food stores until Monday.

Robson was up the mast for most of the morning, fixing this and that. Cameron pumped out the tanks, cleaned out the cabin and worked on the hatch. The hull had quite a few barnacles, but they were loath to get in the water and scrape them off. Almonds worried about them reducing *Kumasi's* speed and tried to get the local youngsters to help, but they were too busy swimming around the boat, splashing in the water. A local seminarist came aboard for a chat. It was market day and a steamer, *Lima*, arrived. The farmers had brought down their cattle, which were duly loaded by means of slings round their bellies. Fresh water (seawater, filtered through lava rock) appeared in a lorry arranged by Senhor Machado Avila. There followed a wonderful time with about fifty villagers and fishermen helping to pump it into *Kumasi's* water tanks.

Then, it was time to accept Manuel's invitation to a vineyard lunch party in Madalena. Almonds went in one car with the port captain and two ladies. Cameron and Robson travelled with Norberto and Maria Antunes, the attractive lady who had met them on arrival. Another three cars followed; also in the party were Luzia and Ilda Vale, Inez Soares de Melo and Maris Raquel Campos. Manuel had an old farm, with a wine still, producing black wine and angelica. Lunch was truly marine, with fish, lobster and all sorts of clams and shellfish, *cracas* (boiled barnacles) and *lapas*.[2] The feast was sumptuous. Almonds made a very good speech, translated by Arturo. Robson also gave an impromptu discourse, saying that their hosts in Lages should not let their guests go until Monday as he was enjoying it so much on the island.

After lunch, they took photographs and sat drinking and singing on the veranda, before returning to Manuel's house for Samovar vodka, whisky and pineapple liqueur. Manuel then presented each guest with a carving made from a whale's tooth and a bottle of angelica. On their way back to Lages do Pico, they stopped for a brief spell in Candelaria to listen to a fiesta in the church square. Two bands of violins and guitars vied with each other, while the villagers ran from one band to the other. Clothes pegs held sheet music onto the music stands. It was late at night, but children and babies were everywhere.

Meanwhile, Almonds was hitting it off with the pilot in the family house of the Portuguese cardinal. They moved on and stopped at the factory. Bettancourt told them that two whales had been caught and were being fleshed. The stink and greasy surface of the yard were striking. It was quite an eerie sight in the dark to see furnaces flaming and men up to their knees in blubber and blood. After pushing one of the cars to get it started, they were soon back in Lages and in their beds at the end of another memorable day.

Robson was the first awake on Sunday 14 August. The arrangements in the hospital-cum-hotel were marvellous. Coffee and biscuits were laid on each evening and the sister in charge went out of her way to make her three guests comfortable. A little servant girl did all their washing and the formerly filthy clothes returned spotless. Cameron went to church, causing quite a stir by genuflecting and crossing himself.

A copy of *Correio de Horta*, dated 12 August 1960, gave a somewhat warped account of *Kumasi's* adventures to date. The local paper, *O Telegrafo*, of 13 August also gave a distorted version of their travels. As Robson was on his way down to the boat, a photographer who had taken their picture on arrival presented him with a set of prints for each of them. Robson did a few jobs on board, including a couple of splices on the main sheet, then had a chat with Manuel Viera Soares, the whaler, who had been so helpful. He showed Robson around his boat, the *Cigana*. The fishermen had caught lobsters, octopus and eels the night before and Robson watched the men making fishing baskets.

The three met at the pension for their usual breakfast. The proprietor, José Joav Soares de Melo, was accompanied by his wife, Mathilde Nazare, a son, Antonio, and a pretty young daughter, Ana Maria. The latter was most anxious that the three guests should remain for the party on Sunday evening. 'A delightful family!' noted Cameron. 'Mother buxom, daughter a rosebud, son and father...' After breakfast, the *Kumasi* crew tried to get down to letter writing. Later, a trip to the whale factory revealed that the entire whale had been cut up and was in the pot. The manager, Maria Antunes's elder son, led Robson through the factory where he photographed some massive whale jaws. Lunch at the pension consisted of cow's tongue, vino and lobster – a guest at the pension had kindly purchased for them the lobster that Robson had seen that morning.

Senhora Avila pressed Robson to come to her house again, so he went. He did not need much pressing with a girl like Helen-Marie around. He was persuaded to play the piano, which he did – not very well. Then, Olga Avila sang to a ukulele-tuned Portuguese instrument, which was good, the children joining in the chorus. Cameron, meanwhile, went with Bettancourt, his three sons and Arturo to a village for some cheese for the boat. Bettancourt seemed to know everyone. At the village, they visited the *fromagerie*. A fat, rosy-cheeked wench wrapped up five cheeses for them, one of which Robson wanted to keep for the UK.

Almonds spent the morning down at the harbour running his hands over boats and 'feeling them'. The dock was full of old whale jaws, which had been left there to rot for a while to facilitate removal of the teeth. Pico would be a wonderful place for a holiday and Cameron resolved to return. It was so peaceful – but about to acquire an airfield. He hoped it would not spoil the island's natural loveliness.

Almonds tried to phone Lockie at Stixwould, but the village postmistress, Elsie Holden, couldn't take a call from the middle of the Atlantic. He talked of the good wind that day and how they had not taken advantage of it. Moreover, they still had a long way to go. They were still in the mid-Atlantic, with the distance to the UK being about the same as that from Port Etienne to the Azores. Robson insisted they all needed a rest. On Monday, they would have been on the voyage for three months, but of all the ports at which they had called, none could beat Lages de Pico for generosity and hospitality. They were sorry to be leaving.

The morning of 15 August was disappointingly grey and rainy. Cameron arranged with Senhor Avila for stores to be brought down to the jetty, while Almonds did all their packing in the hospital and Robson went to the pension to say their goodbyes. Cameron managed to get the hospital matron to accept 3,000 francs as a gift to the hospital staff, who had done so much for the three unexpected guests. That was the only money the Pico Islanders allowed them to spend on the island.

At the jetty, all their new friends were waiting to say farewell. The rain had eased slightly and they ferried their provisions to the boat. These were all free and consisted of: forty-eight tins of tuna fish; twelve tins of peas; five large cheeses; a tin of biscuits; a dozen loaves of bread; a bag of apples; a bag of potatoes and onions; three tins of Nescafé; ten litres of kerosene; a tin of grease; a pair of gumboots; three pairs of socks; two dozen eggs; two bottles of brandy; six bottles of angelica; white wine; cigars; and 2,000 cigarettes and matches. Finally, they embraced their helpers, cast off and were towed out by a launch, followed by two others crowded with their new friends and fishermen.

Out of the lee of the island, they raised sail, hoping that nothing would stick and shame them. Fortunately, nothing did. They waved goodbye and were on their way to the UK. The sea was a little choppy and the wind light. It was 9.30am; the log stood at 2,890 miles. They made for the St Jorge-Terceira Channel, but were becalmed off St Jorge. So they tried for the Pico-St Jorge Channel but, being in the lee of Pico and the wind westerly, were becalmed again. They tacked 6 miles at dusk, but the wind strengthened so they lowered the main in a small squall. Going about again, they made the St Jorge headland and entered the channel just after midnight.

As they set out from the Azores, Robson said to Almonds,

'When we strike land, how will we know which bit it is?'

'If it's cold and it appears to port, it will be Iceland; but if it's warm and sunny and appears to starboard, it will be Portugal,' the skipper replied.

On 16 August, they sailed up the channel on a port tack, cleared the
Terceira headlands and were in open sea. The seas rose with the wind and
by 2pm, they had another storm on their hands. They drifted east under
the staysail, feeling rather uncomfortable at sea again. Almonds considered
anchoring in Villa da Praia, but in a Force 7 wind decided to press on.
After drifting all night, the log read 3,060. During the afternoon, the sea
moderated and they made little progress. With a west wind and course now
north northeast, they enjoyed a supper of tuna fish and angelica. A fair wind
all night saw them more cheerful on the morning of 18 August. It remained
fair all day, but at dusk they were becalmed. They decided to try a course
more to the north to catch the true southwesterly winds and avoid being
dragged into the Bay of Biscay.

On 19 August, it was Cameron's turn to have a birthday – his thirty-
ninth. They celebrated with a bottle of wine at lunch. It brought them no
luck. By 4pm, a real old storm was brewing. Almonds was pooped at the
stern as, without warning, a huge wave broke over it. They lowered all sails,
put out the new sea anchor and sat cooped up in the cabin. Outside, the wind
howled and the sea became increasingly mountainous. Almonds considered
various proposals for improving their sale plan and rigging, so that *Kumasi*
could perform better with a following wind. She had no spinnaker or twin
staysails, so was unable to make optimum use of a strong south wind or
southwesterly. They wanted to go north for a few hundred miles and then
turn northeast towards the English Channel, which would be very difficult if
they couldn't sail before the wind. They could use the spare mainsail on the
main mast alongside the other one in order to sail goose-winged again or
they could try the whisker pole.[3] Cameron was doubtful of using makeshift
gear in the strong winds. They would wait to see what the next few days
brought. He took some cine film of the storm, but it was difficult to prevent
the lenses being soaked. The log read 3,230.

On 20 August, they were in a Force eight gale. The barometer had
sunk so low – to 1,005 millibars – they wondered if it was broken. The
morning was bright and clear, but the wind howled through the rigging,
tossing them back and forward with the occasional comber breaking over
the cabin and hatch. They were not worried about the hull or deck, which
were tremendously strong. However, life was uncomfortable cooped up in
the cabin with only two bunks. One person had to take turns sitting on the
steps down into the cabin. They cursed the poor old brute lying at their feet.

However, they ate well, attacking their Pico bread and cheese. The latter was really delicious and they gorged on it.

The sea grew ever higher. Almonds talked of taking down the masts in order to lessen the wind resistance, but that was not going to be easy in the now Force 10 winds. He got ready the hacksaw, pliers, screwdrivers and hammer just in case. The cabin's Perspex windows were standing up well to the beating of the seas and rain, but he was ready to board them up. At supper, they had three brandies to cheer themselves up. Robson spilt his stew over himself and treated the others to some choice language. Later that evening, they tried to sail with the stay up. It came down very quickly! Next they tried the mizzen – far too dangerous! They wondered how far east they were being driven.

My father always said that this was the most powerful storm of the voyage. Towards the end of his watch, he went below and put on the kettle to make everyone tea. As he did so, the storm struck. He had been watching a big dark cloud with a white spot in it. Invariably, this meant trouble. The boat went right over on its side. Gordon leapt up and went above, just as the boom broke and came crashing down. Then, the large iron stay at the head of the jib snapped. Almonds had a spare and a bolt with which to repair it. And he knew *Kumasi* would always right herself and would not ship much water because no hatches were allowed open.

At the height of the storm, Almonds was on deck and saw a large ship coming past. *Kumasi* was about 40 feet up; the newcomer was down in the hollow between the waves. *Kumasi's* new sea anchor – made of two tightly fastened jerrycans – made all the difference. As the boat came into each swell, she rode easily, gliding to the top of each wave. Without the anchor, she would have been buffeted. The jerrycans were hit by the sea each time and lost from view, but then the air inside them pulled them back to the surface. So *Kumasi* made way more efficiently, while the big ship made heavy weather of it. Almonds revelled in what he knew was his most exhilarating adventure.

Another night cooped up with one on watch at all times meant three hours at a time with one's head stuck out of the cockpit. The barometer was unchanged, while the waves seemed even steeper. According to the pilot, some lows in the area could last six days. The storm had few squalls, but consisted mainly of wind and translucent seas. When the swell was big, Almonds looked through the side of a mountain of water next to the boat and saw sharks swimming inside it with countless small fish. A tanker passed 100 yards away, but did not deign to investigate why a seemingly deserted boat was bouncing up and down in the middle of the Atlantic. Almonds thought they had drifted 60 miles east. After cheese for lunch, they raised the stay without the sea anchor, but had to lower it again.

By 22 August, the sea and wind appeared to have reduced a little during the night. The barometer was up one millibar. While Robson slept off his watch, Almonds and Cameron raised the stay and reefed the main. They took it down again in a hurry, but tried again an hour later and were off under sail, course east northeast. By noon, they had covered 11 miles. Riding huge waves as they swept over the stern was quite an experience. After all, two of them were complete landlubbers. Every time they rode a crest, the helmsman had a continual fight with the tiller. There was always the danger of being pooped or broaching – when the rudder would not be able to compensate and the boat could capsize. However, it was great to be sailing again.

Next day, heavy rain squalls arrived after midnight. They downed the main and all got wet and miserable. Still, by 10am, the log read 3,284. They let out the reefs and drove *Kumasi* as hard as possible. Another day of hard work at the tiller. Various birds paid them a visit, but unfortunately the crew of *Kumasi* were not ornithologists. The wind was northwest, so they steered east northeast. After midnight, during a dark, squally night, they navigated by the Pole Star when it was visible.

They sailed with the stay and mizzen, while heavy seas slapped over the sides, making good speed and riding the crests with a swoop each time. At 4pm, they raised the reefed main. Constantly raising and lowering sails was hard work, but Almonds had more to lose than his crew, so he was careful about the wind and taking the sails down quickly. *Kumasi* could make six knots. But in rough conditions, although the boat could go faster with all her sails up, it was also the way to tear them, break all the gear and go quickly to the bottom.

The night of 25 August was dark, with menacing clouds. A sudden northwesterly squall caught Almonds and he had a few anxious moments handing the main and mizzen. They sailed the rest of the night with just the stay. Despite the bad weather, their mileage was encouraging. They crossed the shipping lane for low-powered steamers from Europe to Gulf posts and New York. They sighted the *Danaland* and another ship. Sailing under the reefed main and mizzen with the stay, dark clouds scudded across a blue sky. They were always more cheerful when the sun shone.

It was cold at the tiller and beginning to be colder in the cabin. The oilskins were much in use and Cameron's began to tear. A turtle swam past. Almonds thought that from the stars they were on the same latitude as Finisterre. Next day, they sailed along breezily until 10am, when the wind became fitful. The seas had moderated considerably. At 3am, Almonds raised the jib for the first time in many a day. The log read 3,495. He repaired the primus stove again; Robson reorganised the front hatch; Cameron refilled the jerrycans from the rusty water tanks. The water now tasted 'lousy'. He tried some alum to see if it would settle it. Their onions were beginning to run out again. In three days, the cigarettes would finish, too. They would be rationed to one cigar a day. 'We are all heavy smokers', noted Cameron. 'We will miss the occasional fag when sitting alone at the tiller at night'.

They enjoyed the fine weather, but were making little progress at about 2 knots. Their course was east since with a wind from the north, more northing would lessen their speed. A steamer passed on the port side. In the evening, they were becalmed and needed blankets at night to cover their feet. Several planes droned in the night sky. On 27 August, there was not a ripple on the water. Robson made coffee. Cameron stayed on watch until 9am. Occasionally, they prolonged their watches in order to give the next man a longer sleep. The tunny for lunch was oily as the tins were intended for the Italian export market. French and BBC radio stations began to come through clearly. They were amused by some popular ditty called 'Itsy Bitsy Teeny Weeny Yellow Polka-dot Bikini'. Becalmed practically all day, they sunbathed. At 9pm, a light breeze arrived from the southeast, veering to south.

Next morning, the wind strengthened and they reefed the main and mizzen. The seas were stronger and heavy rain arrived. Robson sighted a weather station vessel ablaze with light. This gave *Kumasi*'s position as Latitude 45 degrees north; Longitude 16 degrees west, so they were approximately 660 miles from the English Channel. Again, this position proved that their log was under-registering by at least 20 to 30 per cent. All morning, they pressed on in rough seas. Suddenly, the wind veered from south to northwest and they went onto a port tack. That evening, the seas fell. Their course was still east northeast in the cool and misty air.

On 29 August, having been becalmed almost all night, at 10am, the log read 3,710 miles. Day broke with clear blue skies and a warming sun. Seven ships passed during the night. Robson had to flash his torch to warn one of them off. For the last few days they had not lit the navigation lights, but decided they must now do so as they approached the Channel. The port lamp was not very effective as the glass was cracked. Almonds had repaired it, so it worked at least. All morning, they lazed on deck in the sun. At 3pm, Cameron called Robson up on deck to see a cargo ship passing close by. Robson donned a pair of trunks. The ship *Cestos* of Monrovia came within 100 yards. Robson gave a wave and shouted, jokingly, 'Where's England?' An officer on board shouted something and then the ship sailed on.

To Almonds's consternation, the *Cestos* turned in a circle and came up on their port side. This was a great surprise. *Kumasi's* crew downed sail and drifted to within 30 yards of the *Cestos*. Men and cargo passengers lined the deck. Through a loudhailer, *Kumasi* got a fix: Latitude 45 degrees, 35" north; Longitude 13 degrees, 55" west and their distances: 318 miles from Ushant and 364 miles from Land's End.

Cestos's captain asked if they needed anything. Robson replied that they had enough of everything except cigarettes. 'You are welcome to them!' the slow shout floated over the water from the Monrovian vessel. Almonds manoeuvred the boat nearer, but warned Cameron not to accept any kind of line from the *Cestos* in case she claimed *Kumasi* as salvage. Robson fended off and Cameron caught a canvas bag containing 800 cigarettes and a bundle of weather reports. *Kumasi* was also running short of booze, but they preferred not to cadge anything else. The captain said he would report their position to England and then they all waved goodbye. Ships that passed in the night.

The encounter was nearly a catastrophe. As *Kumasi* drifted under the huge bow of the *Cestos*, her mast almost caught it. Some anxious moments had them with their hearts in their mouths as they shoved off with the boathook. They scraped by with about six inches to spare. 'However, all's well that ends well', noted Cameron. They raised sail and the *Cestos* blew a farewell on her siren. The *Kumasi* crew were so grateful to the master of the *Cestos*. She was the only vessel in the whole voyage to show any interest in the homemade ketch. Almonds then revealed that he had saved up to 200 cigarettes for a rainy day. 'Not a bad idea', said Cameron. He knew a bloke who used to hide one-pound notes all over his room, so that he would have the pleasant surprise of finding them again when he was broke.

A light breeze gusted until midnight. Robson and Cameron told dirty stories to pass the time; Robson had a wonderful piece about Tam who had to put it in a splint. Almonds recited a long piece of Kipling fluently. They began to use a masthead lamp at night. On 30 August, there had been hardly any breeze during the night and very little progress. At 10am, the log read 3,735 miles, course NE. The morning was cloudy, but gradually the sky turned a brilliant blue and the sea was calm. Almonds, fearing a gale after the calm, decided to get out the motor and use up their remaining fuel to get into the Channel. Robson and Cameron were in favour of saving the fuel until they reached the enclosed Channel waters, but Almonds felt strongly that it was better to motor now. So out with the Brute, who was a heavy bastard and tore an inch of flesh from Almonds's little finger. The wound was bandaged with some neobacrin jelly, but Cameron thought that it must be very painful.

One of the motor's levers had been damaged in the cabin, so the Brute had to be started on two cylinders. This meant that Almonds had to be on call continually or on watch to start the motor, which also misbehaved and died out about every half an hour. Robson had great antipathy towards the Brute; Cameron felt much the same. But they motored on, the cockpit and deck becoming very greasy and oily. They ran out of linen handkerchiefs for filtering the rusty petrol and began tearing up Robson's fine Indian dhobi. In the afternoon, three ships passed by. By evening, a cold wet mist had descended. They motored all night through some rain squalls.

On 31 August, Almonds was exhausted and his finger was painful. Still, it could not be as bad as Popski's. He remembered a cool evening in the wartime Western Desert, meeting up with Popski between desert raids. His left little finger had caught an Italian bullet and was badly injured. As Popski tried to spread out the map on his jeep bonnet, the mangled finger kept getting in the way. Hardly pausing between sentences, he took out his Commando knife, put the offending digit on the wheel arch of the vehicle and lopped it off. [4]

At 5.30am, they stopped the motor and put up the sails in a light southerly breeze. Frequent mugs of tea or coffee kept them going and 'did them a world of good'. Robson suffered from cold hands while on night watch. They motored for one and a half hours. The skipper wondered if they were heading for the Irish Channel or for the region towards Nantes in the Bay of Biscay. They met a small fleet of two dozen French fishing smacks with colourful hulls and red, russet or blue and white sails. They were under diesel engines with, to Cameron's inexperienced eye, ketch or yawl rigging. Their presence caused some speculation about *Kumasi*'s position. Had they gone too far east? They had seen no steamers or tankers for the previous twenty-four hours. They searched the pilot to see what it said about fishing grounds. It was not very precise. They carried on through the fleet; *Kumasi*'s skipper not wishing to bother the French boats by asking for an exact position.

But the French were interested. One boat chased them up to have a look. So *Kumasi* took down her sails and began a longwinded conversation in French. It was difficult to understand the Frenchmen (from Vannes and Lorien), but the *Perle de Bretagne* drew up her fishing lines and approached. *Kumasi* learned that she was at Latitude 47 degrees, 11" north; Longitude 11 degrees west and 260 miles from Ushant. Almonds was sceptical, but Robson thought the position about right. They said *au revoir* and dawdled on, course east northeast. The sky clouded over; they skirted round a black, ugly-looking one. The clouds looked fiercer than tropical ones, but held mainly rain and little wind. The sea remained calm. The fishing vessels disappeared over the horizon.

Kumasi barely made east on a faint south southwest wind, the jib and staysail flapping slightly as they were caught in the lee of the other two sails. About 50 miles worth of petrol remained and Almonds was in favour of using it to get into the Channel as soon as possible. At 10pm, they woke up the Brute. He coughed in disgust, then got down to the job of chugging away steadily east northeast. It was going to be an exhausting night for Almonds. He was taking four Aureomycin tablets a day against infection of his finger wound. The night was calm, moist and cloudy.

September began with the passage of a large liner at 3am going south southwest. They wondered whether it was on the Africa or South America run. The Brute misbehaved frequently. Then, while Cameron and Robson were on watch and carrying out refuelling, he caught on fire. They extinguished the flames and smothered them with old towels. There is always something to relieve the monotony on a small boat! They took more care about smoking cigarettes. Mugs of hot sweet tea or coffee every two hours helped them all to get through the hours of darkness. At 5am, they stopped the motor and raised the sails, course east northeast. The BBC weather forecast seemed to be missing. The wind continued fair all morning, but in the afternoon, they could only sail east. Almonds rested all morning after his night's labours. At 7pm, they lowered the main as a storm seemed to be brewing on the horizon. They ate no supper, having made pigs of themselves with cheese at lunchtime.

On 2 September, with a fresher wind, they sailed with mizzen reefed and a handed main. At 10am, the log read 3,925 miles, course northeast on a port tack. There was some confusion about their position. On the one tack they might close with Land's End and on the other with Ushant. They wanted to end up bang in the middle of the Channel. After a fairish wind all day, they sighted one ship sailing southwest. They had been expecting to see some of the larger passenger ships. One of the Queens would give them a good course to Cherbourg or Southampton. Robson pointed out that fortune favoured the brave – in other words, 'Who Dares, Wins'. East northeast still seemed their best bet. During a damp night, falling wind and a few squalls, they sailed northeast. At 10am, on 3 September, the log read 4,000 miles! The wind increased quickly from the north northwest. The sky was a hard blue with high, mackerel clouds. All the sails were up, but in a Force 4 to 5 wind, they were forced to reduce to just the main and the stay.

Rough, choppy seas thumped on the hull. After cheese and biscuits for lunch, on a course northeast, they were back in the shipping lane. They saw seven ships, some steaming north, the others on a parallel course on the horizon. They thought this indicated the proximity of Ushant. However, from noon, there were no ships. Were they were getting close to the French coast?

Almonds pondered his future movements. He hoped to meet all of us at Ryde and that his friend, Colonel Keymer, might join him in *Kumasi* to Lincolnshire. John was on standby to meet them as soon as they made a UK landfall, so that he, too, could join the last leg of the journey to the River Witham.[5] Cameron wanted to see family in Portsmouth. By 4pm, another storm was in the offing from the northwest. Cameron and Robson stood by on deck while Almonds rested from his watch. The storm consisted mainly of rain, then some nasty combers smacking under the stern. There was no danger yet. They handed the main and had just started on a hot mug of stew when the seas became more violent; down stay and out with the sea anchor. One wave loosened the engine lashings.

Almonds again considered dismantling the brute and bringing him below the waterline for increased stability. The swell was high, but they had seen worse. So the motor was firmly lashed down and again the three men rode it out in the cabin. The masthead lamp was lit on top of the cabin in case other ships were in the vicinity. One man remained on watch in the Force 7 to 8 gale. 'Just our luck to be caught with this at the entrance to the Channel', Cameron recorded. The clouds disappeared, to be replaced by bright stars, howling wind and the occasional splatters of water slapping on the cabin. They lay a-hull all night.

On 4 September, at 7am, the barometer read 1,010. The gale slackened, so they put up the stay and, at 3pm, the jib and main. They put a reef in; the wind was north northwest, course east northeast. Four ships passed by. They thought they must be well into the Channel. The barometer rose to 1,017 with blue sky and fresh air. The seas were dropping, but still rough. More ships appeared; they kept a sharp lookout. Nobody wanted a mishap at this stage of the game.

Just after midnight on 5 September, they lowered the mizzen and passed groups of trawlers, one of which was the *Torbay*. This raised their hopes of a good landfall. By 5am, all sails were up in a Force 3 NW. The dawn was bright, fresh and clear with quieter seas. Cameron was suffering from a nasty, poisonous rash on his left buttock – the result of sitting for hours on a wet deck in dirty clothes. He tried some synthomycetine tablets. Robson had a recurrence of ear fungus and Almonds's finger was raw and painful. At 7pm, the log read 4,094. Cameron thought they were 40 to 50 miles inside the Channel and heading towards Portland Bill. The wind strengthened. *Kumasi* was cutting beautifully through the water, doing 5 to 6 knots. There was nothing more pleasant than being on a broad reach in a good wind.

Cameron sighted a lighthouse flashing. In a jiffy, Almonds was on deck and they both got out their watches. The light was flashing five seconds every thirty seconds. They had no table of lights, so Almonds pored over all the lighthouses in the vicinity of the Channel, then all the lighthouses of the Channel Islands. Finally, they were certain that *Kumasi* was off the Casquets. They woke Robson. In the dim light of the broken cabin lamp and feebly glowing torch, he rechecked and confirmed their position. To celebrate, they had their last mouthful of brandy, then set a course two points north of northeast. Under stay and mizzen only, they dawdled along, keeping a sharp lookout. They would take no chances of running aground on the islands.

Unluckily, Cameron had to lie on his face on the bunk. He took two Aureomycin tablets and two aspirins – they acted like a Mickey Finn! During the ensuing nightmare, he knocked over the cabin lamp with his hand.

Fortunately, the glass didn't break again. Almonds and Robson covered Cameron's watch, while he strove vainly to get some more sleep. They brewed mugs of piping hot tea, loaded with sugar, then started on coffee. The end was in sight. The morning of 6 September dawned dull and grey – a sure indication that they were near England. At noon, the Royal Navy greeted them by firing dummy shells at a nearby target – a fine welcome for the first yacht from Ghana. On looking at the chart, they found they were sailing through a practice firing range and moved swiftly on.

At 2pm, they sighted England, but they could not identify the headlands. St Catherine's Point? Or the Needles? Or were they near St Alban's Head? As they scoured the pilot and charts, a mist came down. *Kumasi* drifted under sail slowly northwards. As Cameron made tea, there came a loud shout, 'Shambles'! There was the lightship 100 yards away in the rain and mist. Instantly, they knew where they were; they also knew about the dreaded Portland Race. They tacked round the lightship. The skipper decided that their first port of call would be Portland, not Ryde. They crept slowly landwards in the gathering rain, past the headland. Cameron got out the pilot to study the approaches to Portland Harbour. They made out a grim entrance. A grey, sinister-looking frigate swooped past them and a submarine nosed its way in.

Almonds was at the tiller. On a port tack, they slipped in between forbidding walls. The Ghana flag drooped, wet and oily, at their stern. They tacked to and fro towards the yacht anchorage. In the rising wind, they made little progress, so they started the Brute and approached a large motor yacht. Its deckhand told them they would be more comfortable in Weymouth. Off they chugged out of the bleak harbour, edging their way past gleaming yachts and shining motor cruisers, up the river into Weymouth. They tied up at the jetty, stepped ashore in the drizzle and shook hands silently.

Almonds had satisfied his dream. He told me that Cameron and Robson had dreams, too, but they didn't do anything as adventurous, before or after, as crewing on the maiden voyage of the ketch Kumasi. Almonds had overcome every obstacle: mechanical failures, the loss of the sea anchors, the exhausting and perilous refuelling of the Brute and even the cantankerous Brute himself. He did so through skill and determination. After covering 5,000 miles, a man came up and welcomed them with the words, 'Anything to declare?'[6]

A phalanx of press met *Kumasi* and were given a polite but reserved reception from the reeling men (it took a few days for them to get their 'land legs' back). Among the questions was: 'At one point, you were twenty-three days at sea without sight of land. How did you get on with each other?' No doubt sometimes they did get on each other's nerves, but real comrades in adventure always leave out the downsides afterwards. One newspaper headline read: 'The soldier home from the sea'. Another said: 'Bold Major's hazardous trip'. The Scottish press picked up that an Edinburgh man and a Dundee man had made the amazing voyage. Lockie, Gloria and I stayed in Weymouth for a few days to welcome them back. Then, my father sailed on up the Channel and turned north towards Lincolnshire.

A solitary SAS man greeted Almonds on his way up the River Witham to Stixwould. Former wartime 1st SAS Trooper Stanley Hayes from Boston was fishing from the riverbank and saw my father sailing home from Africa.[7]

Chapter Twenty-One

LAST ESCAPE

At 23.59 on 31 December 1960, I was in the kitchen with my father at Stixwould when he left the army for the third and last time. On relinquishing his commission, he was granted the honorary rank of major. Having not bothered at Freetown about the Sierra Leone training job, he had subsequently been offered it. However, before he could think about it, the War Office switched his posting to Chepstow. He did not want a 'pen pushing' job in the UK and was not going to accept an ordinary job at this stage of the game. He hung up his sword.

After the *Kumasi* trip publicity had died down, he continued to receive letters about it. One wartime SAS man, George Mortimer, wrote:

'There can only be one Almonds who came home in a boat the way you did. You're still crazy… you always went hunting alone and carried your rifle in the crook of your arm. My most vivid recollection is of you standing 200 yards from the Officers' Mess before going on one of your hunting expeditions. You were the Duke of Argyle's pet dislike. He, of course, never knew you: one rifle; a hundred rounds; one fighting knife; one axe and you equals one haunch of venison. That it was out of season, we learned too late… I joined the troop at Inverary with Bob Lilley. Duffy is still alive; Doug Margates fell on his feet… SQMS, GHQ Cairo, living the life of riley with a wad big enough to choke a horse. Do you remember Christmas 1940 in that LSI? Cold as hell; we could see Largs on the horizon but no leave.

There were more hangovers than pullovers on Christmas Day morning. Jelly[1] came down and wished us all a Merry Christmas.[2] Do you remember when we went to do that job at Benghazi and something measuring 6 feet, 6 inches was laid aft, spewing its ring up?'[3]

Almonds remained a keen sailor. No thought of risks – for any of us. John, at eighteen, sailed *Kumasi* from Wells-next-the-Sea back across the Wash, one of the trickiest bits of water in the UK, single-handed, with four sails, in rough weather to Boston. On one occasion in the Wash, I took a school friend to help crew. We lost a boathook. I went over the side, swam after it and got it. At Stixwould, on the narrow River Witham, John and Gloria put up one mast and a sail and tacked *Kumasi* up as far as Bardney. Above the riverbank, she caught the wind beautifully. She must have looked a bit odd from the land side, which was below river level, with just the top of a mast and sail going along above the green bank. Turning her round in the confined space at Bardney was complicated. There was maintenance, too. At Cromer, we would red-lead one side of her hull, then sleep in the car until the tide lifted her and went out again, before red-leading the other side. The smell inside *Kumasi* was not unpleasant: creosote, seawater and oilskins.

Dudley Apthorp started a boatbuilding firm and persuaded my father to be a director.[4] He never forgot the way that Almonds had built the garage, workshop and canoe in Dessie. He and his wife, Ann, came to visit and Dudley told Ann he liked my father more than any other man he had met.[5] John was at Sandhurst, but Gloria and I were only fifteen and still at school. Since the boatbuilding firm was in its early days, my father went looking for a job. It was difficult – nobody wanted an ex-army officer – but soon he got one working for the Bardney Sugar Factory. This was the first and (as it turned out) the last Lincolnshire Beet Sugar Co. Ltd.

As children at Stixwould during the holidays, we were woken in the mornings – *very* early in the mornings – to the rumble of massive sugar beet lorries as they tore past our house to Bardney, a few miles away. They continued all day, one after the other, until well after nightfall. A relatively short window of opportunity in the autumn required the beet to be harvested and transported before the winter frosts.

Not for nothing was this highly efficient effort called 'the sugar beet campaign' each season. The factory had been opened in 1927, thanks to the efforts of Mr Henry Beacon and the amazingly rich and productive

Lincolnshire soil. On his first day at Bardney, Almonds worked for Walter Bereken (a former German Army parachutist, so they had jumping in common). For one week, my father was part of a painting gang. In the second week, he joined the engineering department and from there he progressed into the laboratories and the esteemed task of 'sugar boiling'. Alan Spittlehouse, another colleague, asked my father why he was working there after all he had done. He replied, 'It's just a different sort of challenge.'[6]

Kopyt thought his brother-in-law had done a 'Lawrence of Arabia'. After being a major in the army, he would surely feel lost at the factory, but Almonds reverted to country type born and bred. He was useful and versatile. He initiated several successful technical changes and attended courses. Above all, he enjoyed it. Always regretting his lack of formal education, my father did not know whether it had really held him back. He knew he had gifts, but only partly accredited his self-taught knowledge and skills. 'University of Stixwould,' he always said, when asked in the Mess which university he had attended. But it was his country upbringing that had saved him when an escaping POW in enemy territory. As a boy, he would lie in a field and sneak up on 'Colonel Bags' – the cow so called because she had plenty of room on her 'chest' for medal ribbons. He perfected his stalking then; what would it take to avoid startling a pheasant?[7]

A neighbour in the village, Peter Holden, also worked at the Bardney factory. Sometimes, he and Almonds went to work at night together. One evening after they had gone, Peter's wife, village postmistress Elsie Holden, heard a knock at the door. It was Lockie. Elsie invited her in and they talked and laughed all night. It was some kind of companionship they did not know with their husbands. Elsie Holden told me this story when she was dying. She added, 'Your father was always, always the same, a perfect gentleman. He could be pessimistic, but he never panicked. He was totally self-reliant.'[8] At the sugar beet factory, when discussing whose turn it was to carry out a task, Almonds would say, 'Here; if it's a job, give it to me.' He was always busy. At home, he built a large workshop with adjoining double garages and a second summer house.[9]

A work supervisor, a Russian, Ross Muscherness, and another, Ken Dannatt became friends. They all wanted to sail. Nearly every Friday, these *matelots* would go straight from work in my father's old Humber Super Snipe and drive like mad to the *Kumasi*. During the summer, she was moored at Wells-next-the-Sea, Wainfleet Haven, near the bird sanctuary, or at Saxmundham. On return from one sailing trip, the harbour master told them to moor near some fishing boats. They dropped anchor and came in by dinghy. When they went back the next time, the fishermen were up in arms. *Kumasi* was lying over their mussel beds. The weather did not deter them. On one filthy night, with conditions worsening, they had a drink in the local pub with the harbour master.

'You're not going out tonight?' he said.

'Oh yes, we are!' came the response.

He remonstrated with them. The local lifeboat master also advised them not to go. They went out. The storm increased still more to a Force 9 gale. Almonds stood chatting. Nothing bothered him as he moved with the motion of the boat. He was totally confident and self-reliant.[10]

The Brute still lived up to his name. Almonds remained just as patient, pulling and pulling to coax him into life. The day the Brute finally died, *Kumasi* was nearly ploughed under by a huge cargo ship in Boston harbour. Had the Brute not been such an obstreperous beast, they might have felt sorry for him. As John, Gloria and I went off to join the army, I had the sad task of drafting a sales advertisement for *Yachting World*. *Kumasi* sold quickly and sailed away to adventures new.

Almonds and Muscherness were always building something. George North, a welding engineer, used to do bodywork on my father's car. They went to a breaker's yard and chose an old Humber Hawk to renovate. 'Now, George, is this one alright?' my father asked. They were both good at bashing cars around. This one was given a new radiator, a new wing and front bumper. Other men at the factory had said they would never do it, but in due course the car was like brand-new. [11]

When the factory closed in 2001, David Miles compiled a comprehensive history. Among the employees given a special mention was the following:

'1962

On 1 April 1962, Mr John Edward Almonds became an employee of the factory… worked as a Spare man, then went on to the Carbs Evaporators, Vacuum Pans and eventually progressed to become an Instrument Mechanic until he left in February 1973. *It is only in retrospect that Mr Almonds has become renowned for his part in the formation of the elite Special Air Service, started in 1941.* [My italics].[12]

As usual, my father had not mentioned the war to anyone.

He loved an engineering challenge and had always admired the ancient techniques of using rollers, wedges and levers. He used them in one of his last projects: a pair of large double garage doors. Massive, they would have done credit to the Panama Canal lock gates. He manoeuvred them into place and secured them; at this point, he was well into his eighties.

The SAS Association and the annual 'L' Detachment reunion got his full attention. He attended lunches in Hastings and the unveiling of a statue to Paddy Mayne in Newtownards. There, my father was unusually vocal when talking to the press about Mayne. Almonds went on trips to France, teaming up with Stirling, Jellicoe, Fitzroy Maclean and others. They all wore dark glasses in the morning to hide the effects of the previous night's carousing. Stirling was very generous to former SAS men (he set Dave Kershaw up with a fish and chip shop). Sometimes Stirling saw a real need and felt the urge to be generous on the spot. He would ask my father to slip him a £20 note (a lot of money in the 1970s), so my father went well prepared and did not ask for any of it back. My parents were honoured to attend a luncheon when Stirling was knighted in 1990. He died later that year.

Almonds maintained a lively interest in world affairs. One evening, sitting with a friend, TV coverage of Vietnam provoked him to comment, 'Look at that. Every gun in the world's going off. If you're street fighting, it takes one crack. This lot have battered the place to death – and killed civilians, too. They've razed it to the ground and then said, "We've saved you".'[13]

Ray Bell was the local country bobby.[14] In those days, if a village had no pub (Stixwould had none), there was usually somewhere else where men met, smoked and chatted. This was often the workshop of a local tradesman, who had a well-heated workshop and a habit of working long hours. In Stixwould, this was the local mechanic, 'Chipper' Hardwick. He had been at the village school with Almonds and had the job of keeping Bell's police moped on the road (no easy task).

On arrival, Bell asked Hardwick about the important people in Stixwould. Hardwick listed landed gentry and farmers. Bell then asked who the interesting people were. Hardwick described Almonds: 'He went to the village school, joined the army, helped found the SAS, won more medals than a man can shake a stick at, built a boat, sailed it back from Africa and tied it up at Stixwould. He's interesting alright.' Intrigued, Bell knocked at Almonds's door and introduced himself. Lockie immediately invited him in for a cup of tea. She showed Bell some brass cannon Almonds was completing.

Since they both enjoyed making things, they visited his workshop. Bell read the log of Kumasi's maiden voyage. He was stunned by the task of making the boat, then the voyage and all the problems encountered. 'Don't forget,' he said, when I interviewed him, 'this was before the Chichester and Rose voyages.' The log was extraordinary: a Force 10 gale went unremarked upon. Almonds wasted no energy on panicking or worrying. He had no contingency plan other than what was up his sleeve. He relied on great hidden physical and spiritual strength.[15]

The second summer house, *Valhalla*, was in a wood half a mile down the road to Woodhall Spa. Bell noticed that Almonds was 'just as effective building *Valhalla* as he was when marking 1,000th of an inch on his lathe.' They shared the tranquillity of the place; when my father created a pond there, it became a nature reserve. Almonds could hold a tit-bit of food and a robin would take it from his hand. Bell told me, 'He was a gentleman'.

A curious police mobile crew wanted to go and check out *Valhalla*, but Bell persuaded them not to. He threw in words like 'Norse mythology', 'slain heroes who feast for eternity' and 'voodoo'. He had in mind the words of Sir Robert Mark: 'No matter how drastic, there are no circumstances which cannot be made worse by a visit from the Police'. Bell's colleagues agreed to give the place a wide berth.

By 1963, John, Gloria and I had all joined the army: the 'family firm'. John served with the Royal Corps of Signals before passing SAS selection and commanding one of the Hereford squadrons. Gloria was a technical analyst on sensitive work on the Isle of Anglesey. And twenty years after my father's French Picnic in the Forest of Orleans, I was doing my officer training, before also serving with Signals. In a family represented in the army from guardsman to brigadier, rank is immaterial; it is just about different jobs. But when all three of us went home on leave at the same time, my mother noticed something. John's and my kitbag contents were strewn everywhere, while Gloria's bed-space was neat and tidy. 'Hmm,' said Lockie, 'I can see who's living in the Mess with a batting service and who isn't.' In the 1990s, the whole family went to war: John's wife, Marion, and their two daughters all served in the Gulf War.

In 1997 came the greatest challenge. My mother died suddenly. Beautiful, vivacious, articulate Lockie was gone. They had been married fifty-seven years. Loyalty was her strong suit, but he had met his match in her as a young Bristol policeman when she had broken off their relationship. For three months, it had troubled him so much that he lost weight. She did not give in. In the end, her mother had got them back together with a kitten needing a home. After their marriage, Lockie had gone with him everywhere she could and supported all his dreams.

My father was poleaxed. Six years older than her, he lived another eight. The following year, I accompanied him to New Zealand to create some new memories. We visited the New Zealand SAS, where he laid a wreath on behalf of the UK SAS Association and met wartime fellow escapee Merlyn Craw. We sailed, my father helming a yacht again in Auckland Bay. When *Gentleman Jim: The Wartime Story of a Founder of the* SAS was published in 2001, my father and I did many book signings and media interviews. He showed no reaction to becoming well-known.

Early on the morning of 11 September, I was at Stixwould following a book signing in Lincoln. I spotted a postcard from John to my father featuring a picture of the US Pentagon rose garden. I turned it over. On the back, my brother had written that he was there giving a briefing. He added, 'the rose garden in the Pentagon is reckoned to be the ground zero of any international terrorist attack on the US.' By the time I reached London, the attack on the Twin Towers had happened.

Paul Lincoln of the Desert Raiders took some vehicles and weapons to Hereford for the 40th anniversary of 'G' Squadron. He had several pieces of uniform on display, all labelled, including my father's donated Denison jumping smock. Lincoln was amazed by how many past and present members of the regiment stopped, stroked the material and asked him, 'Was this the actual smock that Gentleman Jim wore'? They almost worshipped it.[16]

The fine values and standards of the Guards stayed with my father for the rest of his life. Even a few weeks before his death, he was still concerned with his turnout and the trim of his moustache. His soldiering had taken him to Africa and Asia during the brushfire wars of post-colonialism, on military missions and paramilitary operations, with skirmishes and adventures – some like the boat trips of his own making. He wrote no books and gave no presentations; sufficient for him was the adventure itself. He was also a great engineer, adapting cars and designing and hand building huts, summerhouses, workshops, mess annexes, bandstands and much of the early SAS training facilities without power tools. He built a log cabin in the Forest of Orleans for himself and his men and sangers at Tobruk and in Eritrea. It was, however, as a nautical engineer that he excelled, having made by hand seven craft of varying sizes and descriptions, all of which performed well during the exacting exploits to which he subjected them.

Gloria was his main companion in his later years, in the family home where he had been born. Medically, he remained fit, though gradually less mobile. Kopyt thought the problem was due to the knee he had damaged parachuting into France. As his Italian captors had discovered in 1943, he did not take easily to confined spaces. He remained permanently young at heart, always excited by new adventure or innovation, by guns, bows and arrows, canoes, trolleys, land yachts and all the trappings of perpetual boyhood. Born in August, he died in August, and appeared to live his life in permanent high summer – with a spring foreshortened by the war, a few years of autumn and a mere few months of winter.

He told Bell, 'My life has been a series of unplanned moves.'[17] But they were also escapes and opportunities he exploited to their full potential. Over and above his soldiering, he sought adventure and explored every corner of the world in which he served. Alone, he travelled the deserts of North Africa and the Middle East, the highlands of Ethiopia and Eritrea, the coasts and jungles of Asia, the big rivers of West Africa and took on the wild Atlantic. But of all these adventures, the only exploit ever to reach the media was building and sailing home SS *Kumasi*. Had he stayed in the Coldstream Guards and ploughed one long furrow, he might have gone further in the world's terms, but he was never ambitious that way. He remained boyish, doing his duty but spending a lifetime indulging his creativity. He was a leader, too; men like Apthorp, Calvert, Gould, Robson and Cameron wanted to be part of his adventures. They sought him out.

People and peace mattered to him. A few months before he died, John took my father up to the Lincolnshire Wolds. A patchwork of fields lay spread out in front of them. 'There you are,' said my brother. 'That's what you did it all for'. He meant not only the Second World War, but the savage fighting of the 1950s during the final years of the British Empire. Later, they drove to the New Forest. My father said that the happiest moments of his life had been at the helm of *Kumasi*, nursing her through rough seas. If he could do one thing over again, it would be to build another boat like her. They were sitting on a log at the time and he was eyeing up some newly felled oaks!

Why did he return in 1961 to the house where he had been born until he died in 2005? 'Many people wouldn't understand it,' he said. 'It's quite logical to me… I live in the house my father lived in and my grandfather before him and so on. It's a tradition to live here, so that's where I live.'[18]

Some say old soldiers never die, but just fade away. It was like that for my father. He grew even quieter, ate less and his world gradually became just the house. He had no illness. My brother said,

'One morning he won't wake up for *Reveille*'. John was right. Not long after his ninety-first birthday, my father could not get out of bed. 'I've lost power,' he said to Gloria. He went into hospital for tests. They found nothing, but on 20 August 2005, he did not wake up in the morning. The three of us gathered round his bedside, holding his hands. 'Shout in his ear, if you like,' said a young male doctor. I did not dare, for fear that my father would suddenly rear up and shout back to be quiet! Instead, I whispered in his ear and squeezed his hand. He still had a full head of thick hair, now white, and his massive length and big shoulders filled the bed. All was peaceful. The young doctor said.

'He's got a very good physique.' We said nothing as there was nothing to say. Then, the doctor said, 'In fact, he's got a better physique at ninety-one than I have at twenty-three!' We all laughed. It might seem wrong to have done that around a deathbed. *Gentleman Jim* would not have had it any other way.

NOTES AND SOURCES

PROLOGUE: THE PRISONER

1   Interview with my father, John Edward Almonds, known as 'Gentleman Jim' of 'L' Detachment, 1st SAS. Hereafter 'Interview JEA'.
2   He remained in solitary confinement for seven months. Lorna Almonds-Windmill, *Gentleman Jim: The Wartime Story of a Founder of the SAS and Special Forces*, Pen Sword Books Ltd, Barnsley, 2011, p 155-158. Hereafter, 'Lorna A-W, *Gentleman Jim*'.
3   Ibid, p 142 The Italian warship made a detour to avoid Allied bombing.
4   Ibid, p 159.
5   Ibid, p 156.

CHAPTER 1: MANHUNT

1   Interview JEA.
2   Alfred Edward (Alf) Gould joined the Palestine police on 14 January 1939 as British Constable 21890. Interview 17 March, 2001 Edward Horne, author of *A Job Well Done: A History of the Palestine Police Force 1920-1948*, The Book Guild, Lewes, Great Britain, 1982. Horne was also Chairman, Palestine Police Old Comrades Association (many EPFF members had served in the Palestine police). Hereafter, 'Interview Edward Horne'.
3   '*Shifta*', singular and plural, was the name for bandits and terrorists in Eritrea. It derived from the Amharic for vagabond.
4   Interview JEA.
5   Ibid.
6   It was from weapons similar to the Savage that the US Armalite evolved, followed by other types, including the current British Army rifle the SA80. Most armies now use this small calibre weapon of about 0.22.
7   FO/1015/819, 10 April, 1951.
8   FO/371/90320, 1 May 1951. It was more likely that they were mistaken for Italians since

they were not in uniform and riding motorcycles, a form of transport in Eritrea usually identified with Italians.

9   FO/371/90320, 30 April 195.
10 Ibid, 1 May 1951. US troops in Asmara had accepted responsibility for their own security arrangements on the roads with effect from 8 November 1950. To rub salt into the wound, the State Department also announced its intention to make representations to Britain over the incident.
11 Ibid, 1 May 1951.
12 Interview JEA.
13 FO/371/90320, 1 May 1951.
14 Interview JEA.
15 FO/371/90324, 9 May 1951.
16 Interview JEA.
17 Ibid.
18 FO/371/90322. Closed until 1982, 22 May 1951.
19 A river of southwest Ethiopia, a tributary of the Baro River, which it joins at Latitude 8 degrees, 22', North and 33 degrees, 46' East.
20 JEA letter to Beatrice Noble Almonds (Almonds' mother), 26 May 1951, author's collection.

CHAPTER 2: ESCAPING THE ORDINARY

1   Lieutenant Colonel 'Paddy' Blair Mayne, DSO and 3 Bars, ex 'L' Detachment, to whom Almonds had been troop sergeant at the regiment's founding base at Kabrit, Egypt in 1941.
2   The SAS was disbanded at the end of the Second World War, despite the best efforts of its then commanding officer, Paddy Mayne, who deployed them effectively in Germany in the latter stages of the conflict. Lorna A-W, *Gentleman Jim*, p.227.
3   Interview Albert Youngman, 'L' Detachment, 1st SAS, 12 September 2001.
4   Martin Dillon and Roy Bradford, *Rogue Warrior of the SAS: The Blair Mayne Legend*, John Murray Publishing Ltd, London, 1987, photograph inside the back cover.
5   Lop Nor became China's nuclear testing ground,
6   The location of its terminal lake alternated between the Lop Nur dried basin, the Kara-Koshun dried basin and the Taitema Lake basin.
7   Lorna A-W, *Gentleman Jim*, p.228.
8   He had served with them before being recalled to the colours on the outbreak of war in 1939.
9   Interview, 2 April 2006, Ernest Miller. A Bristolian by birth, Miller was a regular lance sergeant in the Grenadier Guards and later a policeman in the Bristol Constabulary; he became assistant chief constable of the Merseyside Police.
10 Ibid.
11 Interview, Ray Bell, 10 December 2005, a friend and retired Lincolnshire policeman whose area of responsibility included Stixwould during Almonds' later life.
12 Ten years later, my brother went to the same barracks for his army medical before entering Welbeck College.
13 Scott Daniell, David, *Cap of Honour: The Story of the Gloucestershire Regiment (28th/61st Foot) 1649-1950*, George G Harrap & Co Ltd, London 1951, p136.
14 Ibid. Its most striking distinction was the Back Badge, worn at the back of the headdress, awarded for the 28th Foot's gallantry at the Battle of Alexandria in 1801, when simultaneous attacks from the front and rear were met and repulsed.
15 Interview, my brother Brigadier John Herbert Almonds, 26 November 2014. Hereafter, 'Interview JHA'.

16 Father of Alistair Darling, who became Chancellor of the Exchequer, interview JEA, 10 November 2002.

17 My father never mentioned this incident. My brother learned of it years later, when as a brigadier he visited an infantry arms school, from someone who had been an NCO at Eaton Hall and was a witness that night.

18 Interview Ricky Kopyt, 11 December 2005.

19 Letter to his mother Beatrice Almonds, dated 4 March 1949.

20 Iris May Almonds ('Lockie') letter to Beatrice Noble Almonds, 7 May 1949, author's collection.

CHAPTER 3: ETHIOPIA AND THE BRITISH MILITARY MISSION

1   He also wrote to Lockie twice a week. Interview JEA.

2   While not perfect, this arrangement worked – compared with the dismantling of the Iraqi Police after the First Gulf War.

3   *Eritrea: A Colony in Transition 1941-52*, GKN Trevaskis, RIIA, OUP, London, New York, Toronto, 1960.

4   FO/371/73841, 5 January 1949.

5   Interview JEA.

6   Interview Stuart Perry, 2 April, 2015.

7   Wingate's successful Abyssinian campaign was over by June 1941, but these early ideas on the use of unconventional irregular troops in guerrilla warfare were later developed by emerging Special Forces in the Western Desert.

8   Unfortunately, these joint live operations are not documented.

9   WO 32 9640 'Abyssinia (Code O (AK)): British Military Mission, Ethiopia and formation of Ethiopian Army (Text date 1941–1942). Originally closed until 2003; released 1983, 24 March 1947.

10 Ibid, 10 June 1941.

11 Ibid, 2 May 1947.

12 William, Daniel Lascelles, diplomat, born 19 March 1902, son of William Horace Lascelles and Madeline (sic) neé Barton, 1994–2002 *Brian Tompsett Sources*, version: 25 March 2001.

13 WO 32 9640, 4 May 1948.

14 Lascelles joined Dartmouth College in May 1917 (Admiralty No 2625), but left at the end of his fourth term at Easter 1918. Interview Dr Richard Porter, Britannia Royal Navel College, 16 February 2001.

15 He did not escape the class photograph in April 1918, but no picture of him was in the embassy in Addis Ababa when I visited in 2002.

16 In 1945, he was invested as a Companion of the Order of St Michael and St George and promoted in the Foreign Office hierarchy. In 1948, he was appointed Envoy Extraordinary and Minister Plenipotentiary to Addis Ababa and then Consul-General to the Kingdom of Ethiopia.

17 Interview, in Addis Ababa, with Geoffrey Wetherall, *Ambassa Enterprises*, 23 February 2002. Wetherall returned to Addis in 1949 and met the BMME officers playing cricket near the Princess Tsai Hospital. He met Lascelles several times, on one occasion with a visitor, Lieutenant Sandy Curle.

18 WO 32 9640, Minute 214, 6 December 1948.

19 Ibid, 17 January 1948.

20 'Ras' is roughly the equivalent in Ethiopia of a duke.

21 Interview JEA.

22 The booklet, which I found in the British Embassy Archives in Addis Ababa, is undated,

but shows Ethiopian officer cadets in training. Since the first intake of cadets at the reopened college at Holetta was in November 1950, the booklet must date from early 1951. I was unable to find any trace of subsequent editions.

23   Italy annexed it on 9 May 1936, along with the Italian colonies of Eritrea and Italian Somaliland. The Ethiopian Army continued to carry out guerrilla operations after the Italian invasion.

24   When I visited Addis Ababa in 2002, this building had become the Institute of Ethiopian Studies.

25   A type of shawl worn loosely around the shoulders, sometimes covering the head.

26   Interview Sir Wilfred Thesiger, 5 May 2001.

27   Interview JEA.

28   Ibid.

29   Ibid.

30   Ibid.

31   Ibid.

32   Ibid .

33   'Ata' meaning 'Sir' or, more commonly, used as an equivalent to 'Mr' in English.

34   The punishment was usually for taking something and refusing to give it up or for infringing Ethiopian Army regulations.

35   Interview JEA.

36   Ibid.

37   FO/371/80869, 28 December 1949.

38   Ibid, 31 December 1949.

39   Extract from the editorial column of the 'Baltimore Sun', 6 January, 1950.

40   FO 371/80870 Closed until 1981, 7 January 1950.

41   According to the Bank of England, which gives these figures all the way back to the 13th Century.

42   FO 371/80870 Closed until 1981, 17 January 1950.

43   Ibid.

44   The first modern fragmentation grenades used by the British Army.

45   FO 371/80870 Closed until 1981.

46   A movement in favour of an Italian Trusteeship.

47   FO 371/80870 Closed until 1981.

48   A 'concession' was a Government allocation of land for farming.

49   Interview JEA. My brother remembers my father saying, 'One day, the Ethiopians will take the Olympics by storm!'

50   *A Handbook of Ethiopia*, prepared by General Staff Intelligence, Khartoum, Whitehead Morris Egypt Ltd, 1941. The list of birds and animals included the giraffe, but it had disappeared by 1949.

51   Interview JEA.

52   Ibid.

53   I visited it in 2002.

CHAPTER 4: RISE OF THE *SHIFTA* BANDITS

1   From www.measuringworth.com

2   *Ethiopia, Great Britain and the US, 1941-1974: The Politics of Empire*, Harold G Marcus, University of California Press, London, 1983, p.56.

3   WO 216/723 Closed until 1982.

4   *Ethiopia, Great Britain and the US, 1941-1974: The Politics of Empire*, Harold G Marcus, University of California Press, London, 1983, p.77 and minute by Baxter, JA 1201/4 FO/371/80262, 25 May 1950.
5   WO 32 9640, 7 September 1950.
6   Interview JEA. Almonds was fortunate. If he had gone to Korea with the Gloucesters, he would have been at the battle of the Imjin River, where many were killed or captured. The North Koreans treated the POWs very badly.
7   WO/32/9640, 29 October 1950.
8   FO/371/80880, 19 October 1950.
9   The EPFF (Eritrea Police Field Force): a special paramilitary wing of the Eritrea Police with a strength of about 1,800 men specially recruited, trained and equipped to go after the *shifta*.
10 FO/371/90320, 10 March 1951.
11 Many of these reports from Asmara to FO are annotated here and there 'grp missing' as all bear 'Cypher/OTP at the top (meaning that some of the one-time message pad letter groups were garbled).
12 FO/371/80880, 4 November 1950
13 Ibid, 3 November 1950.
14 Ibid.
15 FO/371/80880, 7 November 1950.
16 General Sir Brian Robertson Bt, Commander-in-Chief, HQ MELF.
17 Interview, in Addis Ababa, Geoffrey Wetherall, *Ambassa Enterprises*, 23 February 2002.
18 The emperor spoke perfect English, but during important meetings he used an interpreter to give himself extra thinking time (as told to Geoffrey Wetherall by Lascelles). Interview, in Addis Ababa, Geoffrey Wetherall, *Ambassa Enterprises*, 23 February 2002.
19 WO 32 9640, 10 November 1950.
20 FO/371/80880, 18 November 1950.
21 Resolution 390A (V) (carried by 46 votes to 10 with 4 abstentions), *The UN and the Independence of Eritrea*, Blue Book Series, Volume XII, Department of Public Information, United Nations, New York, ISBN 92-1-100605-8.
22 It also avoided various previously mooted options for partition. There had been proposals for Eritrean inclusion in the Sudan, proposals for an independent Eritrea and proposals for inclusion in Ethiopia. FO/371/73841, text date 1949.
23 WO216//723, 7 November 1950 Closed until 1982.
24 Ibid, 28 November 1950.
25 FO/371/80880, 24 November 1950.
26 Ibid, 3 December 1950.
27 Ibid, 28 November 1950.
28 Ibid, 5 December 1950.
29 Ibid, 11 December 1950.
30 Interview Leonard Dickson, 12 April 2001.
31 Ibid.
32 FO/371/80880, 18 December 1950.
33 WO/216/723, 16 January 1951. This was agreed by the War Office.
34 A major was to remain as acting Head of the BMME until the arrival of a Military Attaché. Two officers wanted the job: the Deputy Head of Mission, Lt Col J. de la M. Herapath and the G2, Harry Hawkes. Neither of them got it and it instead went to Major W. Wingate, RA, who had served with the mission in 1948.
35 Seventy-five years later, Leonard Dickson sent it to me not long before he died in February 2015.
36 Interview Leonard Dickson, 7 August 2015.

37 He kindly sent Lockie nylon stockings, which were sometimes available in Aden but rationed in England. In 1971, my brother and Dickson met, courtesy of the SAS, and in 2001, I tracked him down.
38 FO/371/90319, 30 December 1950.
39 Interview Stuart Perry, 2 April 2015.
40 Interview JEA.
41 JEA letter to Beatrice Noble Almonds, 4 January 1950, author's collection.

CHAPTER 5: ERITREA POLICE FIELD FORCE

1 Interview Edward Horne, 17 March 2001.
2 It began officially on 16 May 1950. FO/1015/478.
3 Interview Edward Horne, 21 February 2001.
4 FO/1015/478, Proclamation 14 of the Eritrea Police Field Force.
5 Ibid.
6 Interview Sir Wilfred Thesiger, 5 May 2001.
7 Ethiopia seemed to make an effort to organise and coordinate the activities of the *shifta* gangs for political ends at the time when the Eritrean question came up for consideration at Lake Success in California, the location of the United Nations General Assembly which adopted Resolution 390A (V).
8 *Plus ca change!*
9 Victor Mallet, HM Ambassador in Rome to Foreign Office, FO/371/80869, 31 December 1949.
10 FO/371/80869, 31 December 1949.
11 FO/371/90319, 10 February 1951.
12 FO/1015/755 Opened 4 January 1951.
13 McGill had come from the Eritrea Police. FO/1015/445.
14 Interview Edward Horne, 17 March 2001.
15 Interview Anne Schlee, Duncan Cumming's daughter, 19 August 2002.
16 'Football Retrospective and Football Characters, 1920' in *The Giggleswick Chronicle*, 1920.
17 FO/371/90319, 9 March 1951.
18 FO/371/90320, 10 March 1951.
19 Ibid.
20 Ibid.
21 The eccentric Count de Bisson established his ill-fated communist settlement there in 1864. Subsequently, it became the Egyptian administration centre for this part of Eritrea and the scene of the bloody battle between Osman Digma and Ras Alula in 1885.
22 FO/371/90320, 10 March 1951.
23 Ibid.
24 WO 216/723, 10 March 1951.
25 WO 32/9640, 18 April 1951.
26 In October 1954, while Emperor Hailie Selassie was in London, he invited Almonds to a reception at the House of Lords. By then, however, he was in Singapore.
27 Lorna A-W, *Gentleman Jim*, Foreword.

CHAPTER 6: NEW 'WILD WEST'

1   At the time, Patrick Joseph McGill was British sergeant 981. He joined the Palestine police on 18 September 1931.
2   FO/1015/445. By August, there was a total establishment (with vacancies) of 1,884, of which thirty-six were UK personnel.
3   'A' Company later moved to Dongollo Camp, a new 'D' Company moved to Adi Caieh and an 'E' Reserve Company was created.
4   Interview JEA.
5   FO/371/90321, 9 April 1951.
6   Ibid.
7   Iris May Almonds' ('Lockie') letter to Beatrice Noble Almonds, author's collection. The letter is undated but must have been in April 1951.
8   Interview JEA.
9   T S Baxendale joined the Palestine police on 1 May 1941 as British Constable 2142. Post Eritrea, he became a superintendent in the Kenya police, then chief superintendent of Cyprus police, commanding a unit like the EPFF. He specialised in close quarter combat for presidential bodyguards. Interview Ted Horne.
10 British Embassy Addis Ababa Residence Library, 590 Series, Professor Edward Ullendorf, Oxford University Press, *The First to be Freed: The Record of the British Military Administration in Eritrea and Somalia 1941-43*, p.30.
11 Interview JEA.
12 Ibid.
13 Ibid.
14 FO/371/90323, 4 July 1951.
15 FO/371/90322, 4 July 1951.
16 JM Wood (but like many called 'Wood', nicknamed 'Timber') always spoke enthusiastically of Almonds. Letter, Elaine Burns, former partner of the late Tim Wood, dated 2 May 2001. Bitmead followed Wood to Rhodesia but died of sleeping sickness.
17 Interview JEA.
18 Ibid.
19 FO/371/90320, 1 April 1951.
20 Ibid, 4 April 1951.
21 Ibid, 31 March 1951.
22 Ethiopian Herald, 21 April 1951.
23 FO/371/90320, 4 April 1951.
24 Ibid.
25 Ibid.
26 Ibid.
27 FO/1015/932.

CHAPTER 7: THE EMPIRE STRIKES BACK

1   FO/371/90320, 17 April 1951.
2   Ibid, 20 April 1951.
3   Ibid, 24 April 1951.
4   Ibid, 5 April 1951.
5   Ibid, 27 April 1951.

6   Interview JEA.
7   FO/371/90322, 5 June 1951.
8   Ibid, 19 June 1951 report on *Shifta* activity, GHQ MELF to WO.
9   Ibid.
10 Ibid.
11 Ibid.
12 Ibid.
13 Ibid, 14 June 1951.
14 Ibid.
15 FO/371/90323, 15 June 1951.
16 FO/371/90322, 20 June 1951.
17 FO/371/90323, 4 April 1951.
18 Ibid, 2 July 1951.
19 Ibid, 20 June 1951.
20 Interview JEA.
21 FO/371/90322.
22 Ibid, 22 June 1951.
23 Ibid, 23 June 1951.
24 FO/371/90323, 19 June 1951.
25 FO/371/90322, 22 June 1951.

CHAPTER 8: OPERATION ROUNDUP

1   FO/371/90323.
2   FO/371/90322, 25 June 1951.
3   FO/371/90323, 26 June 1951.
4   Interview JEA.
5   FO/371/90323, 26 June 1951.
6   Ibid.
7   Ibid.
8   FO/371/90322, 4 July 1951.
9   FO/371/90323, 4 July 1951.
10 FO/371/90322, 6 July 1951.
11 Ibid, 6 July 1951.
12 FO/371/90323, 9 July 1951.
13 FO/371/90322, 10 July 1951.
14 Ibid, 16 July 1951.
15 Ibid, 30 July 1951.
16 FO 371/90323, 25 July 1951.
17 Interview JEA.
18 Interview Gloria Almonds, 17 May 2015.
19 FO/371/90322, 23 July 1951.
20 Ibid, 2 August 1951.
21 Iris May Almonds' ('Lockie') letter to Beatrice Noble Almonds, 11 August 1951, author's collection.
22 FO/371/90322, 21 August 1951.
23 Ibid, 10 September 1951.
24 Ibid, 15 October 1951.
25 Lorna A-W, *Gentleman Jim,* p169.

26   FO/371/96743.

27   Iris May Almonds' ('Lockie') letter to Beatrice Noble Almonds, 5 February 1952, author's collection.

28   FO/371/90320, 28 March 1951.

29   FO/371/96743, 1 April 1952.

30   Ibid, 21 April 1952.

31   Ibid, 20 June 1952.

32   FO/1015/932, 5 August 1952.

33   E Sylvia Pankhurst and Richard KP Pankhurst, *Ethiopia and Eritrea – The Last Ten Years of the Reunion Struggle*, Walthamstow Press Ltd, London, 1953, p.284.

34   On 11 February 1953, he was posted to the Airborne Forces Depot and on 17 March 1953, he sailed for the Far East on the *Empire Halladale*. Disembarking in Singapore on 15 April 1953, he was TOS 22 SAS Regiment the same day.

CHAPTER 9: MALAYAN PICNIC

1   After joining the SAS in 1950, Frank Williams served nineteen years with the regiment and received the British Empire Medal. After leaving the army in 1969, he took over the David Garrick pub in Hereford (now known as 'Watercress Harry's). He decorated the aptly named *Ulu* Bar in jungle style with weapons he had collected.

2   Interview Major Peter Walter, 23 July 2015. Walter went on to be commissioned and became the most decorated service person, post-WWII, earning six awards: an MBE, MC and Bar, the Order of St John and two Mentions in Despatches.

3   Interview JEA.

4   Peter de la Billière, *Looking For Trouble*, Harper Collins, London, 1994, p.116.

5   The red beret was due to Parachute Regiment influence, which 22 SAS wore instead of their sand-coloured beret (which had replaced the original white beret). I do not recall my father wearing the sand beret until John took him to the unveiling of Paddy Mayne's statue in Newtownards, when Tanky Smith, SAS Association Secretary, made them all put one on. John, having served in the regiment and trying to keep a low profile, suddenly felt very conspicuous and kept waiting for the bullet strike!

6   The Gully Gully Man was a magician who visited ships in the Middle East and elsewhere. He would perform coin, rope and card tricks. His speed and sleight of hand would leave sailors puzzled – and poorer.

7   When deployed, the SAS tended not to wear their army issue boots. Instead, they wore locally bought 'hockey boots', which only had six laces, making it much easier to remove leeches.

8   Dugdale-Pointon, T. (26 August 2007), *The Malayan Emergency (1947-1960)*, http://www.historyofwar.org/articles/wars_malaya.html

9   Osprey Men-At-Arms Series 132 *The Malayan Emergency 1948-60*, p6.

10   Another being the non-war in the Yemen in the 1960s, in which British mercenaries received unacknowledged Government support.

11   His predecessor, Sir Henry Gurney, one of the key thinkers behind the broad strategy, had been killed by guerrillas in October 1951.

12   Singapore had become a republic on 9 August 1965.

13   In 1952, their name had changed to '22 SAS Regiment'. They wore the same red beret as the Parachute Regiment, but with the SAS cap badge.

14   Lieutenant Colonel James Michael Calvert DSO and Bar.

15   *Mars & Minerva*, December 2002, p.19, footnote 184.

16 Calvert, Mike, *Fighting Mad*, Airlife Publishing Ltd, London, 1996, p.166.

17 He had had to return to it once before after escaping from an Italian POW camp and finally rejoining the SAS at Darval. He had not parachuted then for nearly three years.

18 Hoe, Alan quoting David Stirling in *David Stirling: The Authorised Biography of the Founder of the SAS*, Little, Brown and Company (UK) Ltd. 1992, front pages.

19 Interview Stuart Perry, March 2011.

CHAPTER 10: DEEP JUNGLE WARFARE

1 Interview JEA.

2 In wartime France, he had jumped at night with a kitbag strapped to his right leg, dangling 25 feet below him. That would not have worked in the tree tops of Malaya.

3 Interview Stuart Perry, 3 July 2015.

4 To the Semang people of the northern part of the Malayan Peninsula, to which the Sakai belonged, *Sakai* was a rather derogatory term meaning something like 'slave'. It is said that at one time the Sultans hunted the *Sakai* for sport.

5 The success of the 'hearts and minds' approach was well taken by the regiment and proved vital in later campaigns, including Borneo and Dofar.

6 Shortt, James G, *The Special Air Service*, Osprey Publishing, London, 1981, p20.

7 Interviews JEA and JHA.

8 Interview JEA. Sadly, Gould also went on to die by the sword, being killed years later at his own homestead in Kenya, probably by his servants.

9 Maps had not improved by the time John was on SAS Ops in the Malayan jungle in 1970.

10 Colonel John Douglas Slim, 2nd Viscount Slim OBE, DL, FRGS Interview Stuart Perry, 3 July 2015

11 Malay name of a large, curved, sharp dagger, very useful for hacking through the jungle.

12 Interview Stuart Perry, 12 July 2013.

13 John Scurr, *The Malayan Campaign*, Osprey Men-At-Arms Series 132, 1984, pp16/17.

14 The Malay for 'mealtime'.

15 Interview Stuart Perry, March 2011.

16 Interview JEA.

17 Interview Stuart Perry, 3 July 2015.

18 Lorna A-W, *Gentleman Jim*, p.69.

CHAPTER 11: SINGAPORE ISLAND

1 In recognition of the heat (and very limited air conditioning in those days), a smart shirt, trousers and no tie.

2 I met John Duck again in Bielefeld, BAOR in 1967 at 1st British Corps where I was serving as a lieutenant and he was a major. When he realised who I was, he said 'I feel old.'

3 Many military families go down the generations: in Cyprus, in 1990, John commanded Major Beattie's son, who was CO of 3 Queens. Then, later still, John's daughter, Claire, served under him when he was a full colonel in the Balkans.

4 Almonds had now started to swear sometimes, but it was usually in fun and never four-letter Anglo-Saxon words.

5 Lorna A-W, *Gentleman Jim*, p.52.
6 Instead, he went to Welbeck College, then to Sandhurst and eventually into the SAS.
7 Estuarine crocodile *Crocodylus porosus* Family Crocodylidae. They were still there when I lived in Singapore again in the early 1970s. Singapore had lizards, too, but these had narrow heads relative to their body size and longer snouts.
8 Pulau Ubin became the source of much of the hard core used later to build the new Singapore and was disfigured by quarrying.
9 *Platurus Pelamis* It is the most widely ranging snake in the world and never sets scale on land or the sea floor in its entire pelagic life.
10 RNAS Sinbang was based at Sembawang, not far from the Sembawang Rubber Estate.
11 Strangely, I never did tell my parents. I was probably too embarrassed.

CHAPTER 12: WHITE MAN'S GRAVE: THE GOLD COAST/GHANA

1 It was rumoured at the time that, concerned about a possible military coup, the Prime Minister, Dr Kwame Nkrumah, delayed the placement of African officers into top leadership roles
2 Unfortunately, accidents were all too common, often involving fatalities.
3 Interview, Iris May Almonds ('Lockie'). Hereafter, 'Interview IMA, 5 January 1997'.
4 The Queen remained sovereign of Ghana from 1957–1960. Nkrumah remained Prime Minister. On 6 March 1960, Nkrumah announced plans for a new constitution to make Ghana a republic and went on to become president.
5 In 1964, when I was an officer cadet, I met him again at the Aldershot Army Physical Training School.

CHAPTER 13: VOLTA RIVER

1 Commander Sir Robert Gillman Allen Jackson, Chairman of the Preparatory Commission for the Volta River Multipurpose Project, Gold Coast, 1953–1956; Chairman of the Development Commission, Ghana, 1956–1961; and Organization of Royal Tours in Ghana, 1959 and 1961. He was the author of *The Volta River Project (1956)*. Born in Melbourne on 8 November 1911, Jackson was appointed principal adviser to Oliver Lyttleton, War Cabinet minister in Cairo in 1941. His work with the Middle East Supply Centre encouraging local food production across many countries fostered his diplomatic and administrative skills. He was responsible for United Nations Relief and Rehabilitation Administration (UNRRA) projects in Europe, parts of Africa and the Far East. Jackson came to specialise in multiple purpose river development schemes and his obituary in *The Times* said, 'He was associated with virtually all major undertakings of this kind in the developing world.' While working on the Volta project in Ghana from 1953 to 1960, Jackson got to know Kwame Nkrumah. His time in Ghana led to the awards of Knight Bachelor in 1956[3] and Knight Commander of the Royal Victorian Order in 1962.[4] He died in London on 12 January 1991.
2 On which this account of the Volta River exploration draws, together with interviews with my brother, Brigadier John Almonds.

CHAPTER 14: RAINFOREST, ROCKS AND RAPIDS

1   Possibly the then Deben River.
2   This must have been a different Akroso, later engulfed by Lake Volta, from the one existing today just northwest of Accra.
3   Three miles north of Akosombo, the dam site.
4   The information about rock-fill dam engineering was useful later on in John's SAS days. He and others planned to blow a dam on another large African river. However, this also turned out to be a rock-fill construction and he was able to point out that such dams cannot be blown easily.
5   The gorge was through the quartzite and indurated sandstone ridges of the Akwapian Hills, with its southern end 30 miles from the sea.

CHAPTER 15: TREKS, TRACKS AND ELEPHANTS

1   Highlife dancing was associated with the local African aristocracy during the colonial period.
2   A local food made from ground sweetcorn flour, mixed with water into a kind of porridge.
3   In due course, they had offspring. We held the eggs as they hatched, then had to protect the pullets from circling black crows, who did manage to snatch some of them.
4   *Onchocerciasis*, an infection caused by the parasite *Onchocerca volvulus* (worm), spread by the bite of an infected blackfly. It was called River Blindness because the transmission was most intense in remote African rural agricultural villages, located near rapidly flowing streams. Boys with heavy infections usually had dermatitis, eye lesions and/or subcutaneous nodules.
5   *Schistosomiasis*: a type of infection caused by parasites that lived in the rivers or lakes. Symptoms included fevers, rashes and a cough. Sometimes the condition became chronic years later and more serious, leading to blood in the urine, vomiting blood and paralysis of the legs.
6   My brother heard it during his time as a director of British Telecom. The narrator, an ex-army quartermaster, found John's name interesting and asked, 'Are you related?' Then out came this story about recruiting and the gun cotton charge. When John retold the story, his daughters were outraged: 'Granddad! How could you treat those poor Africans like that?!' Views and values do change over three generations.
7   Years later, Gloria and my father discussed that night. He told her that he had seen her go out, so he had also gone out a little while later. He observed the same phenomenon, but had no explanation for it.
8   Afadja is the name of the mountain whereas 'to' in the Ewe dialect means 'mountain', therefore it is pronounced 'Afadjato' by Ghanaians. The name was derived from another Ewe word *Avadzeto*, meaning 'at war with the bush', due to the presence on the mountainside of a plant that caused severe skin irritation.

CHAPTER 16: THOSE WHO GO DOWN TO THE SEA IN SHIPS

1   *The Originals: The Secret History of the Birth of the SAS, In Their Own Words*, Gordon Stevens, Ebury Press, London, 2005, p.329.

2   Interview Ricky Kopyt, 11 December 2005.
3   Lorna A-W, *Gentleman Jim*, p.196.
4   Some were easy, consisting of a simple square of one of these primary colours. Others
     were complicated: like the blue and white checked flag for 'N' and the diagonal red and
     yellow stripes of 'Y'. Having first made a flag in the background colour, Lockie then
     appliquéd on the other required colours, double-stitching them on the machine so that
     they would withstand ocean gales.
5   WO letter P/333683/AG14 dated 7 December 1959.
6   *Daily Graphic*, (a Ghanaian newspaper), 27 February 1960, p9.
7   His letter said that he was coming to Kumasi. but sadly they did not manage to meet up.
8   WO letter BR/SP Coord/502, Major RB Parkes, Cameronians, DAAG to Adviser on
     Secondment Policy.

CHAPTER 17: MAIDEN VOYAGE OF THE KETCH *KUMASI*

1   Walt Whitman, *Sea Drift*.
2   *The Originals: The Secret History of the Birth of the SAS, In Their Own Words*, Gordon
     Stevens, Ebury Press, London, 2005, p.229.
3   Log of the Maiden Voyage of the Ketch Kumasi, Skipper Major J E Almonds, MM and
     Bar, Alan V Cameron and Gordon Robson – hereafter, 'Kumasi Log' – in author's and
     Robson family's possession
4   Kumasi Log. Cameron always wore a beard.
5   JEA airmail letter dated 25 May 1960 to Mrs Iris May Almonds ('Lockie'), in author's
     possession.
6   As *Kumasi* was gaff rigged, she had rings around the mast to keep the sail close into
     it between gaff and boom. When the gaff is hauled up, the rings should just slide up
     behind it. However, this is never easy in many a boat (including *Wug*). The answer is
     often to make the rings of a round material and even put beads on them to act as rollers.
     Kumasi's rings were made from copper strip metal, which was not round and had edges
     that tended to stick into the wood of the mast and cause the problem.

CHAPTER 18: LONELY SEA AND THE SKY

1   John Masefield, 'Sea Fever'.
2   Letter WS Pryke, dated 1 Aug 1992 – a friend to whom Almonds had written and who
     had been living in Monrovia at the time of *Kumasi's* maiden voyage.
3   I have experienced having something stolen while in a foreign hotel (clothing), only to
     find it back in its place again after complaining. This might have been what happened in
     this case.
4   He was referring to their possible posting to Freetown.
5   Lorna A-W, *Gentleman Jim*, p.28.
6   Presumed to be King Tom Quay (King Tom was a Koya Temne sub-chief; a Freetown
     cemetery is named after him).
7   The SS *Winneba*, a ship of the Elder Dempster line, in port at the time.

CHAPTER 19: WILD ATLANTIC

1   Lorna A-W, *Gentleman Jim,* p.114.
2   For the full account, see Lorna A-W, *Gentleman Jim,* p.198.

CHAPTER 20: A TRUE VIKING

1   This detail comes from Gordon Robson's diary of the trip.
2   Lapas are mussels eaten live by the people of the Azores, Portugal.
3   We later sailed her many times in the Wash and off the East Coast, on all points of sailing. John could make her run.
4   Major Vladimir Peniakoff, who set up a Special Forces unit in Cairo in 1942. Interview JEA.
5   Sadly, this was not to be as *Kumasi* reached the UK just after John went back to Sandhurst.
6   This was an approximate reading since the last reference to the log was 4,094, a few days earlier. The log only registered distance through the water and took no account of drift when the propeller was not turning. Nor did the log measure the true distance from Ghana to UK without all the tacking back and forth. The distance by sea from Ghana, along the coast, out to the Azores and into Weymouth is approximately 5,000 miles.
7   Letter, Colin Hayes (son of Trooper Hayes), dated 18 August 2001. Stanley Hayes served in 1st SAS from early 1944 until disbandment in November 1945.

CHAPTER 21: LAST ESCAPE

1   The 2nd Earl Jellicoe.
2   Letter from George Mortimer, 3 October 1960.
3   'Spewing your ring up' usually meant having an attack of diarrhoea. 'Six foot six' could be an indirect reference to David Stirling.
4   A.U.I. (LEISTON) Boat Builders and Woodworkers of Leiston, Suffolk.
5   Letter from Ann Apthorp, dated 15 January 2001.
6   Condolence card from Alan and Doreen Spittlehouse, August 2005.
7   Interview Ricky Kopyt, 11 December 2005.
8   Interview Elsie Holden, 10 December 2005.
9   Interview Walter Bereken, 10 December 2005.
10 Ibid.
11 Ibid.
12 *Bardney Sugar Factory 1927-2001 The First & Last Lincolnshire Beet Sugar Co. Ltd.,* Miles, David, Great Britain, 2002, Tucann Books, ISBN 1873257252, p.46.
13 Interview Ray Bell, 10 December 2005.
14 Bell had served in the RAF, leaving as a sergeant. He spent two years making church furniture before joining the Lincolnshire constabulary and becoming a country bobby. When he was offered the Horsington beat, he accepted it immediately.
15 Account written by Ray Bell in August 2005, after Almonds' death, in author's possession.
16 Interview Paul Lincoln, Desert Raiders, 24 February 2007. Not only did Gentlemen Jim wear it, my brother John did, too. Gloria added some rather odd knitted cuffs for him.
17 Interview, Ray Bell, 10 December 2005.
18 *The Originals: The Secret History of the Birth of the SAS, In Their Own Words,* Gordon Stevens, Ebury Press, London, 2005, p.330.

GLOSSARY

2IC	Second in Command
ADC	*Aide-de-camps* (a senior military personal assistant)
Amah	Chinese or Malay house servant
BAOR	British Army of the Rhine
Basha	An improvised shelter of poncho-type capes and a few saplings
BMH	British Military Hospital
BMME	British Military Mission to Ethiopia
CIA	Central Intelligence Agency (of the United States)
C-in-C	Commander-in-Chief
CIGS	Chief of the Imperial General Staff
CO	Commanding Officer
CQB	Close Quarter Battle
Kris	Malay dagger
CTs	Communist Terrorists (during the Malayan Emergency)
DO	District Officer
EPFF	Eritrea Police Field Force
FOAAT	Foreign Office Administration of African Territories
GHQ	General Headquarters
HQ	Headquarters
HQ MELF	HQ Middle East Land Forces
IRA	Irish Republican Army

JGs	Jungle Greens (uniform)
LO	Liaison Officer
Ladang	Patch of cleared jungle (in Malaya)
Laterite	Red earth or dust, rich in iron and aluminium
LMG	Light Machine Gun
LSI	Landing Ship Infantry
LZ	Landing zone
MBTC	Malay Basic Training Centre
MCP	Malayan Communist Party
ME	Middle East
MO	Medical Officer
MRC	Medical Reception Centre
MTO	Motor Transport Officer
NCO	Non-commissioned officer
NTs	Northern Territories (of Gold Coast and Ghana)
OC	Officer Commanding
OETA	Overseas Enemy Territory Administration
OGs	Olive Greens (uniform)
Op(s)	Operation(s) (armed forces)
OR	Other rank
OSS	Office for Strategic Services (of the United States)
PE	Physical Education
PJI	Parachute Jumping Instructor
PTI	Physical Training Instructor
POW	Prisoner of War
PR	Public Relations
QARANC	Queen Alexandra's Royal Army Nursing Corps
QM	Quartermaster
QMSI	Quartermaster-sergeant Instructor
RAPTC	Royal Army Physical Training Corps
Recce	Reconnaissance
RMO	Regimental Medical Officer
RSM	Regimental Sergeant Major
RTU	Return(ed) to Unit
RHQ	Regimental Headquarters
RNAS	Royal Naval Air Station
R&R	Rest and Recuperation

RWAFF	Royal West African Frontier Force
SDO	Senior District Officer
Sanger	Makeshift but robust temporary shelter with low walls
Sitrep	Situation Report
SMLE	Short Magazine Lee-Enfield rifle
SOP	Standard Operating Procedure
SOS	Struck of strength (of an army unit)
SSM	Squadron Sergeant Major
SQMS	Squadron Quartermaster Sergeant
TOS	Taken on strength (of an army unit)
TSMG	Thompson Sub-Machine Gun
Ulu	Jungle
UN	United Nations
USMC	United States Marine Corps
VCIGS	Vice-Chief of the Imperial General Staff
WE	Working Establishment
White area	Area cleared of CTs and known to be safe
WO	War Office (the present Ministry of Defence)
WT	Wireless telegraphy

NAUTICAL TERMS

Aft	At or towards the rear of a vessel
Backing	Change of wind direction against the sun, or anticlockwise in the northern hemisphere
Beam	The measurement of a vessel at the widest point
Bermuda(n)	A rigging with a triangular mainsail
Binnacle	The housing the ship's compass rests in
Blocks	Pulleys through which ropes or wires are led
Bobstay	Standing rigging running fore and aft to the bowsprit to stop it lifting
Boom	A wooden spar used to keep the foot of a sail extended
Bowsprit	The spar projecting forward out over the bows
Broach	Carried by a big sea, with the stern high and the bow dipped, the bow is pushed aside and the vessel goes over onto its side
Bulwark	The sides of a vessel above the level of the deck
Centreboard	A wooden 'fin' lowered and raised through the bottom of a boat to reduce sideways movement and heeling
Cleat	A fastening for ropes with two hooks pointing in opposite directions
Clew	The corner at the foot and aft edge of a sail where sheets are attached
Cockpit	The well, aft of the cabin, from which a boat is steered
Draught	The measurement under water to the deepest point of a vessel

Fore	Forward or towards the bows of a vessel
Freeboard	Height of a deck above the waterline
Gaff	A boom which extends the head and foot of a four-sided sail
Gimbals	Ringed bearings which keep an article horizontal at sea
Go About	To change direction by bringing the bows through the eye of the wind
Goose-winged	Running before the wind with sails set on either side of the vessel
Gunnel(s)	The top edge(s) of the sides of a vessel
Gybe	To change direction by bringing the stern through the eye of the wind
Halyard	A rope for raising sails or flags
Hand	Holding a sheet or halyard in the hand instead of making it fast
Hawser	A large cable or rope, usually of steel or thick wire
Horse	A wire running across a vessel's deck at the stern holding a sheet block
Horse scissors	Scissor-like supports that prop up the two booms when in harbour
Ironbound	A rocky coast without harbour or a place to anchor
Jib	The foremost sail
Ketch	A two-masted vessel with a shorter after mast (mizzen)
Lazy guys	Makeshift lines to steady the booms and stop them crashing about
Lee	The side away from the direction in which the wind is blowing
Luff	The forward edge of a sail
Mizzen	The after mast in ketches and yawls and the sails attached to them
Pooped	A following, heavy sea overtakes a vessel and lands on board
Pulpit	The rail, above deck level, around a vessel's bows
Reach	Sailing while having the wind between aft and close to the wind
Scuppers	Drainage exits in the bulwarks through which deck water runs away
Sea anchor	A bucket-shaped drogue of canvas usually narrowing to an open end used to slow down the movement of a vessel and improve stability

Sennit	Cordage made by plaiting several strands of similar width fibres
Sheet	A rope from the bottom corner of a sail used to control it
Stanchions	Supports for the wire lifeline that runs around the deck of a boat
Tabernacle	The housing for the bottom of a mast when it is lowered
Tack	To make headway against an opposing wind by sailing alternate short stretches, close to the wind, to port and starboard
Throat	The end of a gaff or boom near the mast
Thwarts	The seats in a rowing boat, which run across it
Transom	Planking at a square-shaped stern
Warp	A rope for pulling something along or making a vessel fast

BIBLIOGRAPHY

UNPUBLISHED SOURCES

Blackwood's Magazine, August 1946, *The Intelligence Man's Guide*, Gwyn Griffin

British Embassy Addis Ababa Residence Library, 590 Series Liberation and BMA, H R Wilson, *For Want of a Nail: Britain's Aid to Ethiopia*

British Embassy Addis Ababa Residence Library, 650 Series The Hailie Selassie Years, H Lockot, *The Mission, Life, Reign and Character of Hailie Selassie I*

British Embassy Addis Ababa Residence Library, 590 Series, Professor Edward Ullendorf, Oxford University Press *The First to be Freed: The Record of the British Military Administration in Eritrea and Somalia 1941-43*

Britain in Ethiopia: The Centenary 1896-1996, Foreign and Commonwealth Office, The British Embassy Centenary, PO Box 858, Addis Ababa, Ethiopia

Log of the canoe *Discovery*, by Brigadier John Herbert Almonds, from 27 August 1956 to 4 September 1856, recording the exploration of the then existing Volta River, in author's possession.

Correspondence of John Edward Almonds (*Gentleman Jim*) and Iris May Almonds (*Lockie*), in author's possession.

Farrell, Brian P, *Mind and Matter: The Practice of Military History with Reference to Britain and Southeast Asia, The Journal of American History*, Vol. 93, No. 4 (Mar., 2007), pp.1146-1150, Oxford University Press

Ship's Log of The Maiden Voyage of the Ketch *Kumasi*, by Alan Cameron, from 15 May 1960 to 6 September 1960 and signed by the Captain, John Edward, and crew (Alan Cameron and Gordon Robson). Three bound copies exist, one each in the possession of the Almonds, Cameron and Robson families.

Hack, Karl, *"Iron Claws on Malaya": The Historiography of the Malayan Emergency*, Journal of Southeast Asian Studies, Vol. 30, No. 1 (March 1999), pp.99-125, Cambridge University Press, on behalf of Department of History, National University of Singapore

Handbook of Eritrea Volume II Communications, General Staff (Intelligence), Headquarters Troops, Sudan, July, 1943, in author's possession.

Handwritten account of the Maiden Voyage of the Ketch *Kumasi* by Gordon Robson, in his family's possession.

Mars & Minerva: The Journal of the Special Air Service

Ethiopia Star 1940-1942, Imperial War Museum, J class 486

Ethiopia Review 1957-1961, Imperial War Museum, J class 347

New Times & Ethiopia News: For Liberty, Justice, Democracy, Imperial War Museum, J class 2589

Taylor, Don, *The Commonwealth and the British Empire, 1945-1958*, Frederick A. Praeger, New York, 1960

Van Wingen, John and Tillema, Herbert K, *British Military Intervention after World War II: Militance in a Second-Rank Power*, Journal of Peace Research, Vol. 17, No. 4 (1980), pp. 291-303, Sage, Publications, Ltd Stable URL: http://www.jstor.org/stable/424467

The National Archives (formerly The Public Record Office)

PRO/FO/371/73841

PRO/FO/371/80869

PRO/FO/371/80870 (closed until 1981)

PRO/FO/371/80880

PRO/FO/371/90319

PRO/FO/371/90320

PRO/FO/371/90321

PRO/FO/371/90322 (closed until 1982)

PRO/FO/371/90324

PRO/FO/371/96743

PRO/FO/1015/445

PRO/FO/1015/478
PRO/FO/1015/755
PRO/FO/1015/819
PRO/FO/1015/932
PRO/WO/216/723 (closed until 1982)
PRO/WO/32/9640 (originally closed until 2003, released 1983)

SECONDARY SOURCES

Almonds-Windmill, Lorna, *Gentleman Jim The Wartime Story of a Founder of the SAS*, Pen & Sword, London, 2011
Barber, Noel, *The War of the Running Dogs: Malaya 1948-1960*, Cassell Military Paperback, London, 7 October 2004
Barker, AJ, *Eritrea 1941*, Faber & Faber, London, 1966
Buxton, David Roden, Travels in Ethiopia, Lindsay Drummond Limited, London, 1949
Calvert, Mike, *Fighting Mad*, Airlife Publishing Ltd, London, 1996
de la Billière Peter, *Looking For Trouble*, Harper Collis, London, 1994
Dillon, Martin and Bradford, Roy, *Rogue Warrior of the SAS: The Blair Mayne Legend*, John Murray Publishers Ltd, London, 1987
Dugdale-Pointon, T. (26 August 2007), *The Malayan Emergency (1947-1960)*, http://www.historyofwar.org/articles/wars_malaya.html
General Staff Intelligence, Khartoum, *A Handbook of Ethiopia*, Whitehead Morris Egypt Ltd, 1941
Hoe, Alan, *David Stirling: The Authorised Biography of the Founder of the SAS*, Little, Brown and Company (UK) Ltd, 1992
Horne, Edward, *A Job Well Done: A History of the Palestine Police Force 1920-1948*, The Book Guild, Lewes, Great Britain, 1982
Marcus, Harold G ,*Ethiopia, Great Britain and the US, 1941-1974: The Politics of Empire*, University of California Press, London, 1983
Department of Public Information, United Nations, *The UN and the Independence of Eritrea*, Blue Book Series, Volume XII, New York, ISBN 92-1-100605-8.
Ethiopia – The Biblical Cush, Transaction Publishers, New Brunswick, NJ08903
Eritrea and Ethiopia: The Federal Experience
Ruth Lyob, *The Eritrean Struggle for Independence: Domination, resistance, nationalism 1941-1993*, CYP, Cambridge, 1995

John L Noyce, *Eritrea: A Bibliography*, John L Noyce, PO Box 450, Brighton, 1978

Kinnock, Glennis *Eritrea: Images of War and Peace*, Chatto & Windus, London, 1988

Dr David Pool, *Est Movement and Hegemony: The Eritrean People Liberal Front and the Cities 1977*, University of Manchester Ap. 1992

Pakenham, Thomas, *The Mountains of Rasselas*, Weidenfeld & Nicolson, London, 1998

Pankhurst, E Sylvia, *Ethiopia and Eritrea: The Last Phase of the Reunion Struggle 1911-1952*

The Ethiopian Orthodox Church, Editors Aymro Wondmagegnehu and Joachim Motovu, The Ethiopian Orthodox Mission, Addis Ababa, 1970

Sandford, Christine, *Ethiopia Under Haile Selassie*, JM Dent & Sons Ltd, London, 1946

Scott Daniell, David, *Cap of Honour: The Story of the Gloucestershire Regiment (28th/61st Foot), 1649-1950*, George G Harrap & Co Ltd, London, 1951

Scurr, John and Chappell Michael, *The Malayan Campaign: 1948-60*, Osprey Publishing Limited, London, 1982

Shortt, James and McBride, Angus, *The Special Air Service*, Osprey Publishing Limited, London, 1981

Trevaskis, GKN, *Eritrea: A Colony in Transition 1941-52*, RIIA, OUP, London, New York, Toronto, 1960

Wrong, Michela, *I Didn't Do it For You*, Harper Perennial, London, 2005

Smith E D, *Counter-Insurgency Operations: 1 Malaya and Borneo*, Ian Allan Ltd., Shepperton, 1985

Work, Ernest, *Ethiopia: A Pawn in European Diplomacy*, Macmillan, London, 1935

INDEX

Abbai, Haile, 51
Abdalla, Hagai, 57
Abia, 83
Abidjan, 176-178, 180, 182, 183, 195
Abidjan Canal, 177
Aborigines, 92
Abuna Marcos, 43
Abyssinia, 19
Accra, 125, 126, 129, 130, 152, 153, 167, 169, 178, 188, 189, 209, 210
Accra Airport, 172
Ackele Guzai, 69
Ada, 129, 131, 152
Addis Ababa, 14, 22, 23, 25, 28, 36, 84
Aden, 44, 47, 72
Adi Caieh, 12, 31
Adi Laghan, 41
Adi Nefas, 42
Adi Quala, 65
Adi Quitta, 31
Adi Ugri, 33, 40, 47, 54, 57, 78, 79, 84
Admiralty, 167
Adomi Bridge, 153
Adowa, 43, 51
Adua, 80
Afadjato (Mount Afadja)
Africanus, Leo, 157
Agumatsa, 163
Agordat, 53, 65
Airborne Forces, 95
Air Officer Commanding, 72

Air Operations, 76
Air Station, 112, 113
Ajena, 152
Akele Guzai, 40, 71, 73, 76, 80
Aklilou, 65
Akroso, 149
Alban Hills, 176
Alexandra Grammar School, 109, 113
Almadies, 197
Almonds, Gloria, 11, 19, 81, 94, 109-114, 116, 117, 119, 121-124, 128, 154, 156-158, 161-163, 165, 167, 231, 233, 235, 237, 239, 240
Almonds, Gwendoline, 19
Almonds, Iris May ("Lockie") 16, 17, 19, 58, 82-84, 90, 110, 112, 115, 116, 119-122, 126, 154, 155, 158, 159, 162, 165, 166, 178, 182, 190, 219, 231, 234, 237
Almonds, John H, 11, 94, 99, 101, 105, 106, 109, 111, 112, 114, 116, 118-120, 123, 124, 130-135, 140, 143-150, 154, 158, 163, 165, 172, 233, 235, 223-7, 239, 240
Almonds, John Edward, "Gentleman Jim", MC & Bar, Croix de Guerre, POW, 3
    Closure of SAS, joining 'Glorious Glosters' 14-20
    British Military Mission to Ethiopia, 21-48
    Eritrea Police Field Force, 5-13, 49-85
    SAS Malayan Emergency, 89-97

Jungle warfare, 98-108
Singapore, 109-123
Gold Coast/Ghana 124-129
Volta River expedition, 130-154
Trekking in Northern Territories, 155-163
Building the ketch *SS Kumasi*, 164-170
Maiden voyage of *SS Kumasi*, 171-231
Almonds-Windmill, Lorna
  Childhood, 13-20, 17-20, 90-94, 99, 105, 109-128
  Running away from home, 122
  Trekking in Northern
  Territories, 155-163
  Joining the British Army, 237
Ambassador Hotel, 188
America, American, 8, 32, 33, 44, 46, 51, 57, 165, 187-190, 196, 210, 238
Amharic, 25, 32, 41
Amnesty, General, 68-70, 72, 77, 81
Ampang Road, 105
Angelsey, 237
Antunes, Senhora, Maria, 218, 219
Appollonia, 191
Apthorp, Major, Dudley, 28, 30, 31, 33, 35, 36, 44, 233, 239
Apthorp, Ann, 233
Appiah, 159, 163
Arab, Arabic, Arabs, 52, 65, 68, 190
Ardennes, 14
Argylle, Duke of, 232
Ark of the Covenant, 55
Armenia, Armenian, 157
Army Air Corps, 17
Army School of Tropical Medicine, 114
Arosdidier, Monsieur, 178
Artists Rifles, 103
Artur, Senhor, 216, 217
Arturo, Senhor, Brun, 216, 218, 219
Asfaha, Tecle, 10, 11, 55, 78, 81
Asfaha, Grazmac Ilfai, 10, 55, 79
Ashanti, 124, 126
Ashanti Wars, 155
Askari, 6, 62, 75
Asmara, 8, 11, 13, 22, 31, 33, 36, 42, 44, 46, 47, 50, 51, 53, 54, 56, 57, 59, 60, 61, 65, 67, 70-72, 74, 77, 79, 80, 83-85
Assab, 42, 46, 47
Assaorta, 70, 73, 74, 77
Assay, 46
Assembly, 65

Atbarah River, 13, 60
Atillo, Della, Sante, 65
Atlantic Hotel, 196
Atlantic Ocean, 182, 197, 201, 202, 208, 209, 219, 239
  Mid Atlantic Ridge, 214
Atuabo, 174
Auld Lang Syne, 123
Australia , Australian, 104
Aureomycin, 227, 229
Auster aircraft Autocrat5J1, 8, 9, 10, 11, 52, 53, 59, 62, 103, 104
Avila, Senhor, Machado, 217, 220
Avila, Senhora, Olga, 216, 219
Avila, Senhorita, Helen Marie, 216, 219
Awareh, 48
Awati, Hamid Idris, 12, 32
Azores, x, 202, 205-216, 220

Balliol College, Oxford, 25
Baltic Sea, 196, 199
Banana Islands, 192
BAOR (British Army of the Rhine), 115
Baraka River, 72
Baraka, 60
Barati, Abdulla, 75, 77
Bardney, 233, 234
Barentu, 11, 53
Bath, 28
Bather, Mr 148, 154
Bathurst, 194, 195
Batie, 46, 47
Batu Caves, 94
Baxendale, Stanley, 51, 59, 63
Bay of Biscay, 182, 221, 226
BBC, 205, 207, 224
Beacon, Mr, Henry, 233
Beattie, Major, 111
Beaulieu Boy, 118
Beit Gherghis, 75
Belgium, Belgian, 39, 189
Belgian Congo, 211
Belize, 18
Bell, Sergeant, Raymond, 236, 237, 239
Bell's Palsy, 121
Benghazi, 3, 233
Beni Amer, 8, 12, 52, 65, 72, 76
Benin, Bight of, 173
Bennett, Sergeant, Robert ('Bob'), 14, 89
Bereken, Walter, 234
Bergen, 14

Bermuda, 202
Bermuda sloop, 116
Bessie & Co, 46
Bettancourt, Senhor, 216-219
Bevin, Ernest, 54
Bewitched, Bothered and Bewildered, 114
Biggles, 30
Bijagos Islands, 194
Bilai, Ata, 29
'Birmingham screwdriver', 116
Bitmead, William, ('Titch'), 63
Blackbushe Airport, 125
Blocco di Indepenza, 33
Bohame, Adum, 76, 79
Bolgatanga, 129, 161, 162
Bolivia, Bolivian, 8
'Bombay Fornicator', 106
Bora's Leap, 45
Borchenna River, 35, 45
Borling, Fred, 196
Bostik, 150
Boston, 165, 168, 179, 231, 233, 235
Bottomless Pit, 177
Bournvita, 210
Boy Named Sue, 114
Boy Scouts, 105
Boys Company, 124, 128, 156, 158-160, 163
Branksome Towers Hotel, 28
Brans, 63
Brazier-Creagh, Brigadier, Rupert, 95
Bren Light Machine Gun, 11, 71, 90, 104
Brierly, 196
Briggs, Lieutenant General, Sir Harold, 94
Bristol, 83, 124, 238
Bristol Police, 15
Bridewell, 15
  City Police Headquarters, 16
  Trinity Road, 16
  Britain, British, 8, 10, 21-43, 45, 48, 50, 51, 54, 57, 62, 65, 66, 68, 70, 71, 75, 76, 78-80, 84, 90-94, 99, 101, 102, 105, 122, 124, 126, 152, 154, 156, 165, 166, 178, 190, 192, 196, 198, 206, 211, 214, 219, 220, 228, 232, 233
British Empire, 90
British Empire Medal, 56
British Military Attaché, 85
British Military Hospital (BMH) Singapore, 121, 122
British Overseas Airways Corporation (BOAC), 125, 165

British Palestine Police, 49, 52, 57, 59, 94
British Military Mission Ethiopia (BMME), 7, 19, 21, 23-28, 30, 36, 39, 44, 46, 48, 54
Brooke, Lieutenant Colonel, Oliver, 48, 97, 105
Bruku, Sergeant, Emmanuel, 168
Brownies, 114
Browning, 48, 100
Brute, the, 179, 180, 182, 188, 193, 194, 198, 202, 203, 226, 227, 230, 235
Bugatti, 19
Burma, 9, 94, 124
Butler, Brigadier, 24
B-29 Super Fortress, 15

Cabinet, Government, 206
Cairn Court Hotel, 108
Cairo, 232
California, Californian, 129
Calvert, Daniel, 60, 61, 96, 168, 239
Calvert, Michael, 60, 96, 107
Cameron, Alan, 168, 170, 172-186, 188-191, 193-198, 200, 202-204, 206-213, 215-230, 239
Canada, Canadian, 42, 46
Candelaria, 218
Campos, Senhor, Maris Raquel, 218
Canary Islands, 200, 203, 208, 213, 215
Cap Blanc, 199, 200, 202
Cape Bald, 195
Cape Canaveral, 211
Cape Coast, 173
Cape Mount, 187, 191
Cape Palmas, 181-184, 186
Cape Roxo, 195
Cape Shilling, 192
Cape Sierra Leone, 192
Cape Three Points, 174
Cape Timirist, 198, 199
Cape Verde Islands, 196
Cape Vert, 197
Capomazza, 72
Carabinieri, 3, 22
Carbine, M. 30, 6
Casquets, 229
Cashi, Haile, 51
Catch, 73
Cestos of Monrovia, 225
Challa, 30
Chambers, Lieutenant, 40, 41, 52, 53
Changi, 109

Changi University, 106
Changi Point, 119
Chapman, Colonel, Spenser, 93
Charrington, Angus, 99, 102, 103
Chelmsford, 15
Chepstow, 232
Cherbourg, 228
Chester, 19
Chief of Police, 157
China, Chinese, 21, 62, 91, 92, 94-96, 102, 109, 114, 120
Chichester, Sir Francis, 237
Christian, Christians, 27, 28, 50, 65, 84
Christmas, 209
CIA (Central Intelligence Agency), 15
Ciao Hotel, 34, 59
Cigana, 219
(CIGS), Chief of the Imperial General Staff 25, 43
Civil Power, 122
Clifton, Bristol, 15
Cofit, 53
Colditz, 15
Cold War, 8
Coliseum, The, 93
'Colonel Bags', 234
Colonial Service, 172
Colt .45 automatic pistol, 34
Columbus, Christopher, 198
Commandos, 226
  8 Guards, 4, 21, 115
  Commonwealth, 101
Communism/Marxism, 25, 39, 72, 93, 102
Community bonds, 69
Conakry, 187
Conservative Party, 109
Constellation, 58
Constitution, 65, 72, 78
Consul Chart see Portsmouth
Cooper, John ('Johnny'), 89, 107
Coptic, Copts, 12, 33, 42, 46, 50, 51, 54, 57, 65, 69, 70, 72, 74, 75, 78
Correio de Horta, 218
Corranacudo, 10
Corinth Canal, 4
Cousteau, Jacques, 185
Court of Appeal, 68
Court Martial, 4
Cox, Lieutenant-Colonel, 74, 84
CQB (Close Quarter Combat), 99, 101
Craw, Merlyn, 238

Croix-de-Guerre, 21
Cromer, 233
Cruel Sea, The, 116
CT, Communist Terrorist(s), 93-96, 100-103
Cumming, Duncan, 6, 8, 52-54, 58, 63, 64, 66, 68-78, 80, 82-85
Cummings, William ('Bill'), 173
Cyrenaica, 22
Czechoslovakia, 25, 39

Da Costa, Senhor, Manuel Augusta, 217, 218
Daily, Express, The, 195
Daily Herald, The, 46
Dakar, 190, 194-196, 205, 207, 212
Dakota, 9, 47
D'Arguin Sea, 199
Damas, 67
Danakil, 42, 46, 47, 58
Danaland, 223
Dankyi, Kwadjo Amure, 169
Dannatt, Kenneth, 234
Darling, Lieutenant Colonel, 18
Dartmoor, 18
Dartmouth, Royal Naval College, 25
Davies, Commander, 193
Dayang, 118
Debra Berhan, 29
Decamere, 42, 73, 74, 78
Degun, Corporal, Samuel Kwame, 168
Deki Dasheim, 76
De la Billière, General Sir Peter, 89, 168
De Melo, Senhor Manuel Viera Soares, 219
De Melo, Senhora, Inez Soares, 218
Del Mahari Hotel, 125
De Melo, Senhor José Joav Soares, 219
De Melo, Senhora, Mathilde Nazare, Soares, 219
De Melo, Senhor Antonio Soares, 219
De Melo, Senhorita Ana Maria Soares, 219
Denison jumping smock, 239
Denmark, Danish, 190
Desert Locust Survey, 45
Desert Raiders, Long Range Desert Group Preservation Society, 238
Dessie, 23, 28-30, 33-35, 44-46, 233
Dettol, 186
Devil's Cauldron Rapids, 154
Devon, 168
Devonshire, HMSS, 123, 124

Dhagati, Abinama, 157
Dhagati, John, 157
Dhagati, Leo, 157
Dickson, Pilot Officer, Leonard, 44-47
Diplomatic Service, 25
Diredawa, 61
Discovery, 129, 131-136, 138, 140-142, 145, 147-151, 153
Dodecanese Administration, 62
Donnollo Basso, 8
Doody, John, 63
Dorfu, 12
Dorman, Maurice, Sir and Lady, 193
Dothée, General, 39, 40
Drew, Brigadier, Grenville, 33, 43, 51, 52
Ducal Palace Hotel, 188
Ducambia, 8, 9, 12
Duck, Lieutenant, John, 110
Duffy, Frank, 169
Duffy, Sergeant, 232
Dundee, 168, 231
Durham, 105
Dutch Baby, 115

East Africa, 48, 52, 97
Eaton Hall, 17, 18, 19
Edinburgh, 168, 231
Ein topf, 180
El Mahairjât, 198
El Manghar, 198
Elder Dempster, 193
Emba Soira, 11
Embatkalla, 12, 44
Embae, Amaré, 43
Embae, Asserassie, 41, 43, 51, 67
Embei, 42
Enfield rifle, 22
Empire, 36, 66, 239
Empire Ken (Ubena Ken), 21
Empire Windrush, 90, 91
England, English, 59, 91, 114, 116, 124, 125, 151, 164, 166, 178, 189, 225, 230
English Channel, 221, 224-229
Eridist, 83, 84
Eriforce, 84
Eritrea, Eritreans, x, 5, 19, 21, 22, 30, 31-33, 39, 42-44, 47, 49-53, 55-58, 63-66, 70, 75-79, 82, 85, 93, 239
Eritrea Nuova, 51
Eritrea Police Field Force (EPFF), 7, 9, 6, 10, 12, 13, 40, 41, 45, 49-51, 53-57, 59-

63, 67, 69, 71, 73, 75, 76, 80, 82-85, 94
Erta Ale, 35
Eskimo, 110
Ethiopia, 5, 19, 21, 23, 24, 27, 32, 35, 36, 39, 41-48, 50, 51, 53-55, 58, 61, 62, 64-68, 70, 73, 75, 78, 80, 84, 85, 239
Ethiopian Herald, 22, 54, 64
Ethiopian Imperial Guard, 24
Ethiopian Orthodox Church, 43
Everard, Captain, 178
Executive Officer, 123
Egypt, Egyptian, 178

Facism, Fascist, 32, 61, 62
Far East, 96, 123
Federal Act, 78
Federation of Ethiopia and Eritrea, 66, 68
Federation of Malaya, 92, 94
Federation Police Field Force, 94
Fellowship, The, 58
Fender, David, 114, 118-120
Fenwick, Major, Ian, 90
Fiennes, Sir Ranulph, OBE, ix
Fioux, Monsieur, 178
Firestone, 189
Fitzpatrick, T W, Commissioner, 32
FOAAT, 51
Force 8 Gale, 209
Forest of Orleans, 90, 97, 237, 239
Foreign Office, 8, 22, 32, 39, 43, 66, 69, 70, 72, 73, 78, 79, 83
Fort Shean, 103
Fotheringham, Colin 103
France, French, 6, 21, 34, 72, 93, 134, 177-179, 189, 196, 199, 200, 209, 212, 224, 227, 228, 236, 239
Forte Baldissera, 84
From Here To Eternity, 109
St Francis of Assisi, 82
Freeman, Peter, MP
Freetown, 170, 182, 184, 187-190, 193, 195, 232
Freetown Bay, 192
Freetown Sailing Club, 211
Frihed, 199, 200

Gabre-Heywot, Ato Saude, 46
Gambia, 206
Gander, James ('Jim'), 62
Garrard, Monsieur, 179
Garrison Engineers Department, 168

Gash River, 52, 53

Gendarmes, 178

Geneva Convention, 7

Gentleman Jim: The Wartime Story of a Founder of the SAS, 238, 240

German, Germany, 50, 81, 134, 189, 212, 234

Gerunchi, Danyata, 131, 132, 134-139, 142-144, 146-150, 154

Ghana, see Gold Coast/Ghana

Gheresghir, Chelete, 32

Ghido Railway Station, 40

Ghinda, 22, 77

Ghurkha, 105, 106, 120, 121, 165

GHQ MELF, 46

Gibraltar, 212

Gibraltar, Rock of, 90

Gideon Force, 24

Giggleswick School, 52

Gillray, 106

Gillman Barracks, 109

Glenlivet, 216

Glenroy, HMS, 192

Gloucesters Regiment/Glosters, 17, 40, 85

Goshes, 196, 197

Gold Coast/Ghana, 8, 125-127, 130, 131, 146, 147, 155, 159, 163-169, 172, 180, 189, 200, 209, 230

Gold Coast Regiment, 124

Gondar, 46

Gordonstoun, 203

Gould, 5, 10, 11, 51, 59, 94, 101, 103, 119, 120, 239

Grand Bassam, 177

Grand-Bérèbi, 182

Grant's Standfast, 207Gravina, 3

Great Bitter Lakes, 4

Great Circle, 202

Great Rift Valley, 30, 35

Greece, Greek, 46, 156

Green Spot, 105, 120

Greenwich, 211

Greenwich Meridian, 173

Guards

  Coldstream, 107, 114, 239

  Grenadier, 16, 62

  8 Guards Commando, 192

Guinea fowl, 160

Guinea, Gulf of, 129

Habtit, Georgio, 77

Hadendowa, 12

Hadgu, Zaggai, 42

Hagos, Beine, 79, 83

Hamasien, 12, 55, 72, 75, 76, 80

Harar/Duke of, 28, 35, 58

Harding, General Sir John, 96

Hardwick, George, ('Chipper'), 236

Harewood, 4th Earl, 25

Harmattan, 127, 159

Hass, Hans, 185

Hastings, 236

Hausa, 158

Hawkes, Harry, Major, 23

Hayes, George, Staff-Sergeant, 127

Hayes, Trooper, Stanley, 231

Haynes, Corporal, 51

Hazimo, 54

Heden, Sven, 14

Heineken beer, 166

Heinz Maria Restaurant, 188, 189

Henco brandy, 182

Hereford, 99, 237, 238

Highland Light Infantry, 60

'Highlife' music, 156

Himberti, 47

Hiroshima, 15

Hogarth, 106

Holden, Elsie, 219, 234

Holden, Peter, 234

Holetta, Imperial Military College, 26, 46

Holland, Dutch, 14, 190

'Horace', 158

Horfield, Bristol, 17, 19

Horne, Edward, OBE, 59

Horsington, 19

Horta, 214, 216

Hotel de Parc, 178

Hotel Ambassadeur, 188, 189

House of Commons, 33

Howard, Michael, Baron Howard of Lympne, 109

Humber, 33,

Humber Hawk, 128, 235

Humber Super Snipe, 234

HBWR&Co, 169

Iceland, 220

Iksander, 103

Il Quotidiano, 68

India, Indian, 92, 124, 168

Injera, 29

International Maritime Code, 166
IRA (Irish Republican Army) 16
Irish Channel, 226
Island in the Sun, 206, 209
Isle of Wight, 25
Isle de Gorée, 196
Ilse de Los Lighthouse, 194
Italian, Italy, 22, 23, 28, 32, 33, 39, 41, 42, 47, 50, 51, 53, 54, 56, 58, 59, 64, 65, 68-72, 78-80, 83, 84, 96, 110, 164, 168, 188, 189
Ivory Coast, 176, 179, 239

Jackson, Sir Robert, 130
Jaffa, 56
JGs (Jungle Greens), 92
Jahore, 92
Jahore, Straits of, 13, 117-120, 123, 172
Jalan Kamuning, 92
Japan, Japanese, 14, 93, 95, 111, 113, 120, 124, 196, 205
Jellicoe, Brigadier, George, 2nd Earl, 55, 236
Jerusalem, 56
Jew, Jewish, 72, 190
Jikawo River, 13
Job, 168
Johnson's Seahorse Outboard motor, 165
José, 216
Joss stick, 120
Johnson, Trooper, ('Jigger'), 104

Kablake Lighthouse, 182
Kabrit, 4, 95, 99, 116
Kagnew Station, 8
Kano, 125
Kedah, 92
Kelantan, 92, 94, 103
Kenya, 24, 189
Keren, 7, 8, 9, 10, 11, 22, 42, 44, 53, 55, 57, 59, 60, 65, 71, 75-77
Kershaw, David ('Dave'), 236
Kessie, Kobina, 189
Ketah, Second Lieutenant, Alf, 163
Kete-Krachi, 140, 144, 147, 148, 153, 154
Keymer Colonel, 193, 228
Khartoum, 13
Khormaksar, 44
Kitchener, Lord, 97
King Tom, 193
King's Own Scottish Borderers, 130

Kintampo, 129, 162
Kipling, Rudyard, 21, 206, 226
Kopyt, Richek ("Ricky"), 19, 165, 234, 239
Koran, 156
Kordofan, 52
Korea, 40, 42
Korean War, 106
Kpong Rapids, 154
Kuala Lumpur, 89, 91, 93, 107
Kumasi, 125-128, 130, 131, 138, 152, 154-156, 165-167, 179, 181, 182, 184
Kumasi, SS, x, 165-169, 172-184, 187-191, 193-200-202, 203, 206-209, 213-219, 222-233, 235, 237, 239
Kunama, 53, 72
Kus-Kus River, 46
Kunama, 11, 12

Labadi Beach, 129
Lages de Pico, 214, 215, 218, 220
Lake Haik, 45
Lake Lop, 14
Lake Success, 42
'Layforce', 192
Lalibella, 35
Land Rover, 45, 128, 152, 157
Land's End, 225, 228
La Palma, 203
La Pergola, 178
Largs, 232
Lascelles, Daniel, William, 25, 36, 39, 40, 41, 43, 44, 46, 54, 66, 70, 80
Lascelles, Henry, 25
Las Palmas, 189
Lawford's Gate, Bristol, 16
Lawra, 129
"Layforce", 21, 56
Leonard, 199
Liberia, 183, 188-190, 196
Liberty ship, 177
Lij, 46
Lilley, Warrant Officer I, Ernest, Thomas, ('Bob'), 232
Lima, 217
Lincoln, Lincolnshire, 17, 19, 35, 107, 168, 200, 207, 211, 228, 233, 238, 239
Lincolnshire Beet Sugar Co. Ltd., 233
Lincoln Bomber, 94
Lincoln, Paul, 238
Lion of Judah, 27, 55
Lipton's, 199

Lison, 214
Liverpool, 124
LMG (Light Machine Gun), 79
Lobi, 162
Loch Ness Monster, 184
Lock, Iris May, ("Lockie") (see Almonds, Iris May)
Log see Ship's Log
London, 72
Long Ships, The, 206, 209
Lorimer, 56
Lorien, 227
Lower Road, 110, 112, 116
Lumley, Joanna, 109

Maadi Grundi, 45
Maby, Chief Constable, 16, 17
Maclean, Fitzroy, Major-General Sir, Hew Royle, 236
Mark, Sir Robert, 237
McBain, QMSI, Royal Arm Physical Training Corps (RAPT), 128
MCP (Malayan Communist Terrorists) see Communism
Madelena, 217, 218
Madeiras, 208, 213
Mai Altal, 13
Maiden Voyage of the Ketch Kumasi, 168, 171
Makalle, 40, 44, 51, 66
Mahado, 42
Makara, 76
Malacca, Straits of, x
Malaya, Malaysian, 89, 92, 94-96, 99, 101, 102, 106-108, 117-120, 122
Malay Basic Training Centre (MBTC), 107, 109, 122
Malayan Emergency, 95
Malayan Scouts, 95
Malpas, 17
Mandai Jungle, 111
Man O'War Bay, 192
Maquis, 212
Mareb River, See Gash River
Marfik, 203
Margates, SQMS, Douglas, 232
Martin, 40, 41, 43
Maria Theresa, 7, 55
Martell Brandy, 207
'Martha', 159
Marxism, see Communism

Massawa, 8, 13, 19, 21, 22, 42, 44, 61, 67, 70, 71, 73, 84
Masses Movement (Min Yuen), 93
Mastagata, 15
Matienzo, Edouard, Anze, 8, 63-65, 72, 84
Mauritania, 197
Mayne, Colonel 'Paddy', Blair, 14, 15, 81, 107, 119, 236
McGill, Paddy, 51, 56, 57, 67, 81, 85
McGregor, Alistair, 89
Mederic, Mohammed, 57
Mediterranean Sea, 90, 209
Meerut Square, 111
Melotti beer, 62
Melotti, Adolfo, 65
Melotti Signora, 65
Merson, William, 46
Mexico, Mexican, 217
Mickey Finn, 229
Middle East, 90, 115, 171, 192, 239
Middle Road, 115
Miles, Mr, David, 235
Milli, Ingide, Sheik, 62
Mills bomb, 33
Military Medal and bar, 21
Miller, Ernie, Assistant Chief Constable, 16
Miniferi, 73, 74
Min Yuen, see Masses Movement
Mohammed, Azimatch, Ahmed, 57
Monkey Head Rock, 151
Monrovia, 182, 183, 187-190, 196, 225
Monserrat, Nicholas, 116
Montgomery, Field Marshal, Sir Bernard, ('Monty') 96
Morocco, 206
Mortimer, George, 232
Motte d'Angels, 198
Mount Afadja see Afadjato
Mount Road, 115
Mount Pico, 216
'Monty', 112
Moriatis, 46
Mosasghi, Berhe, 31
Mosasghi, Voldegabriel, 51
Mowgli, 106
Much Ado About Nothing, 114
Mueller, Olaf, 196, 199-201, 204
Mullins, Vernon and Dana, 46
Munn, Commodore, 118
Muscherness, Ross, 234, 235
Muslim, 12, 42, 44, 50, 51, 54, 57, 65, 69-71,

74, 78, 80, 84, 92, 158
Mussolini, 29, 61

NAAFI, 110, 123
Nadia, 189
Nagasaki, 15
Nairobi, 23
Nancray-sur-Rimarde, 15
Nantes, 226
National Service, 90
Navrongo, 162
Nazis, 14, 15, 46, 82, 83, 190
Nebrid of Axum, 43, 44
Nee Soon Garrison, 99, 109-113, 120, 122
Nefasit, 71, 73
Negga, Colonel, 80
Negri, 92
Nelson Street, 15
Neptune, 91, 192
Nescafé, 220
Newell, Dare, 107
New Forest, 239
New Times and Ethiopia News, 32, 51
Newton Abbot, 168
Newtownards, 236
New York, 223
New Zealand, 238
Nigeria, 125
Nissen, 17
Nkrumah, Dr Kwame, 128
Noberto, Senhor, 218
North Africa, 90, 208, 239
North East Trades, 207, 208, 210
North, Mr, George, 235
Northern Territories (NTs), 159, 160
Norway, 14, 81

O Telegrafo, 218
Obel, 40, 54
Obuasi, 126
Octavious, Emperor, 205
Offences and Criminal Responsibility, 69
Ogaden, 40
OGs (Olive Greens), 92
Okehampton, 18
Okinawa, 211
Om Hager, 65
Operation Boxer, 98
Operation Roundup, 74
Orang Asli, 101
Orchard Road, 109

Orkney Islands, 214
Orleans, Forest, 166
Ooto, 189
OSS (Office of Strategic Services), 15
Ovaltine, 188
Pahang, 92, 98, 103
Palestine, 5, 42, 49, 50
  Palestine Police, see British Palestine Police
Panama Canal, 236
Pankhurst, Miss, Sylvia, 32, 33, 51, 84
Parachute Regiment, Para, 107
Paul, Sandra, 109
Peace Delegation, 57, 80
Peacock, 40
Pentagon, the, 238
Pearce, Sir Frederick, 40, 83
Perak, 92
Perle de Bretagne, 227
Perlis, 92
Perry, Stuart, Lieutenant, 23, 48, 97, 98, 103-106
Pentagon, 8
Penzione Belvedere, 57
Peyton Place, 128
Pico Island, 214-216, 219, 220, 222
Pico St Jorg Channel, 220
Pierre, 46
Pimms, 156
Piton de Chedallah, 198
Players Navy Cut, 113
Pole Star, 223
Polish Army, 19
Polizia Africana, 22
Poole, 28
Ponto Delgardo, 216
'Pontius', 208
'Popski', Peniakoff, Major Vladimir, 226
Port Dixon, 106
Port Etienne, 197, 198, 199, 210, 215, 220
Portland Bill, 229, 230
Portland Harbour, 230
Portland Race, 230
Port Said, 90
Portugal, Portuguese, 196, 208, 209, 214, 216, 218-220
Portsmouth, 215, 228
  Consul Chart, 215
Poulton, 17
Prince Mekonnen, Haile Selassie, 35, 36
Proclamation, Public Security, 63, 68, 69,

71, 74, 75, 77, 79, 84
Public Relations see PR3
Pulau Benai, 104
Pulau Punggol, 118
Pulau Saletar, 118
Pulau Ubin, 118
Punggol Point, 120

Queen Alexandra's Royal Army Nursing
    Corps (QARANC), 122
Queen Elizabeth II, HM, 166
Queen of Sheba, 27

Radio Australia, 211
Radio Marina, 8
Radio Montreal, 208
Radio Switzerland, 211
Raffles Hotel, 91
Range Rover, 33
Rashitu, 199
Red Cross, 3
Redda, Ghindia, 83
Red House Sailing Club, 116, 118-120
Red Sea, 11, 13, 22, 23, 47, 61, 63, 73, 76,
    77, 80
Remington .22 rifle, 57
Residenti Courts, 50
Reuters, London, 51
Rhodesia, Rhodesian, see Special Air
    Service, 22 SAS, 'C' Squadron
Riley, Pat, 18
Rio de Orio, 201, 203
RMO (Regimental Medical Officer), 106
Robertson, General, 41-43
Robson, Lieutenant, Gordon, 130, 132-
    139, 143, 144, 146-150, 152-154, 168,
    170, 172, 173, 176-178, 180, 181, 183,
    185-187, 193, 197, 198, 200, 202, 203,
    205-220, 222, 224-230, 239
Rockton Point, 183
Roman Catholic, 216
Rome, 70, 83
Rose, Sir Alec, 237
Rose's lime juice, 173
Royal Air Force (RAF), 44
Royal Air Force Seletar Sailing Club, 120
Royal Army Service Corps (RASC), 40, 89
    Company, 152
Royal Berkshire Regiment, 41, 44, 53, 54,
    75, 82
Royal Corps of Signals, 237

Royal Naval College, Osborne, 25
Royal Navy, 116, 118, 167, 184, 193, 230
Royal Norfolk Regiment, 28, 30
Royal Palm Avenue, 126, 157
Royal Sierra Leone Military Forces, 170,
    193
Royal West African Frontier Force
    (RWAFF), 124, 128
RTU (Returned to Unit), 89
Russia, Russian, 234
Ryan, Trooper, 103
Ryde, 194, 230

Sabderat, 70
Sadler, Sergeant, Mike, 14, 15
Sageneti, 71, 73
Sahara Desert, 125, 127, 146, 199, 203
Saint Paul River, 187
Sakai, see *Orang Asli*
Salmon River, 154
Sam Browne belt, 35
Sam, Kwesi, 168
Samovar, 218
San Jorge, 214
Sandhurst, Royal Military Academy, 26,
    163, 165, 233
SAS see Special Air Service
Savage.22 rifle, 6, 7, 35
Saxmundham, 235
Scium, Ali, 12, 78
Scotland, Scottish, 153, 168, 231
Scott, Kenneth, 45
Scranton Corner, 181
Second World War, 59, 82, 124, 171, 239
Secretary of State, 80
Selangor, 92
Selassie, Hailie, Emperor, 24, 26, 27, 28, 36,
    43, 44, 55-57
Seletar, Pulau, See Pulau
Seletar Reservoir, 115
Sembawang, HMS, 112
Sembawang, Royal Naval Base, 116-118,
    120
Sembel Camp, 57
Sembilan, 92
Senafe, 73
Senchi, 152, 153
Senegal, Sengalese, 196
Serae, 12, 40, 41, 53, 69, 72, 76, 80
Setit River, 6, 8, 11, 13, 61
Shakers, 106

Shakespeare, 114
Shambles Lightship, 230
Shell Quay, 179
Sherbro River, 191
Shetland Islands, 214
Shevlin, William ('Bill'), 63
Shifta, 6-13, 22, 31, 39-47, 50-55, 57, 59-61, 63-67, 69-78, 80, 81, 83-85
Sidi Barrani, 210
'Simon', 159
Shinfa River, 60
Ship's Log, 168
Sierra Leone, 170, 187, 190, 191-193, 232
Slim, Viscount, John, 104
Sinatra, Frank, 114
Sinbang, Royal Naval Air Station, 120
Singapore, 10, 13, 90, 91, 95, 99, 109, 116, 117, 120-123
SMLE (Short Magazine Lee Enfield), 79
Société Industrielle de Pêche, 200
Solomon, 27
Somalia, 22, 24
Somaliland, 23, 39, 48
Somerset Light Infantry, 90
South Africa, South African, 189
South America, 213
South East Asia, 106
Southampton, 90, 228
South Pole, 15
South Wales Borders, 74, 75, 79, 82, 84
Southwest Winds, 208
Soviet (Union), 39
Spain, Spanish, 189, 199
Special Air Service (SAS), 40, 62, 85, 89, 91-93, 95-103, 105-107, 120, 123, 134, 192, 210, 212, 231, 235, 236, 237
  'L' Detachment, 1st SAS, 1, 3, 4, 89, 100, 107, 164, 231, 236
  'D' Squadron, 1st SAS, 90
  'A' Squadron, 22 SAS, 95, 98, 102
  1 Troop, 105
  'B' Squadron, 22 SAS, 89, 92, 93, 95, 98, 100, 102, 107
  'C' Squadron, 22 SAS, 95, 98, 102
  'D' Squadron, 22 SAS, 95, 98, 102
  17 Troop, 103, 105
  'G' Squadron, 238
  'Selection', 237
  New Zealand SAS, 238
Special Court, 82, 83
Special Forces, 102

SS, 46
Staffierne, Mrs, Ellen, 165, 169
Star of David, 55
Sten gun, 99
Stirling, Colonel Sir David, 15, 18, 21, 89, 107, 116, 171, 236
Stixwould, 14, 17, 48, 165, 166, 169, 200, 231-233, 236
St Alban's Head, 230
St Andrews, University of, 172
St Catherine's Point, 230
St Jorg-Terceira Channel, 220
St Jude's, Bristol, 16
Strato-cruiser see BOAC
St Werburgh's, Bristol 15
Sudan, Sudanese, 13, 24, 52, 70
Suez Canal, 78, 90, 106, 156
Sumatra, Sumatran, 98, 118, 119
Sungei Betram, 103
Sungei Besi, 89, 99-101
Sweden, Swedish, 14, 24
Suffrage Movement, 32
Switzerland, Swiss, 46, 156, 196
Sydney Harbour Bridge, 153
Sykes-Fairbairn knife, 34, 100
Synthomycetin, 229

Tagliero, 72
Takoradi, 10, 125, 167-169, 172-175, 178, 182, 193, 195
Takoradi Sailing Club, 169, 172, 173, 211, 215
Tamale, 129, 131, 159
Tamil, 92
Taranto, x
Tarim River, 14
Tasek Bera, 103, 105
Techeste, Haile, 42, 51, 76, 79
Tedessa Makonnen, 44
Tedj, 29
Tef, 29
Teferi, Private Tebde, 29
Tel Aviv, 49
Temeloh, 98
Templer, General Sir Gerald, 95
Tenerife, 203
Terceira headland, 221
Teroa, 75
Teroa Beit Sareh, 74
Terror, *HMS*, 116
Texaco Petrol, 131, 139

Thessiger, Sir Wilfred, 28, 50
The Times, 51
Tiger beer, 105
Tigrai, Tigrean, 24, 41, 43, 50, 52, 69, 71, 84
Tigre, 43
Tigrinya, Tigrinian, 6, 51, 68, 78
Titanic, 114
Tobruk, Siege of, 9, 192, 239
Togoland, 163
Tommassi, Guiseppe, 83
Torbay, 228
Transit Road, 113
Treble Chance, 209
Trengganu, 92
Trinity, 153
Tropic of Cancer, 91
TSMG (Thompson Sub-Machine Gun), 79
Tripolitania, 59
Tesemma, Dedjatch, Abraha, 41
Tubman, President, 187, 188
Tucul, 40
Tukul(s), 30
Turnbull, General, 40, 41, 59
Turner, Lieutenant, Crawford, 110
'*Tusker* time', 140
Twin Towers, 238
Tzenadegle, 74, 77, 78

UK, (United Kingdom) See Britain, British
UNESCO, 72
Union Flag, 85, 127
Unionist Party, 50, 70
United Africa Timber Company, 165, 169, 175
US see America
US .30 Carbine, 101
Ushant, 227, 228
USMC (United States Marine Corps) Camillus knife, 34, 96, 100, 116, 119, 133, 168
United Nations (UN), 8, 11, 22, 32, 33, 41, 42, 46, 63-65, 68, 71, 75, 85

Vale, Senhora, Luiza, 218
Vale, Senhora, Ilda, 218
Valhalla, 237
Vannes, 227
VCIGS, (Vice Chier, Imperial General Staff), 84
Verey pistol, 10, 120
Victorian, 216

Vidal, Captain, 187
Vietnam, 102, 236
Viking, 214
Villa de Praia, 221
Virgin Soldiers, The, 115
Voice of Eritrea, 51
Volta Region, 163
Volta River, x, 129-131, 133, 135, 142, 153, 154, 168
Volta River Dam, 152
Volta River Project, 152

Wainfleet Haven, 234
Wales, Welsh, 105
Wall's, 211
Walter, Peter, 89, 101
Watson, Captain, 97
War Diary
War Office, 7, 24, 39, 43, 46, 84, 124, 168, 169
    PR3 (Public Relations), 168
Wash, The, 233
Washington, 70
Waterloo Dispatch, 17
Wat, 29
Wavell, General, 24
Welbeck College, 165
Wellington, Duke of, 17
Wells-next-the-Sea, 233, 234
West Africa, 164, 179, 239
Westerlies, 202, 211
Western Area, 62
Western Desert, 62, 92, 93, 99, 100, 107, 168, 210, 226
Western Province, 59, 61, 62, 65, 67, 68, 76, 80-82, 84
Westmorland, 'Rusty', 98
Wetherall, Geoffrey, 41
Weymouth, 230, 231
Wiaga, 129
Williams, 'Burglar', 63
Williams, Frank, 89
Whitehall, 31, 32, 46, 51, 78, 12
Witham, River, 169, 228, 231, 233
Wild West, 56, 59, 61, 74
Willis, Bruce, 17
Wingate, Orde, General, 24
Winneba, 193
Winters, Sergeant ('Paddy'), 105
Woldmikael, Asfaha, 57
Wollo Region, 30

Wood, Edward Joshua, ('Timber'), 62, 63
Woodhall Spa, 237
Wug, 116-119, 120, 150

Yachting World, 235
Yates, Colonel ('Daddy'), 110
Yedhego, Kifleghi, 57

Yeji, 131, 133, 137, 140, 153
Yellow-Bellied Sea Snake, 119
Yemen, Yemeni, 70
Yes Minister, 55
Youngman, Albert, 1st SAS, 14
York Street, Bristol, 16

ABOUT THE AUTHOR

Lorna Almonds-Windmill is the daughter of the subject of this book, 'Gentleman Jim' Almonds, who was a founder of the SAS with David Stirling. After resigning her Regular Army Commission, Lorna was a Whitehall career civil servant. While serving in HM Treasury, she won the European Union of Women/IBM Award for European Woman of Achievement.

Lorna has a BA with First Class Honours in Politics, Philosophy and History (PPH) from the University of London.

Her first book, *Gentleman Jim: the Wartime Story of a Founder of the SAS and Special Forces* was published in hardback by Constable Publishing in July 2001 and is now in its fourth edition. Her second book, *A British Achilles: the Story of George, Second Earl Jellicoe*, was published in hardback by Pen & Sword Publishing in January 2006 and is now in its third edition.